GO WITH THE FLOW OF POWER

Deep within our subconscious minds is buried the ancient knowledge that the Moon has a real power over our moods, actions, and lives. Unfortunately, many of us—even those who may have secretly wondered about the Moon's powers—have convinced ourselves that the Moon has no influence on anything but the tides.

But evidence shows that the Moon does affect our behavior. For example, it's no coincidence that incidences of suicide and deadly violence rise consistently during a Full Moon. It only makes sense to conclude that the Moon impacts us differently at different times.

Now you can find out how the cycles of the Moon affect you, and how you can successfully ride their tides of power. Moon Magick describes dozens of ways you can work with the Moon to constructively channel your energy instead of expending it uselessly, thereby saving yourself a lot of time and frustration. What's the best time for making personal changes? Or for undertaking high-energy tasks? Moon Magick will tell you.

Just how do you immerse yourself in the flow of Moon energy that our ancestors knew so well? After you read the chapters on each lunar month and phase, you'll discover how each period's unique characteristics manifest themselves in your life. Then you'll actually learn how to take advantage of this ever-changing flow of energy to empower your magickal workings and day-to-day activities.

With the Goddess coming into Her own once more, the Moon is being more openly recognized for its influence in the lives of humans. Life can be difficult at times—why not use Moon magick to smooth the way?

About the Author

I was born on a Beltane Full Moon with a total lunar eclipse, one of the hottest days of that year. Although I came into an Irish-North Germanic-Native American family with natural psychics on both sides, such abilities were not talked about. So I learned discrimination in a family of closet psychics.

I have always been close to Nature. As a child, I spent a great amount of time outdoors by myself. Trees, herbs, and flowers become part of my indoor and outdoor landscapes wherever I live. I love cats, music, mountains, singing, streams, stones, ritual, and nights when the Moon is full. My reading covers vast areas of history, the magickal arts, philosophy, customs, mythology, and fantasy. I have studied every part of the New Age religions from Eastern philosophy to Wicca. I hope I never stop learning and expanding.

Although I have lived in areas of this country from one coast to the other, I now reside on the West Coast. I am not fond of large crowds or speaking in public.

I live a rather quiet life in the company of my husband and my two cats, Callisto and Finnigan, with occasional visits with my children and grandchildren. I collect statues of dragons and wizards, crystals and other stones, and of course, books. Most of my time is spent researching and writing. I have published eight books. Before I am finished with one book, I am working on another in my head. All in all, I am just an ordinary Pagan person.

To Write to the Author

If you wish to contact the author or would like more information about this book, please write to the author in care of Llewellyn Worldwide, and we will forward your request. Both the author and the publisher appreciate hearing from you and learning of your enjoyment of this book and how it has helped you. Llewellyn Worldwide cannot guarantee that every letter written to the author can be answered, but all will be forwarded. Please write to:

D.J. Conway
℅ Llewellyn Worldwide
P.O. Box 64383-K167, St. Paul, MN 55164-0383, U.S.A.
Please enclose a self-addressed, stamped envelope or $1.00 to cover costs. If outside the U.S.A.,
enclose international postal reply coupon.

Free Catalog from Llewellyn

For more than 90 years Llewellyn has brought its readers knowledge in the fields of metaphysics and human potential. Learn about the newest books in spiritual guidance, natural healing, astrology, occult philosophy, and more. Enjoy book reviews, New Age articles, a calendar of events, plus current advertised products and services. To get your free copy of *Llewellyn's New Worlds of Mind and Spirit,* send your name and address to:

Llewellyn's New Worlds of Mind and Spirit
P.O. Box 64383-K167, St. Paul, MN 55164-0383, U.S.A.

Llewellyn's Practical Magick Series

MOON MAGICK

Myth & Magick, Crafts & Recipes, Rituals & Spells

D.J. CONWAY

1995
Llewellyn Publications
St. Paul, Minnesota 55164-0383

FIRST EDITION
Second Printing, 1995

Cover painting and interior art elements: Karen Wann
Cover design: Anne Marie Garrison
Line drawings on pages 46, 82, 88, 120, 121, 174, 175, 212: Anne Marie Garrison
Book design and layout: Pamela Henkel
Clip art: Dover Publications, except where noted

Library of Congress Cataloging-in-Publication Data
Conway, D.J. (Deanna J.)
        Moon magick : myth & magick, crafts & recipes, rituals & spells /
D.J. Conway
        p.   c.m. -- (Llewellyn's practical magick series)
        Includes bibliographical references and index.
        ISBN 1-56718-167-8
        1. Moon--Miscellanea. 2. Magic. 3. Ritual. I. Title.
II. Series.
BF1623.M66C66   1995
133.4'3 --dc20   95-18474
                                                       CIP

Printed in the United States of America

Llewellyn Publications
A Division of Llewellyn Worldwide, Ltd.
P.O. Box 64383, St. Paul, MN 55164-0383

About Llewellyn's Practical Magick Series

To some people, the idea that "Magick" is practical comes as a surprise.

It shouldn't. The entire basis for Magick is to exercise influence over one's environment. While Magick is also, and properly so, concerned with spiritual growth and psychological transformation—even the spiritual life must rest firmly on material foundations.

The material world and the psychic are intertwined, and it is this very fact that establishes the Magickal Link: that the psychic can as easily influence the material as vice versa.

Magick can, and should, be used in one's daily life for better living! Each of us has been given Mind and Body, and surely we are under Spiritual obligation to make full usage of these wonderful gifts. Mind and Body work together, and Magick is simply the extension of this interaction into dimensions beyond the limits normally conceived. That's why we commonly talk of the "supernormal" in connection with the domain of Magick.

The Body is alive, and all Life is an expression of the Divine. There is God-power in the Body and in the Earth, just as there is in Mind and Spirit. With Love and Will, we use mind to link these aspects of Divinity together to bring about change.

With magick we increase the flow of Divinity in our lives and in the world around us. We add to the beauty of it all—for to work Magick we must work in harmony with the Laws of Nature and of the Psyche. *Magick is the flowering of the Human Potential.*

Practical Magick is concerned with the Craft of Living well and in harmony with Nature, and with the Magick of the Earth, in the things of the Earth, in the seasons and cycles and in the things we make with hand and Mind.

Other Books by the Author

Celtic Magic
Norse Magic
The Ancient & Shining Ones
Maiden, Mother, Crone
Dancing with Dragons
By Oak, Ash, & Thorn
Animal Magick
Flying Without a Broom
Falcon Feather & Valkyrie Sword
Dream Warrior (fiction)

Forthcoming

Soothslayer (fiction)
Astral Love
Magickal, Mythical, Mystical Beasts

To Esther, my sister-priestess from Greece,
and especially to all the Pagan children
who will one day change the world.

Moon Song

I raise my arms in greeting
As She slips up through the night,
The rounded Moon of Mystery,
A glowing silver disk of light.

My spirit answers to Her call
And longs for wings to fly,
That I might seek Her secret place
Whose symbol is the sky.

A place of hidden secrets,
Of sacred Mysteries old,
A place I knew in other times,
In temple wisdom no more told.

I struggle to remember
All the things I learned before,
The forgotten Mysteries of the Moon,
The Goddess and Her lore.

Although my arms reach skyward,
I turn inward toward Her voice.
I tread the inner labyrinth,
Trusting in my choice.

"Seek not without, but deep within."
The words are soft and clear.
"Keep faith with Me for thirteen months,
The Mother's Sacred Year."

I watch Her through Her cycles,
As I did in lives before,
And follow down Her moonbeam path
To the secret, inner door.

Table of Contents

PART ONE: THE MOON'S INFLUENCE ON OUR LIVES

PART TWO: THE LUNAR YEAR

APPENDICES: MOON DIETIES AND SYMBOLS

PART ONE

The Moon's
Influence on
Our Lives

Chapter 1

MOON TOUCHED

*Moon struck or Moon touched: affected by the Moon;
distracted; bemused; given to unnatural fantasies (as when one is psychic
and those about the person are not).*

No one knows exactly when humans began to observe the Moon but it must have been very early in our development. The carving of the Great Goddess of Laussel, dating back to about 20,000 BCE, shows the Goddess holding a bison horn with thirteen marks for months on it. In a cave at the Abri du Roc aux Sorciers at Angles-sur-l'Anglin is a massive carving of three women, very likely goddesses. This carving dates from between 13,000 and 11,000 BCE. These three figures, standing on a bison, may well represent the three phases of the Moon.

The Sun was a constant factor to early humans, except for its seasonal rise and fall on the horizon, but the Moon was mysterious, changing Her faces and shapes, withholding and giving light during the dark hours of the night. It wasn't long before menstruating women learned to count Moon cycles, thus creating the first calendar. However, the Sun was no help in dividing time into smaller portions than seasons. Counting from one Moon phase through the cycle and back to the same phase enabled clans to plan gatherings and religious ceremonies.

For centuries, women were the calendar-keepers, priestesses, healers, and advisors of the clans because of their ability to communicate with the powers of the Moon Goddess. Men learned to read the Moon's seasonal passages for use in hunting and farming. All early people knew that no human was unaffected by the Moon and Her mystical powers.

I was born on a Beltane Full Moon, with a total lunar eclipse. The Moon has always been important to me, long before I knew what She symbolized. As a small child, I would stand under the light of a Full Moon, reaching toward Her and yearning for something I couldn't put into words. Some in my family called me Moon touched, to them a derogatory term, but little realizing how right they were under another definition.

Everyone is Moon touched, or influenced, some just more than others. About one-third of all people have a Full Moon in their natal astrological chart. These people are highly sensitive and emotional, with intense reactions each time the Moon re-enters its natal sign. For those whose religious views do not permit emotional and psychic sensitivity, these Moon phases can be miserable, upsetting experiences, particularly if a person's sensitivity takes the form of seeing non-physical beings, having precognitive dreams and visions, or recalling past lives.

Humans cannot escape the influence of the Moon, whether they believe in it or not. The Moon touches the lives of all people in one way or another. Some individuals, who make little effort to obey the social laws or take responsibility for their lives anyway, who are either unstable or on the edges of being so, allow Her influence to lead them into violence, robberies, overindulgence in alcohol or drugs, or antisocial, harmful behavior. Even the best of us may snap and snarl when the Full Moon is in certain astrological signs. The more unaware we are of Her influences, the more we tend to react.

The police, firemen, paramedics, bartenders, and hospitals know that Full Moons bring more dramatic, dangerous problems. A team of psychiatrists in Florida compiled a report on murders in Dade County and Greater Cleveland, Ohio, over a fifteen-year period; they found there was a sharp increase in deadly violence at the Full Moon. A similar study done in New York charted peaks in robbery, assault, and car theft when the Moon was full. Research in Buffalo, New York, discovered an increase in suicides during a Full Moon. Another study done by the Department of Psychology at Edgecliff College in Ohio found that ten categories of crime are affected by the Full Moon: rape, robbery, assault, burglary, larceny, theft, auto theft, drunkenness, disorderly conduct, and offenses against children or family members.

It isn't only the Full Moon that seems to stir up human emotions and irrational behavior, although the Full Moon appears to have the most influence. The New Moon also affects humans, especially those with mental instability. As far back as the sixteenth century, Paracelsus wrote that the New Moon made mentally unstable people worse. The New Moon is the second, albeit lesser, time in a lunar cycle when authorities see an increase in strange and dangerous behavior.

Being aware & working with the energies with the Help from the work through the good & influences

The influences and power of the New and Full Moons need not be all negative. Fishermen in Nova Scotia have passed down the information for many years that the largest catches of herring can be taken at the Full Moon. The grunion (smelts) of California spawn according to the Full Moon and high tides. Those in magick have long used various lunar cycles to increase their powers for manifestations.

Aristotle and Pliny both insisted that earthquakes usually occurred on the New Moon. An M.I.T. geophysicist was curious about the effects of the Moon on earthquakes and did a study on over 2,000 of them in Turkey. Dr. Toksoz discovered that twice as many earthquakes happened at the New and Full Moons, during the two highest daily tides. Perhaps if this information were taken more seriously, we would not be caught unaware by earthquakes.

Lady Luna

Everyone complains about the weather and the inaccuracy of weather reporting. A Leningrad geophysicist, Sergei Timofeyev, decided to investigate old folk sayings that the Moon affected the weather; scientists now believe that only the sunspot cycle does this. However, Timofeyev found some very interesting facts by monitoring the air temperatures, in comparison with Moon phases, for a number of years over various places in Russia. Sunspot activity runs on an eleven year cycle; Timofeyev discovered that changes in air masses and temperature had a nine and nineteen[1] year cycle, that of the Moon. By checking Moon phases, he discovered a parallel with historical catastrophic weather phenomena around the world.

The greatest proportion of the human body is made up of water. If the Moon affects the oceanic tides, the lowly grunion and herring, and possibly the weather through the moisture in the atmosphere, it is logical to concede that humans are directly affected also. Some scientists and medical experts will grudgingly agree because of the accumulating data on violent crime and mental upheavals during certain Moon phases.

But what has all this to do with the average law-abiding person, stable in mind and emotions? History tells us that there were other influences of the Moon, mystical influences that most people once knew and used to better their lives. This knowledge was forgotten when the modern religions gained control and either forbade their practices or ridiculed them into near-extinction along with the ancient deities that represented and symbolized the Moon.

These powers of the Moon phases were ancient knowledge in a great many cultures around the world and that same Moon knowledge is being used today by Pagans, Ceremonial Magicians, and the Wiccan groups. Certain phases of the Moon produce unique energies which can be tapped by humans through rituals large and small. In simple terms, spellworking for banishing, decreasing, or removing problems takes place from after the Full Moon until the New Moon, with the day or night of the New Moon being strongest. Spellworking for increase, growth, and gain takes place from after the New Moon until the Full Moon, with the day or night of the Full Moon being the most powerful. This use of Moon magick is ancient, and it still works.

But actual Moon magick is a little more involved than this simple explanation. The Moon month has traditionally been connected with three aspects of the Triple Goddess: Maiden (Crescent Moon), Mother (Full Moon), Crone (Dark Moon). These three aspects are further joined by specific energy paths: waning (decreasing) and waxing (growing). There are thirteen Moon months in a calendar year. Each Moon month is directly connected with a different type of seasonal energy flow.

With the Goddess coming into Her own once again, the Moon is being more openly recognized for Her influence and importance in the lives of humans. Anne Kent Rush, in *Moon, Moon,* wrote that the importance and position of women in a

The Moon's Phases, designed by Hans Holbein II, from Sebastian Münster's Canones super novum instrumentum luminarium, *printed by Andreas Cratander, Basel, 1534*

society can be judged by the importance that society gives to the Moon. Hidden in that statement is the religious fact that where the Moon is ignored or denigrated to the role of fantasy and fairytale, so the Goddess is ignored, forbidden, or cast in the role of the wife/mother of a deity. Women, the Moon, and the Goddess are inextricably bound together. What is doubly sad is that the patriarchal societies have concealed the fact that men also are caught up in the weaving of the Goddess and the Moon.

Women subconsciously know their connection with the Moon through their bodies and menstruation. Men do not have such obvious physical connections. However, a Japanese taxi company would tell you that men are not immune. They began a study to understand the unusual monthly cycles of accidents by their all-male drivers. They found that each male seemed to have periods that affected his reactions, and these periods corresponded to certain lunar positions. When schedules were changed to fit around these lunar cycles, the rash of accidents ceased.

The entire Chinese philosophy of Yin and Yang is linked to the waxing and waning of the Moon and the rise and fall of life-energy in humans. This would place the New and Full Moons as times of extremes in energy. Hindu astrology places great importance on the Moon phases as well, saying that people born during a waxing Moon live longer.

So, of what use is watching the Moon and Her phases? Being aware of the Moon and Her influences upon your life can save you a lot of frustration, time, and wasted energy. The Crescent, sometimes called the New,

A Gnostic emblem showing the moon goddess—Luna Regia—from Jacob Bryant's "Analysis of Antient (sic) Mythology"

Moon is a time for introversion, of starting new projects and plans, and making personal changes in general. It is an excellent time for self-examination in everything from your love life, career, moving into a new house, and breaking habits, to spiritual intentions. The Full Moon, the most powerful phase, is a time of extroversion, high-energy tasks, and work with other people.

Are you letting the intense Moon energy lead you by the hormones, and are you really seeing your lover as she/he is, not a fantasy-person? Are you suddenly restless in your career? Watch out for those Moon phases! Are you making quick decisions to move or join a religious group? Back off, and let the Moon slide into another phase before you make a commitment. Check the Moon cycle before you shop for any item that requires you to sign a contract. You can be more easily swayed emotionally during a Full Moon. If you must deal with someone you really don't get along with, stay away from Full or New Moon meetings. Chances are you both will be edgy and the communication will be off. If you must undergo surgery of any kind, check the Moon before setting the date. Simply, don't set a surgery during a Full Moon or for four days before or after it. Bleeding will be more profuse at this time.

There are benefits to being in tune with the Moon as well. By cutting your hair and nails during a waxing Moon, they will grow back stronger and faster. Planting by the Moon has been known for centuries; certain plants grow better when planted during certain phases. There are Moon sign almanacs, such as the excellent one by Llewellyn Publications, that give you all the information on this you need.

This is all interesting information on the Moon but hardly of much practical use unless you combine it with magickal techniques. And magickal techniques are of little use unless you apply them in practical ways to your personal life. After all, magick is for improving your life physically, mentally, emotionally, and spiritually.

To do this throughout a lunar year can be a challenge. The lunar year consists of thirteen months, the old calendar reckoning. I have divided Part Two of this book into these months, filling each lunar division with old sayings about the Moon, ancient religious information, recipes, practical rituals and spellworkings, and a great many other things to make your lunar year one of interest and enthusiasm. By working with the Moon's energies, instead of against them, you should find yourself in greater harmony with yourself, others, and the universal spiritual rhythm.

Part Three includes a list of Moon goddesses and gods from around the world. This can be used to find an appropriate deity if you wish to add a name to your rituals. Or it can be an interesting overview of world Moon deities and how long the Moon has been important to humans.

We can't escape the influence of the Moon and Her powers, even if we don't consciously believe in them. The collective unconscious, or universal mind, still holds all the old information from our own past lives and those of our ancestors. The Moon knowledge of all those ancient civilizations still can affect our subconscious thinking, and our lives, in subtle ways. Each human, however, can learn to deliberately access this portion of the mind through deep meditation and, therefore, be more aware of how it is influencing life. Add this to the fact that the physical Moon affects our bodies and emotions, and it seems rather absurd not to work with the flow of power instead of against it. Life is difficult enough. Why not use Moon magick to smooth the path a bit?

Endnotes

1. This is called the Meton cycle after its discoverer, Meton of Athens, who lived in the fifth century BCE. It takes the Moon nineteen years for Her phases to repeat themselves on the same days.

Chapter 2
HISTORY OF LUNAR CALENDARS

The word "calendar" comes from the Latin *calendae* or *kalendae*, which was the title of the first day of each Roman month. The Indo-European root words for "moon," "mind," and "month" are *mati-h, manas, mana,* or *men;* all are connected in meaning to the menstrual blood of women and the Goddess. In Greek, *mene* means Moon, while in Latin the word for Moon was *mensis* and *mensura.* These same root words are found in measurement. Even today there is a remnant of the Moon in our present calendar under the name Monday, or Moon Day. The word "create" comes from the word "crescent," or New Moon. In modern French this survives openly in the word "croissant," or crescent cake.

There are three types of calendars: solar, lunar, and luni-solar. Calendars are used to establish dates, both secular and religious. They help to mark the times of the Solstices, Equinoxes, eclipses of Sun and Moon, etc. They are a way of dividing the seasonal year. The most ancient calendars were lunar, those based on the Moon.

The solar calendar which most of the world now uses is a rather modern innovation, when compared to the length of time humans have inhabited this planet. There are a great many archaeological finds and historical documents which reveal that the first cultures lived their lives around the Moon and its phases. Certain holidays are still figured according to the Moon phases. A few cultures even retain the use of the lunar calendar.

The earliest Chinese calendar was based on lunar cycles, with observations of both the Sun and the Moon. The twenty-eight divisions of the Chinese lunar year were called Hsiu, "Houses"; each House was inhabited by a warrior-consort of the Moon goddess. Such a calendar was also used in Japan, Korea, and Vietnam. The calendar of the early Hindus was lunar; still today they speak of the "28 mansions of the Moon."

The very early Egyptians had a lunar calendar; in fact, the hieroglyph for "month" was a crescent Moon. In about 4236 BCE, they set up their solar calendar consisting of twelve months of thirty days each. Their weeks were ten days long. At the end of the last month, they added five additional days, which were known as the birthdays of special deities. This calendar was based on observations of the rising of Sirius (or Sothis, the Dog Star).

The early calendars of Chaldea, Babylonia, Mesopotamia, Greece, Rome, and the Celtic clans were also lunar. Babylonian priests taught that the god Marduk counted holy days and the seasons by the movements of the Moon. The Chaldean "Moon-worshippers" believed that movement of the Moon through the zodiacal signs determined a person's fate. The Gaelic words for "menstruation" and "calendar" are almost identical: *miosach* and *miosachan*.

The Babylonian god Marduk counted holy days by the movements of the Moon

Even today the Moslems use lunar months and years. Because the Islamic year is only 354 or 355 days long, their religious feasts, such as Ramadan, proceed through the seasons.

The Jewish culture uses a combination lunar-solar calendar, with the years as solar and the months as lunar. Each month begins when the first sign of the crescent Moon is seen.

The Moon never has just one form or size to present to the Earth and its inhabitants. She changes her form as She makes a complete cycle from crescent, through Her phases, back to crescent, in approximately 29½ days.

Sometimes the Moon appears to be larger than at other times. This is caused by the elliptical orbit of the Moon around the Earth. When She is closest to the Earth (at perigee), She appears about 15 percent larger than She does when She is farthest away (at apogee). When a planetary body like the Moon is even a little closer to us than usual, its visual size increases dramatically. Magickally, the Moon would be 25 percent stronger at perigee than at apogee. This is a time when we have much higher tides than normal because of the increased influence of the Moon upon the Earth. Theoretically, the available power for magick would increase also.

Also, because of the variation in the Moon's angle at its zenith, She rises higher at some times than at others. This happens because the Moon's orbit is not exactly at the Earth's

The lunar barge of the ancient Egyptians, on which the moon travels over the sky to the west, and returns through the nether world to the east

equator. Magickal common sense tells you that the higher the Moon rises, the more directly Her rays or powers fall upon the Earth, and the more energy is available for ritual and spellworking. Most of this energy is wasted, as the vast majority of people struggle against the psychic flow instead of putting it to beneficial use.

As the Moon moves through the seasonal year, Her energies also change subtly, for She is influenced by the Sun and the angles She makes between the Sun and the Earth. To use the Moon's energies to the fullest throughout the year, one must not only be aware of Her phases, but of the seasons themselves.

I have divided the lunar months in the following calendar according to the solar months with which most of us are familiar and live our lives. However, the thirteenth month, which I have chosen to list only as the end of October and the beginning of November, is not a full twenty-nine days here. It is very confusing to try to divide the solar months equally into thirteen Moon months, which may begin and end in the midst of a solar month. People have spent centuries living to the rhythms of the solar division of time. For convenience of use, I have chosen to use this unorthodox division system.

A Blue Moon, or the second Full Moon contained in a month, can come at any time of the year. I have chosen to insert it in October-November, a time of year in Northern European tradition that brought remembrances of the ancestors and the Thin Veil between the worlds (a celebration now known as Halloween).

All of the ancient dates of celebration are not listed in this lunar calendar for two reasons: one, other sources already provide this information[1]; two, the exact dates of many celebrations cannot be agreed upon. When in doubt, I used what seemed reasonable to me. I also listed only a sampling of ancient rituals, ones which are practical and have modern meaning for today's practitioners.

Endnotes

1. Pennick, Nigel, *The Pagan Book of Days;* Budapest, Z., *Grandmother of Time* and *Grandmother Moon;* Stein, Diane, *The Goddess Book of Days.*

PART TWO

The Lunar Year

Chapter 3

INTRODUCTION
TO THE LUNAR YEAR

The following list of Moon months contains information that I feel will help the reader understand many of the ancient mystical mysteries, ideas, festivals, and lore about the Moon. The list of correspondences may differ from those of other writers; most lists do. They are not engraved in stone and can be changed to suit individual needs.

The Recipes and Crafts sections of each lunar month was produced out of my personal files and recipe box. Although I like to collect authentic recipes, I invariably change them, whenever possible, into easier methods. Few people have the luxury or time to fuss with hours of cooking. The foods and beverages can be used during ritual or when entertaining friends in mundane situations. Some of the recipes can be made and given as gifts, as can the crafts. I included them as fun projects.

In making the colognes, use unscented rubbing alcohol; this releases the scent as it evaporates. Distilled water is important since the impurities have been removed. The glycerin is a fixative which holds the scent. If the recipe calls for solid ingredients, let the cologne set for several days, then strain out the solid particles.

Many practitioners of magick prepare for their rituals by taking a bath first, using special salts. Some magicians use only sea salt, but I see no reason that regular salt could not be used. All salt comes from the Earth. Add about a tablespoon of the blended salt, herbs, and/or essential oils to the bath before slipping in for a pleasant soak. Any solid particles should be of a fine grind that will wash down the drain. If you have allergies, test a little of the essential oil (which is an ingredient in the bath salts) on the inside of your elbow before using it for bath salts. Store the bath salts in a container with a tight fitting lid.

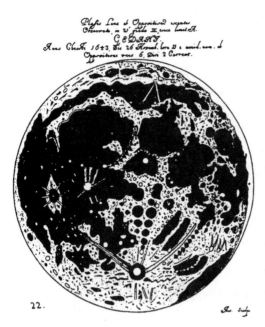

One of the earliest topographic views of the moon, from Johann Hevelius' Selenographia, *Danzig, 1647*

All the potpourris and sachets use dried ingredients unless it says otherwise. If the recipe says "Hot Pot," the mixture is to be used in the small pots which gently heat this type of potpourri. Potpourris can be stored in fancy boxes or jars; the lids are removed for short periods of time to perfume the room.

The myths related here are only a sampling of what exists. If you are really interested in a particular cultural pantheon, you should visit your local library. They have or can get for you books on any particular pantheon.

Although I have tied in various rituals with the ideas behind ancient festivals and celebrations, I have made no attempt to reproduce the old rituals. Instead I have written modern ones. First, reproduction of ancient rites would be impossible since we have few, if any, records telling us exactly what went on. Second, we live in a totally different era. It would not be logical to perform ancient rituals (including use of the language) as they were once performed. Many of the dates are debatable since there have been several drastic calendar changes. The ancient festivals and rituals listed are the ones I felt would be of most interest today.

Rituals should be fun as well as serious. I'm sure the deities and other supernatural beings have a sense of humor; they must since they work with us mortals. Therefore, not every ritual in this book is somber and serious. We should be celebrating the joy of life besides taking care of what we need and desire.

Each lunar month has rituals for the Crescent, Full, and Dark Moons. Most Pagans are quite familiar with the Crescent and Full Moons and use rituals for at least the Full Moon. However, a great many people are either outright frightened or at least wary of the Dark Moon and Dark Moon deities. These people really don't understand how to use the power of the Dark Moon, or, if they do have a little knowledge, are afraid that using such power might be "wrong." Protection of yourself and your family is not "wrong"; using a spell to force someone to love you or give you their personal money is wrong and unethical.

As I have often said, though, using magick to bring about the capture and conviction of rapists, murderers, child and spouse abusers, stalkers, terrorists, drug dealers, and others of similar ilk is perfectly correct; just don't use a name since you possibly might have the wrong person in mind. And never specify how you want them punished. Ask that they be caught by their own mistakes and arrogance. As a citizen, you wouldn't allow such a person to continue their evil activities if you have information that would bring them to justice. As a magickal person you have the same responsibility.

To understand the complexities of the three phases of the Moon, the spiritual secrets hidden in Moon myths, and the Moon deities (particularly goddesses) would require a whole book[1]. The rituals given here should open a few mental and spiritual doorways, enabling the reader to dispense with erroneous ideas and gain a glimmer of what really lies behind the three powerful faces of the Moon.

The Crescent Moon is when the first sliver of light is seen; the Full Moon when Her complete face shows; the Dark Moon when no light is seen at all. A good astrological and/or Moon calendar, such as the ones printed by Llewellyn, will help you to time your rituals.

Traditionally in magick, the waxing or Crescent Moon is for invoking the things you want, a time to start new projects. The Full Moon is used for integrating and perfecting ideas and projects, casting spells for positive things to happen; it is the high tide of psychic energies. The waning or Dark Moon is for causing things to decrease or banishing them entirely from your life. The Dark Moon is also a time of high psychic energies, although completely different from those of the Full Moon.

In personal life energies and activities, the Moon reflects her increase and decrease within the human body and psyche. The New Moon is a period of controlled energies and growth; the Full Moon a time of creation and high energy; the Dark Moon a cycle of retreat, conservation of energy, healing, resting, and dreaming of the future.

The three phases also symbolize the three main areas of the cycle of human life. The New Moon is from birth to puberty; the Full Moon from puberty through adulthood; the Dark Moon through growing older and into death of the physical body.

In the yearly pattern, the phases of the Moon are again seen. The New Moon is from the date of your birthday through six months. The Full Moon is the last five months, approaching another birthday. The Dark Moon is the month just before your birthday. This Dark Moon phase in connection with birthdays may be one of the reasons why most people do not anticipate this yearly celebration. Personal emotions are often scattered and extremely sensitive.

In addition to all this, we can see the Moon phases in events of our lives, particularly the Dark Moon phase. We enter a Dark Moon cycle whenever we experience a personal loss of any kind. We must allow ourselves the necessity of disruption and grief

Man in the Moon

when we suffer these events, for ignoring and denying ourselves this period of grieving and coming to terms will only make us out of rhythm with life.

As you follow the Moon through her three monthly faces and her thirteen lunar months of the year, you should be able to bring yourself into synchronization with the flow of the seasons and the rhythms of the Moon. By accomplishing this, you will find you are more at peace with yourself and those around you.

Endnotes

1. The three phases of the Moon correspond to the three faces of the Goddess. My book, *Maiden, Mother, Crone*, is entirely on this subject. It can be obtained through Llewellyn Publications.

Chapter 4
WOLF MOON
January

*Also called: Quiet Moon, Snow Moon, Cold Moon, Chaste Moon,
Disting Moon, Moon of Little Winter.*

The Full Moon of January honored Ch'ang-O, Chinese goddess of the
bedchamber and protector of children.

The New Year in China begins on the first day of the New Moon when the
Sun is in Aquarius. This can be as early as January 21 and no later than
February 19.

Jan. 1: Celebration of the Seven Deities of Luck in Japan and the goddess
Fortuna in Rome.

Jan. 2: The birth of the goddess Inanna in ancient Sumeria.

Jan. 5-6: Night-time ritual to honor Kore; held in the Koreion in Alexandria.
The fifth day of the first month was the birthday of the Chinese god of
wealth, Tsai Shen, or Ts'ai-Shen.

Jan. 6: Celtic day of the Three-Fold Goddesses: Maid, Mother, Crone.

Jan. 10: Day of Freyja, the Norse Mother Goddess.

Jan. 12: Besant Panchami, or Dawat Puja, the Festival of Sarasvati in India; or on the closest New Crescent Moon. In Rome, the Compitalia to celebrate the Lares, household gods.

Jan. 18: The Theogamia of Hera, a women's festival for all aspects of this goddess.

Jan. 20: In Bulgaria, the Baba Den, or Grandmother's Day for the goddess Baba Den, or Baba Yaga. In China, a day of the Kitchen God.

Jan. 24: In Hungary, the Blessing of the Candle of the Happy Women, a ceremony of purification honoring Fire goddesses.

Jan. 27: The Paganalia, a day of the Earth Mother in Rome.

*T*he word January comes from the Roman name for this month; it was named after the god Janus, who had two faces. This deity ruled over beginnings and endings, the past and the future. Since January is reckoned as the first month of a new year, this connection with the god Janus is appropriate. It is an excellent time to work on putting aside the old and outdated in one's personal life and making plans for new and better conditions.

The Chinese use this concept in celebrating their New Year, which occurs on the first day of the New Moon when the Sun is in Aquarius. They considered this celebration a time for settling debts, honoring ancestors, and having family reunions. They carry paper images of dragons through the streets and set off fireworks to chase away evil entities and misfortune.

Tsao-Wang was the Chinese kitchen god or deity of the hearth and domestic comfort; his picture hung above the stove. He was the protector of the family and recorder of their actions and words. His report at the end of each year to the Heavenly Jade Emperor was said to determine the family's coming fortune. Because of this, the Chinese burned the old picture-image and put up a new one a few days before New Year. His wife had the task of reporting on female family members.

Even the people of Tibet, whose year began about the end of January, had a celebration for expelling the Old Year. They made a dough image for the demons to inhabit, then worshipped them for seven days. At the end of that period, they took the image outside the village to a crossroad and abandoned it. The idea behind this seems to have been that the negative beings, who had accumulated during the Old Year, received recognition for their existence, but also received a firm statement, by the action of leaving their image outside the village, that they were not welcome to hang around.

Most cultures had some ceremony for ending an old cycle of the calendar and celebrating the beginning of a new cycle. Physical activity acknowledging the end and beginning of cycles sets off similar changes in the subconscious mind. This change in the subconscious is necessary in order for actual physical changes to come about. Such rituals are helpful when one faces the end of cycles in relationships, career, residence, or other life situations.

During the Feast of Kore, which was held at night with much feasting and dramatics, a group of initiates bearing torches went down into the goddess's underground chamber. With much ceremony and reverence, they brought out the wooden statue of Kore, naked except for her golden jewelry. The statue was placed on a decorated litter and carried seven times around the temple. The Greeks considered that the number seven brought luck and success.

The Incan festival of Camay Quilla was held at the New Moon.

The Seven Deities of Luck in Japan were honored during a three-day festival called San-ga-nichi. To avoid good luck being swept away, there was no sweeping during this festival. These Seven Deities are also called Shichi Fukujin or Shichi-Kukujin, which means "Seven Gods of Happiness." There are six gods and one goddess that make up this little group: Ebisu, patron of work; Daikoku, god of prosperity; Benzaiten or Benton, goddess of love, music, eloquence, fine arts; Bishamonten, god of happiness and war; Fukurokuju, god of happiness and long life; Jurojin, god of happiness and long life; Hotei Osho, god of good fortune. They sail about in a treasure ship called a *takarabune*.

Tsai Shen, the Chinese god of wealth, is said to rule over money and wealth in general. A number of Moon symbols are connected with him, such as the bat, frog, and the number three.

Correspondences

Nature Spirits: gnomes, brownies

Herbs: marjoram, holy thistle, nuts and cones

Colors: brilliant white, blue-violet, black

Flowers: snowdrop, crocus

Scents: musk, mimosa

Stones: garnet, onyx, jet, chrysoprase

Trees: birch

Animals: fox, coyote

Birds: pheasant, blue jay

Deities: Freyja, Inanna, Sarasvati, Hera, Ch'ang-O, Sinn

Power Flow: sluggish, below the surface; beginning and conceiving. Protection, reversing spells. Conserving energy by working on personal problems that involve no one else. Getting your various bodies to work smoothly together for the same goals.

Old Sayings & Lore

- Whatever the weather is like the first twelve days of January indicates what the weather will be like for the next twelve solar months. Each day equals one month in succession.

- To wish on the Moon in order to see a specific person soon, say while looking at the Moon:

    I see the Moon, the Moon sees me.
    The Moon sees (name of person) who I want to see.

- To get rid of warts, take a slice of apple. While looking at the New Moon, rub the flesh side of the apple against your wart and say:

    What I see is growing,
    What I rub is going.

    Bury the piece of apple or throw it away. As it rots, the wart will disappear.

- If a New Moon falls on a Saturday, it was said there would be twenty days of wind and rain.

- In prophesying marriage, one must look at the first Moon of the new year through a silk handkerchief. The number of Moons showing through it represent the number of months (Moons) of single life.

Recipes

Indian Spiced Tea

The people of India like spices in their tea, not only for the taste, but for the body heat they create in cold weather. They also like milk in their tea; if you feel the need to be very authentic, add one cup of low fat milk during the last simmering process. A very good beverage to serve after a ritual or celebration. Serves six.

7	cups cold water	1	¼"-piece fresh ginger root, peeled and chopped
6	green cardamom pods		
1	cinnamon stick	¼	cup light brown sugar or honey
6	cloves	2	tablespoons black tea leaves

In a large pot, bring the water to a boil. Stir in the spices and brown sugar. Boil gently for five minutes. Turn off the heat, cover the pot with a lid, and let the mixture steep for ten minutes. Add the tea leaves and bring to a boil. Lower the heat, cover the pot, and simmer for another five minutes. Strain the tea and serve.

Herb Mustard

One of the delightful ways to use herbs everyday is in your cooking. Since I am usually a very busy person, most of my personal recipes have been altered to use mixes and prepared foods. This recipe not only makes a great addition to your personal recipe collection, it can also be an unusual but welcome gift. It uses the standard summer condiment yellow mustard. The amount of herbs can be adjusted to suit individual taste.

2 cups prepared mustard	1 teaspoon dried oregano leaves, crumbled
¼ cup parsley flakes, crumbled	1 teaspoon dried basil leaves, crumbled
½ teaspoon dried tarragon leaves, crumbled	1 teaspoon dried dill weed
	¼ cup cider vinegar

Pour the mustard into a large bowl. Add the dried herbs and mix thoroughly. Gradually stir in the vinegar. Put in a covered jar and refrigerate for two to three days before using. NOTE: Several recipes in this book call for Herb Mustard.

Deviled Egg Sandwich Spread

Trying to come up with casual lunches for guests and family can sometimes be frustrating. This spread is tasty in regular sandwiches, on toast squares, or on English muffins. It can be made ahead, wrapped, and ready to eat at the end of ritual. Makes 2 cups of spread mix.

4 hard-cooked eggs, chopped	¼ teaspoon pepper
½ cup finely chopped celery	¼ teaspoon dried basil leaves, finely crumbled
2 tablespoons Herb Mustard	2 tablespoons mayonnaise
¼ teaspoon salt	

Blend the ingredients together thoroughly and chill.

Crafts

Basic Potpourri Spice Mix

½ oz. broken cloves
½ oz. crushed gum benzoin
½ oz. powdered orris root.
½ oz. powdered allspice,
    with a few whole berries

½ oz. powdered mace
½ oz. whole coriander seeds
½ oz. cinnamon stick crushed
    or cinnamon powder

Lightly mix together the above ingredients to make the spice mix. Choose a pretty jar with a lid to hold your potpourri. Into the jar place a layer of dried flower petals, such as rose, lavender, lemon verbena, or tiny rose buds. Over each layer sprinkle some of the spice mix. Continue layering and sprinkling until the jar is filled. To freshen a room, simply remove the jar's lid.

Shaman Bath Salts

1 cup salt
3 drops verbena oil

8 drops rose oil
2 drops cedar oil

Aura of Venus Bath Salts

— For Love Spells —

1 cup salt
4 drops rose oil
4 drops synthetic musk oil

8 drops jasmine oil
4 drops lavender oil
4 drops frangipani oil

Cernunnos Bath Salts

1 cup salt
6 drops amber oil
4 drops patchouli oil
3 drops rose geranium oil

8 drops synthetic musk oil
8 drops synthetic ambergris oil
2 drops pine oil
2 drops clove oil

Pan Bath Salts

1 cup salt
2 drops cedar oil
4 drops juniper oil or
    ¼ teaspoon juniper tincture

2 drops pine oil
8 drops patchouli oil
3 drops vervain oil

Satyr Bath Salts

1 cup salt	8 drops patchouli oil
4 drops carnation oil	8 drops vanilla oil
4 drops synthetic musk oil	2 drops cinnamon oil

Moon Magick Bath Salts

1 cup salt	⅛ teaspoon powdered orris root
8 drops sandalwood oil	8 drops lotus oil

To make the bath salts in this chapter and throughout the rest of the book, lightly mix together the ingredients indicated and place them in a pretty jar for storage. NOTE: Never ingest essential oils.

Myths

Freyja and Seidr Magick

In the ancient Norse myths, the best known of all the goddesses was the independent, beautiful Freyja. Unfortunately, not many stories of her have survived. This may be because of the Christian-influenced scholars who recorded the myths; these men would have been fiercely against any excessive recording of Freyja, goddess of divination and sexual independence. Although Freyja is not called a Moon goddess, many of her attributes connect her with both the Full and Dark Moons.

There are several facts we can deduce from the preserved myths. Freyja was the sister of Freyr and the daughter of the sea god Njord by his unnamed sister, possibly Nerthus. A Vana-Goddess, she was at one time married to the mysterious god Od, or Odr, who disappeared. For him she wept tears of gold; tradition says that the tears which fell into the sea became amber. Except for this one vague mention of a husband, Freyja is never paired to any other god as "wife."

Her cats pulled her chariot in battle, thus making her mistress of cats, the same title given to the Egyptian Bast and the Greek Artemis. In addition Freyja was the leader of the Valkyries and a shape-shifter, the Sage or "sayer" who inspired all sacred poetry. Wise women, seeresses, rune-mistresses, and healers were closely connected with Freyja, as she was the goddess of magick, witchcraft, and love affairs.

Freyja's form of magick was shamanistic in nature, as represented by her falcon-skin dress or cloak which enabled her to shape-shift into a bird, travel to any of the worlds, and return with prophecies. Loki borrowed this falcon skin on several occasions, usually to spy on people and cause trouble. Present-day shamans still count this astral traveling ability as necessary in order to predict the future and gain knowledge. Among the Norse people, this magickal ability, given by Freyja, was called seidr.

Seidr was a form of magick, trance, and divination that was primarily a feminine mystical craft. Although tradition says that the runes originated with Freyja, and were used by her priestesses, the major portion of seidr was the practice of shapeshifting, astral body travel through the Nine Worlds, sex magick, healing, cursing, and other techniques. The female practitioners, called volvas and sometimes seidkona, were priestesses of Freyja. They were consulted on all types of problems. In the *Elder Edda,* three poems, "Voluspa," "Baldrs Draumar," and "Svipdagsmal," are accounts of deceased volvas being called upon to give knowledge to the gods or protection to humans.

Women were not the exclusive workers of Freyja's seidr. There are hints in the poems and prose that at one time seidr was also practiced by men wearing women's clothing. Odhinn, for instance, is the only male god listed in the myths as having practiced this type of magick; he was taught by Freyja herself. However, this was not a popular male occupation and those practicing it were ridiculed and some killed. Cross-dressing is a very ancient tradition that has its roots in the belief that a man had to spiritually become a woman in order to serve the Goddess. This would not have been well received in a patriarchal society.

The female volvas went freely from one clan to another; their skills were in high demand. They did not tend to marry, although they did take lovers. These women carried staffs with a bronze cap or mounting and wore capes, hoods, and gloves of fur. In *Eiriks Saga* there is a very detailed account of seidr practiced by a volva. There is another story in *Landnamabok* telling of a volva who actively brought prosperity to the fishing activity of the people through her use of seidr.

Shamanism requires knowledge of the four Elements which influence every aspect of life and how to use them. The story of how Freyja obtained her famous necklace Brisingamen from four dwarves is really a tale of learning how to use the four Elements.

As Freyja was out walking one day, she came across four dwarves who were crafting a most beautiful necklace. These smiths, called the Brisings, were named Alfrigg, Dvalin, Berling, and Grerr. Freyja decided that she must have the necklace, but the dwarves wouldn't sell. They would, however, give it to her if she spent a night with each one of them. Without hesitation, Freyja did just that and became the owner of Brisingamen, a powerful balance to the Midgard Serpent and a symbol of fertility. These attributes correspond to the Full Moon.

Since the Christian monks took this to be a story of loose morals, it's a wonder it was left in the Norse myths. It isn't a story of sex, however, but one of gaining magickal knowledge (something considered just as evil by the monks). The four dwarves represent the four Elements. Brisingamen symbolizes the beauty, power, and richness that come from knowing how to correctly use and balance these building blocks of matter.

Odhinn's jealousy and anger over this piece of jewelry and how Freyja obtained it caused him to order Loki to steal the necklace. In order to get it back, Freyja had to agree to a dark command of Odhinn: that she incite war between kings and great armies, then reincarnate the dead warriors to fight again. This aspect of the goddess, who was also known as leader of the Valkyries, connects her to the Dark Moon.

The Norse Mani

In the beginning of the world, Odhinn and his brothers killed the giant Ymir and made the Nine Worlds from his body. The myths say that great disks of fire sprayed out of Muspelheim, creating the Sun and the Moon. To the Norse, the Sun was female, the Moon male. These celestial bodies had no fixed courses until the gods had the elf-smiths, the sons of Ivalde, make chariots of fine gold to pull them across the heavens.

The giant Mundilfore, who took care of the World-Mill, considered himself a rival of Odhinn. Mundilfore named his two beautiful children Mani (Moon) and Sol (Sun). His boasting about these children caused the gods to take them from him. They made the girl Sol drive the chariot of the Sun, while they made the boy Mani drive the chariot of the Moon.

The handsome Mani grew lonely in his home on the Moon. One night he saw two children go to the well or fountain of Byrgir ("the hidden"), which sprang from Mimir's well. They had been sent by their father Vidfinn to draw a bucket of song-mead. The boy Hjuki and the girl Bil filled the bucket and put it on a pole to carry home up the mountain. As they trudged up the hill, Mani snatched them away to his home on the Moon. Our nursery rhyme about Jack and Jill comes from this myth.

The Norse said that the spots seen on the face of the Moon are Hjuki and Bil, their water bucket and pole. The skalds invoked the girl Bil to sprinkle the magick song-mead on their lips, so they would be eloquent and skilled.

The Moon god Mani is said to regulate Nyi (the New or Crescent Moon) and Nithi (the waning or Dark Moon).

The Norse god Odhinn on his throne in Asgard, the divine world

Blodeuwedd of Wales

The Welsh goddess Blodeuwedd was known as the Ninefold Goddess of the Western Isles of Paradise, a connection with both the Moon (nine is a Moon number) and death and reincarnation (aspects of the Dark Moon). Robert Graves writes that Blodeuwedd had nine powers; nine is also a multiple of three, a Goddess and Moon number. Owls were sacred to Blodeuwedd. She dealt with lunar mysteries and mystical initiations.

Welsh myth says that Blodeuwedd was created from blossoms of the oak, the broom, and meadowsweet by Gwydion and Math as a wife for their nephew, the young god Lleu. Her name actually means "flower-face." However, after a time Blodeuwedd lost interest in Lleu and fell in love with the dark hunting god of the forest. When she asked Lleu how he could be killed, he told her. She told her lover, the hunting god, who killed him. However, Lleu's uncles resurrected him. Lleu in turn killed his rival. Gwydion changed Blodeuwedd into an owl, a bird that prefers the night and hunts by light of the Moon.

The owl, also a creature of Athene and other Moon goddesses, is a symbol for wisdom and lunar mysteries. To fly at night is to understand and use the powers of the Moon.

Andraste of Britain

Little is known of the goddess Andraste, except that she was worshipped by Queen Boadicea, the British warrior-queen who nearly overthrew the conquering Roman legions. We know that Andraste was connected with the Moon, for the hare or rabbit was sacred to her. History says that just before Boadicea's last battle with the Romans, the queen loosed a hare and watched its running pattern as a method of divination (divining from the actions of animals was used in a great many cultures besides the Celts). There is no record of what Boadicea thought she saw in the movements of the hare. History records that she led her armies in a massive assault against the trained Roman legions and nearly defeated Roman rule in Britain. When captured, the Queen took poison, thereby defeating Roman plans to march her in a victory parade in Rome.

A possible later version of Andraste may be Eostre, who was also connected with hares and eggs and the Spring Equinox.

Rituals

Good Fortune & Change of Luck

On January 1, the Seven Deities of Luck were honored in Japan, as was the goddess Fortuna in Rome. The only way to have good fortune, though, is to change your luck from bad or mediocre to good. Changing your luck is sometimes the only way to obtain prosperity. The same goes for maintaining your health.

This spellworking is best done on the night of a Full Moon. You will need several candles for this spell: an astral candle to represent yourself; an orange to represent sudden change; a silver or light gray to represent neutralization of the bad luck; a black to represent the bad luck itself; and a magenta to hurry the luck-changing process.

One of the Seven Dieties of Luck

Anoint the candles with a good purification or blessing oil, such as lotus, and set them in holders on a safe surface. Anoint the black candle from the end to the wick; by this action you are moving bad luck away from you. Anoint the others from the wick to the end; this brings in what you desire. The candles will be allowed to burn completely out, so be sure that you can leave them safely.

Light the astral candle representing yourself, and say:

This is me, everything that represents me.

Light the black candle, and say:

This is my bad luck. It now leaves me. I shed no tears over the parting.

Light the gray candle, and say:

This will neutralize any remnants of bad luck. They will dissolve into nothingness.

Light the orange candle, and say:

This represents the changes for good that are coming into my life. I welcome them with open arms.

Light the magenta candle, and say:

This is the astral energy that I need to speed up the change.

Now sit for several minutes, repeating to yourself:

I welcome change. I welcome the incoming good.

Leave the candles to burn out completely. Dispose of the wax afterward.

You may find that certain friends will drop away after this ritual. This merely indicates that the friendship was not to your good. Be prepared to release whatever moves out of your life.

Household Protectors

January twelfth was the Compitalia in Rome, when the Lares were honored for their help. The Lares were the household gods said to reside with each family as a type of protection.

Everyone has a protector, individual and family-collective. If you think you don't get help from yours, perhaps you should consider giving them a little attention and praise. Some Pagans provide a statue, bowl of stones, or other focal object as a habitation for the family protectors.

One of our household protectors resides in a statue of a Chinese watchdog, given to us by friends. The other lives in a Buddha statue found in a little shop that moved to parts unknown soon afterwards. Children are fascinated by both statues, but we learned that the protectors have their own methods of protecting themselves. One little fellow confided to me that the "Buddha bit me." Since neither statue is metal, this rules out static electricity.

I have had a yearly ritual in praise of our household protectors for some time. I usually include it as part of one of our regular monthly rituals, but it could be done separately.

Perform this ritual during the waxing Moon. Gather the following items on your tray or altar. Choose an incense that reminds you of herbs, forests, and green growing things. Put a green candle in a holder, and lay your wand beside it.

Decorate the immediate area around your symbol of your guardian with pine cones, small statues of deer or other forest animals, ivy, holly, or something similar. Although having real holly, etc., is nice, it is not absolutely essential. There are very nice artificial substitutes that can be used, then kept to use for other rituals. Clean the guardian symbol so that there is no dust or dirt on it. If the symbol is small enough, set it on the altar; if not, place it close by.

This rite could be considered a kind of birthday party, so feel free to include food and drink as part of it.

Light the incense and candle. Stand before your altar and say:

> *Guardian spirits, I invite you to join me here at this altar.*
> *You are my friends, and I wish to thank you.*

Take the incense and circle the guardian symbol three times, moving clockwise.

> *I thank you for the atmosphere you help to keep clean*
> *and pleasant in this home.*

Move the candle clockwise around the symbol three times.

> *I thank you for the light you send to purify and dispel the darkness.*

With the wand in your power hand, encircle the symbol again three times clockwise.

> *I ask for your continued help and protection for me, my family, my pets,*
> *and my property. I ask that you drive away trouble-makers, thieves, and*
> *others, physical and non-physical, who are bent on evil disruptive purposes.*
> *I thank you for your friendship and love.*

Stand with your arms upraised. Say:

> *Lovely Goddess, Lord of the Greenwood, I present to you the guardian of*
> *this house, the special spirit I have invited into my home. I honor this*
> *guardian in this symbol of its being. Bless this guardian. And to your bless-*
> *ings, I add my thanks for its protection and friendship.*

If you have more than one guardian, change all the "its" to "their" and so on. Spend a few moments lovingly caressing the symbol, mentally expressing that the guardian is important to you.

If you have provided food and drink, invite your guardian friends to party with you. Talk with them, being sensitive to feathery caresses and mental whispers. When you are finished, thank them for their presence at your ritual.

Crescent Moon during The Wolf Moon (handwritten)

Festival of Sarasvati
—Crescent Moon—

The Besant Panchami, sometimes called the Dawat Puja, is the Festival of Sarasvati in India. Sarasvati is the goddess of learning, writing, and account books. She is also a river goddess who pours forth a flood of energy. She is pictured as a beautiful woman dressed in white; on her forehead is the Crescent Moon. She rules over the arts of civilization, such as music, mathematics, the alphabet, calendars, magick, the Vedas, and of course all branching of learning.

In India they begin this festival by cleaning up the inkstand and pens. In the modern age of typewriters and computers, one should clean and dust electronic instruments thoroughly. In fact, cleaning your entire writing space, dusting all your books, and getting personal papers in order would fall into this category.

The Hindus perceive all of life as a participation in cosmic harmony. They consider that all actions are forms of divine worship; this is thought to be internal worship. In external worship, their rituals consist of sounds, rhythms, gestures, flowers, light, incense, and offerings, all of which help to direct the mind away from the physical and toward the spiritual. This is said to draw the desired deity nearer. Individual worship is called puja. Ritual is considered necessary in order to establish and maintain contact with a particular deity.

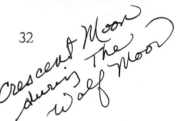

To honor Sarasvati, clean your writing space and instruments. Get fresh flowers, or if unable to obtain these, at least have a nice bouquet of silk ones. Arrange these in a vase or nice glass. Have ready sandalwood or lotus incense; sticks will work just fine. Set out a clean piece of paper and a pen, and a white candle in a fireproof holder.

Take a leisurely bath, and anoint yourself with your favorite perfume or aftershave. Go to your worship place dressed in a nice robe or nude. Don't slouch in wearing some worn old bathrobe and your hair uncombed! You are going to be talking with a goddess.

For an altar you can use whatever you already have, or you can set up a tray large enough to hold your equipment. Arrange the vase of flowers; a statue or picture of Sarasvati (if you are fortunate enough to have one), or at least her name written nicely on a card; the paper and pen; the candle; and the incense on the tray. Play a recording of Indian music or some music that reminds you of India.

Light the incense and gently, using your hands, wave its fragrance over the altar and yourself. Light the candle. Sit or stand before your altar and begin to intone the "OM" used by the Hindus. Chant the OM until you feel its power vibrating through your body and mind.

Put your hands together as in prayer and bow[1] toward the statue, touching the tips of your fingers against your forehead. Do this three times. Say:

> *I stand at the center of this spiritual universe,*
> *Within the heart of the sacred mandala.*
> *Gentle Sarasvati, I come to you for aid and blessings.*

Now write out what you wish to accomplish, what aid you need to make a new project successful. Remember, Sarasvati helps with the creative arts, science, music, poetry, learning, and teaching. She also helps with account books, but not necessarily the work end of business itself. She gives inspiration, diligence, and knowledge, all necessary ingredients to success.

Place the paper on your altar before the statue. Sit for a short meditation, keeping yourself open to any inner voices that may bring suggestions. Visualize the thin Crescent Moon in the night sky, the same crescent that adorns the brow of Sarasvati. If nothing comes at this time, don't despair. She will send something later, perhaps in a dream.

Chant the OM again. Bow with clasped hands toward the statue and say:

> *Beautiful Sarasvati, goddess of light and inspiration,*
> *Reveal to me the knowledge I need.*
> *Grant my requests in a manner that benefits me.*
> *Thank you, lovely goddess.*

Leave the altar set up, and let the candle burn out by itself. The next day go back to the altar and light more incense. After chanting the OM and meditating briefly, burn your paper in a metal bowl or cauldron. When the ashes are cold, scatter them outside.

Ritual for the Protection of Battered Women & Children
—Full Moon—

This was a time of a Chinese Moon festival for Ch'ang-O, who was honored for her rule over the bedchamber and who was considered a protector of children. Since the Moon's energy flow in this month is one of ending old cycles and planning new ones, communication with Ch'ang-O is appropriate. After all, when she was threatened by a dictatorial, physically-aggressive husband because she drank his magickal potion, she cut off her old life and went to the Moon to begin another one.

Ch'ang-O, sometimes called Heng-O, was offered Crescent Moon cakes called Yue-ping during her festivals. Her palace on the Moon was known as the Great Cold.

The designs on the face of the Moon are said to be the form of Hare, who took Ch'ang-O to that celestial body to escape her rampaging husband. Therefore, hares were sacred to her, as were toads, both symbols of fertility.

The week preceding the Full Moon of Wolf month, spend as much time as necessary contemplating needed changes in your life. If you find nothing of great consequence that needs to be changed, choose instead a social wrong that needs to be corrected, such as children's rights, medical care for all, the homeless, women's shelters. Ch'ang-O primarily is concerned with people issues, particularly those of women and children. When you go to your altar, have a special desire in mind, one that really means something to you. Remember, no concern or emotion, no results. Simple enough. The trick is to release those emotions at the end of the ritual. As an example, I will use the theme of shelters for battered women in this ritual.

Set up your altar with a central white candle; sandalwood incense; a round mirror; a white bowl with some salt; a glass or goblet with a little water; a wand or willow twig; a white bowl containing round, white cookies; a glass of a pale beverage. Place four white candles in holders around your ritual area, one marking each cardinal direction. Be sure that you leave ample room to move about without running the risk of setting your robe on fire!

Stand before your altar and breathe deeply, centering your mind on the reason for this ritual. Visualize the Full Moon above you; breathe its white light down inside your body. Feel its tingling energy spreading out from your lungs into your blood, your bones, your flesh. When you feel ready, say:

> *The Moon arises! The Goddess draws near!*
> *Her powerful presence is with me!*

Hold your power hand over the salt:

> *Blessed be this salt.*

Move your hand over the glass of water:

> *Blessed be this water.*

Add a pinch of salt to the water and swirl the glass three times clockwise. Hold the glass up toward the visualized Moon.

> *Cold fire of the Moon, purify this altar with your power.*

Sprinkle a few drops at each corner of the altar. Then, moving clockwise, sprinkle around the edges of your ritual area. Replace the glass on the altar.

Light the white altar candle, saying:

Beloved Moon, lamp of the night, let this be a symbol of your light.

Using the altar candle and beginning in the east, light each perimeter candle, saying:

Behold, the Lady's light appears to guide Her children.

Replace the candle on the altar, and take up the round mirror. Begin in the east and move clockwise around the area. Hold the mirror at heart level, reflecting surface pointing outward.

Lands and people of the East, heed my desire.
Let there be freedom for your women!

Move to the south:

Lands and people of the South, hear my words.
Give your women respect!

Move to the west:

Lands and people of the West, listen to my warning.
Grant your women equality!

Stand facing the north:

Lands and people of the North, be aware.
Protect your women and give them safety!

Return to the altar and turn the mirror so you see your own face reflected in it. Look deeply into your own eyes. Feel the indignity deep within you that demands that this problem be solved.

I am a daughter/son of the Moon Goddess, She who sees all. My heart weeps with Her over the injustices we do to each other, especially to women and children. I call upon the Goddess of the Moon to aid these women and little ones. Shelter them with Your hands, Lady. Guide them with Your wisdom. Lead them out of terror and pain and darkness into Your Light!

Lay aside the mirror. Close your eyes and reach skyward. Let your body be a pipeline for the healing, balancing energy of the Moon Goddess. Let this energy flow down through you into the Earth. Feel it soak through your feet, right down through the floor and into the ground.

When you feel the timing is right, open your eyes and look about your lighted ritual area. If you can, without having some nosy neighbor calling the police, shout:

> *Freedom! Protection! Equality! Respect! Safety!*

Put all your feelings into these words. Shout them as long as you need to release your emotions.

When you feel pleasantly exhausted, the intense emotions gone, do something that makes you feel happy about what you have done: laugh, sing, dance, whatever. Then eat your Moon cookies and drink your Moon beverage. This is a good time to quietly commune with the Moon and the Goddess on a more personal level.

When you wish to close your ritual, go to the perimeter candles, beginning with the east and moving clockwise. As you extinguish each candle, say:

> *Carry my message to all people.*
> *Let the Moon's light open their eyes to truth and justice.*

Stand once more before the altar and raise your arms skyward.

> *Lovely Lady of the Moon, bless and purify me with Your Light.*
> *Thank you for empowering me this night.*

Throw a kiss up to the Moon. Extinguish the altar candle.

Dark Moon Meditation

In Bulgaria, on January 20, they held the Baba Den, or Grandmother's Day, for the goddess Baba Yaga, sometimes called Baba Den. Baba Yaga was a Slavonic goddess described as a tall, gaunt hag with dishevelled hair. They said she ate humans and built her revolving house and stockade out of their bones. Her ally was a snake called Zmei Gorynich.

The revolving house may well be a metaphor for the Moon which seems to turn through its phases. The hag[2] goddesses were almost always connected in some manner with the Dark Moon. The snake, a lunar and goddess creature, symbolized immortality through reincarnation. To be eaten is another way of saying that one dies to an old way of life. To begin a new life or rebuild, one first must get to the bare bones of one's actual being. When you learn who you really are, underneath the facade you have built around yourself, then you have all the power you need to rebuild and reform your life.

Dark Moon rituals are more intense, often more physically draining, than other rituals. You are dealing with a type of energy that most people are not used to handling. However, it is important to spiritual growth that you understand the Dark Moon and the deities connected with it. The Hindus say of the goddess Kali that if one cannot accept, understand, and love her, as the Crone aspect of the Goddess, then one cannot truly accept, understand, and love the Maiden and Mother aspects. The same applies to the God aspects, which are the Light-Bringer, the Lord of Fertility, and the Dark God of the Wild Hunt.

Baba Yaga

The Maiden and the Light-Bringer correspond to the Crescent Moon; the Mother and the Lord of Fertility to the Full Moon; and the Crone and the Dark God of the Wild Hunt to the Dark Moon. The three phases of the Moon and the three aspects of deity are all part of a cycle, a cycle that is repeated in human life and spiritual growth.

The deities of the Dark Moon never seek us; we must seek them. They dwell in the black void beyond the Full Moon deities, a place that can be frightening and exhilarating at the same time.

You should have definite personal goals in mind when seeking these Dark Moon deities, for they tolerate no frivolous wanderers in their realm. And understand before you seek them that their solutions to problems may not be accomplished in a gentle manner. Oftentimes we find relationships and friendships swiftly ended, ongoing problems solved in unusual ways, our personal lives turned upside-down and reformed. Communing with the Dark Moon deities is not a path for the timid or indecisive.

The Dark Moon tears down in order to rebuild. She is the third of the trio of Fates who cuts the thread of life to its karmic length; She balances the scales of justice and karma regardless of how long it takes. Without the Dark Moon and Her deities, we cannot learn the deepest of spiritual mysteries, we cannot truly know ourselves or gain any semblance of control over or order in our lives.

This ritual-meditation of cleansing and renewing should be done during the dark of the Moon when there is not even a sliver of light showing. For maximum effect, it is best to repeat it for three nights. To be certain that you are timing this ritual correctly, check with a good astrological calendar and begin on the night of the Dark Moon.

You will need a black candle in a holder; patchouli incense; a black or dark colored hooded robe, or at least a large towel or scarf to drape over your head. Choose music (instrumental) which is slow and heavy, yet pleasant to listen to: music that will help you to sink deep within yourself. If you know how to use the sound of a drum to reach the deep realms of meditation, you might want to either use a drum or a drumming tape.

The day of this ritual, eat lightly and take special note of your emotions. Take a cleansing bath and dress in a dark robe. Avoid speaking to anyone between the time you take the bath and the time you begin the ritual. You may be meditating for some time so bring a chair or comfortable cushions for sitting before your altar.

Light the incense and carry it counter-clockwise around the entire room. Counter-clockwise, widdershins, or against the Sun is the path of the Dark Moon, the spiraling down into the cauldron of rebirth, the unwinding of formed matter so that it can be reformed into a new shape. Place it on your altar when you are finished.

Light the black candle and carry it around the room in a counter-clockwise path also. Replace the candle on the altar. Turn out the lights, leaving only the candle for illumination. Sit before your altar and pull up the hood or drape the towel over your head so that much of the view of the room is hidden. Don't wrap anything around your face as you don't want your breathing restricted in any way.

Start the music or begin drumming. Close your eyes, and let your thoughts sink deep down inside yourself. Relax your body. Don't push to reach your inner paths, but relax and let your thoughts sink downward into the inner darkness.

Visualize yourself standing in a dimly-lit tunnel carved entirely out of rock. The path underfoot has been worn smooth by the feet of seekers who have gone before you. The walls are rough and set at intervals with glowing lamps. You hear chanting in the distance and move toward the sound.

After many twists and turns of the tunnel, you find yourself at the entrance to a vast cavern. The ceiling and the far walls are shrouded in shadow. In the center of the cavern is a huge cauldron, with tall candles lining a path toward it. Behind the cauldron is a throne carved out of glistening black stone. On this throne sits a silent figure wearing a black robe, the hood pulled far forward over the face. The pale hands hold a gleaming sword. One white hand beckons you to come forward.

You pass between the lines of candles until you stand before the cauldron. The figure opposite you rises and lets the hood slide back, revealing the strong face. Waves of great power emanate from this deity. The eyes are deep-set pools of darkness that see through to your true being. Nothing can be hidden from this Dark Moon deity.

When you are asked, and you will be asked, you can explain why you have come to this realm and before this powerful deity. Explain exactly what you want changed in your life, why you are dissatisfied or unhappy with things as they are. But don't detail how you want the changes to be done! Be ready to accept however the Dark Moon deity brings about the changes.

Listen closely to anything that is said to you. You may well be asked to step into the cauldron. This is a major spiritual experience so be certain you are prepared to undergo what will happen. The cauldron experience differs from person to person and is very personal. If you decide to enter the cauldron, the Dark Moon deity will likely touch your heart with the sword, then take your hand to help you enter and again take your hand to help you come back out.

What each person experiences in the cauldron is different. You may undergo initiation, see visions of the future, and/or even see your physical form melted away to the bare bones, then reformed. You may relive old happenings, a forced viewing to make you understand what you did wrong and how to avoid the same thing in the future. Some experiences, such as loss of loved ones and pets, will be very emotional for you, but necessary. Most of the time these loss-experiences are immediately followed by contact with the loved one or pet, to show you that nothing is totally destroyed and gone.

When you rise from the cauldron and stand once more in the cavern before the Dark Moon deity, you may be shown symbols or objects that will have personal meaning to you. Some of these symbols may not be quite clear to you at this time, either in meaning or sight. Just accept them. Clarification will come later.

At last the Dark Moon deity salutes you with the shining sword and you feel yourself spiraling away through the darkness back to physical consciousness. You will probably find yourself taking deep gulps of air when you surface once more into this realm. The kingdom of the Dark Moon is vibrationally much different from this physical plane of existence. You may even be a little disoriented for a time.

Lower your hood or towel and look about the room. You may well see or feel the presence of supernatural beings who are there to help you assimilate what you saw and learned. Sit for a while longer, thinking about your experiences. Thank the Dark Moon deity for her/his help.

Pay close attention to your dreams through the rest of this Moon period, particularly until the next Full Moon. It is a good idea to write down all the dream details you can remember, as dream messages are primarily in symbols. A few, such as prophetic dreams, are literal.

Above all, you must be prepared to accept and flow with the changes that will come to your life. The Dark Moon deities break down and reform energies, lives, and goals. We cannot grow unless we allow change. Since we humans tend to be afraid of and dislike change, the Dark Moon deities often must perform drastic spiritual surgery to get us back on track. It is better to ask for the changes and be willing to work through them than to have them thrust upon us. Stubborn refusal only makes the necessary transitions that much harder.

After you have made several inner journeys to commune with the Dark Moon deity, you will find yourself better understanding and more at peace with your true being. Changes will always be difficult; that is human nature. But you will have a stronger sense of order within those changes.

Endnotes

1. This gesture and bow is not groveling. It is a form of respect to the goddess.
2. The word "hag" in many cultures seems to come from a similar word which means "holy."

Chapter 5
ICE MOON
February

Also called: Storm Moon, Horning Moon, Hunger Moon,
Wild Moon, Red & Cleansing Moon, Quickening Moon,
Solmonath (Sun Month), Big Winter Moon.

Feb. 1-3: The Lesser Eleusinian Mysteries in ancient Greece; a
celebration of the Returning Daughter: Demeter and Persephone,
Ceres and Proserpina.

Feb. 7: Day of Selene and other Moon goddesses.

Feb. 9: The Chingay Procession, the Singapore New Year, which is a
celebration of Kuan Yin and the promise of coming Spring.

Feb. 12: Festival of Diana, Divine Huntress (the Greek Artemis) in Rome.

Feb. 13-18: In Rome, the Parentalia and Feralia, a purification festival
honoring the goddesses Mania and Vesta; devoted to the ancestors,
peace, and love.

Feb. 14-15: In Rome, the Lupercalia, when women petitioned Juno-Lupa
for children. Also honored the god Faunus, an aspect of Pan.

Feb. 14-21: Aphrodite's Festival of Love in Rome.

Feb. 17: Fornacalia, or Feast of Ovens, in Rome.

Feb. 20: In Rome, the Day of Tacita (the silent goddess), who averts harmful gossip.

Feb. 21: Lantern Festival in China and Taiwan. Also a celebration of Kuan Yin; Full Moon.

Feb. 22: In Rome, the Carista, a day of family peace and accord.

Feb. 23: In Rome, the Terminalia in honor of Terminus, god of land boundaries.

Some say that the name of the month of February comes from the Roman goddess Februa, who was also known as Juno Februa. Others say that the name came from the god Februus, who was later identified with the Roman Pluto or Dis.

The month of February, truly a month of ice in many parts of the Northern Hemisphere, is a dormant time, when all activity and life appears to be low-key or below the surface movement. In both the Celtic and Roman cultures, it was a time of spiritual purification and initiation. The country of Tibet celebrated the conception of Buddha and the Feast of Flowers during this time of year.

February can be an ideal time for dedicating or re-dedicating oneself to whatever deity or deities one worships. It is also a wise practice to cleanse and purify yourself, your dwelling place, and even your property lines before the dedication. Purifying changes the vibrations by removing negative ones and inviting in positive ones. The month of January was a time of ending old cycles and preparing for new ones. February prepares the environment and the body, mind, and spirit for receptivity of new spiritual and life experiences.

Hatun-pucuy, or the Great Ripening, was celebrated among the Incas.

The Lesser Eleusinian Mysteries of Greece was also called the Festival of the Returning Daughter. This was a celebration of the Kore's return from the Underworld and the rebirth of earthly vegetation. This ceremony, unlike the Greater Eleusinian, was open to many people and was a time of initiation into the lower Mysteries. Initiation into the Lesser Eleusinian Mysteries was open to all free men and women who were not guilty of murder and similar crimes. All initiates were bound by an oath of silence so effective that the secrets of the Mysteries were never told. Today we know very little about the actual ceremonies, except what was performed in full public view.

Kuan Yin is the Great Goddess of the Oriental people. She has been known to offer her aid primarily to women and girls, but there is no reason why men cannot honor her and ask her help. She is said to guide lost travelers, protect from attack by humans or animals, bless a family with children, and heal. She is called the Compassionate and is revered for her wisdom and love. Oriental women offered oranges and spices before her statues.

The Roman Lupercalia festival was a time of purification and fertility. A priest of the god Pan signaled the beginning of the Lupercalia with sacrifices of a goat and a dog. The skins of these animals were made into whips which chosen young boys used to strike people, particularly barren

Kuan Yin

women. This was thought to bring good luck in conceiving and having a healthy baby. It is quite possible that our present Valentine's Day has seeds of its beginnings in this ritual.

The Roman Parentalia and Feralia celebrations were a time to honor the ancestors. It was a period of solemnity with no feasting or marriages; all the temples were closed. Houses were cleaned thoroughly and food offerings made to the spirits of the dead. The goddesses Mania and Vesta were honored with solemn rituals.

The priestesses of Vesta (the Vestal Virgins) were accorded great respect and trust. They kept the wills of the citizens of Rome and saw that they were properly fulfilled when the maker died. At a word or appearance of any Vestal, any condemned criminal was set free without question or argument.

Later in the month, the festival of Carista was held as a family celebration for peace and accord. This festival was also known as the Concordia. Concordia, or Caristia, was the goddess of harmony. It was a time for exchanging gifts with family members and resolving problems. Differences and feuds were not to be carried within the family beyond this date.

The Roman god Terminus was the deity of land boundaries. His festival was the Terminalia. Boundary stones marking the property lines were anointed and blessed by the head of the household. This ceremony is rather like the one honoring the household guardians, as the Nature spirits residing in the boundary stones were asked for protection and prosperity for the land and family. This ritual could be adapted for today by blessing the boundaries of your property, stones or not.

Correspondences

Nature Spirits: house faeries, both of the home itself and of house plants

Herbs: balm of Gilead, hyssop, myrrh, sage, spikenard

Colors: light blue, violet

Flowers: primrose

Scents: wisteria, heliotrope

Stones: amethyst, jasper, rock crystal

Trees: rowan, laurel, cedar

Animals: otter, unicorn

Birds: eagle, chickadee

Deities: Brigit, Juno, Kuan Yin, Diana, Demeter, Persephone, Aphrodite

Power Flow: energy working toward the surface; purification, growth, healing. Loving the self. Accepting responsibility for past errors, forgiving yourself, and making future plans.

Old Sayings & Lore

- A snowy February was said to bring a good spring, while a mild month meant stormy weather.

- To see the crescent Moon over the right shoulder was consider lucky, but seeing it over the left shoulder was unlucky.

- In Cornwall, if a boy was born during a waning Moon, they said that the next birth would be a girl.

- They said in Wales that if you moved from one house to another during the Crescent Moon you would have more than enough prosperity in your life.

- When anyone spoke of Mountains of the Moon, it simply meant white mountains. The Arabs call white horses "Moon-colored."

- Mt. Sinai was probably originally named after the Chaldean Moon god Sinn, which would make it another Moon mountain.

- In certain areas of England there was an expression that if a Dark Moon came on Christmas, a fine harvest year would follow. Other areas declared that a waxing or New Moon on Christmas portended a good year, but a waning Moon a hard year.

- In Italy they say that if the Moon changes on a Sunday, there will be a flood before the month is out.

Recipes

Savory Corn Muffins

These are great on a cold day, served with a soup or stew and sweetened with honey drizzled over them. For a different flavor, try adding ½ cup grated Longhorn cheese to the mixture before baking. Makes 8 muffins.

1   8½-ounce package corn muffin
    mix (about 1⅔ cups)
⅓   cup milk

1   egg
¼   teaspoon dried summer savory,
    finely crumbled

Combine the corn muffin mix, milk, egg, and savory. Mix until the dry ingredients are just moistened. Spoon into greased muffin tins, filling each half full. Bake at 400° F for 20 minutes.

Mulled Herb Wine

Although this recipe calls for grape juice, you can use wine instead, omitting the sherry. Great for an evening at home during cold weather. Serves four.

1   cup boiling water
⅛   teaspoon rosemary leaves,
    crushed
¼   teaspoon mint flakes,
    crushed

4-5   whole cloves
1   cup grape juice
1   cup dry cocktail sherry
1   stick of cinnamon

Pour the boiling water over the rosemary and mint; steep for 15 minutes. Add the cloves and continue to steep the mixture for another 15 minutes. Strain; mix this liquid with the grape juice and sherry in a pan. Place over low heat until hot. Strain, add the cinnamon stick, and serve hot.

Crafts

Heart Pincushion

Heart is 2½" deep and 3" across. Pattern can be enlarged.

2   pieces of felt
    Sewing thread and needle
2   lace flowers
    Tracing paper and pencil

    Polyester stuffing
4"   piece of narrow ribbon
2   colors embroidery thread

Heart Pincushion

Trace a heart pattern and cut out two of them in felt. On one piece embroider a line of running or decorative stitching about ¼" from the edge. With a contrasting color of thread, embroider another line of running stitches next to the first. Sew on the flowers, one in each rounded upper corner of the heart.

Stitch the two hearts together (embroidery on the outside) with tiny overhand stitches, leaving an opening for the stuffing. Stuff firmly, then sew up the opening. Fold the ribbon in half and stitch to the top center of the heart to make a loop.

Egyptian Oracle Bath Salts

1　cup salt
6　drops patchouli oil
2　drops cinnamon oil

3　drops acacia oil
8　drops sandalwood oil

High Priestess Bath Salts

1　cup salt
8　drops wisteria oil

8　drops lavender oil
4　drops rose oil

Crystal Temple Bath Salts

1　cup salt
4　drops frankincense oil
8　drops lotus oil

¼　teaspoon powdered orris root
4　drops sandalwood oil

Spirit Blessings Bath Salts

1　cup salt
8　drops violet oil
4　drops ylang ylang oil

8　drops wisteria oil
4　drops sandalwood oil

Druid Curse Bath Salts

1 cup salt
⅛ teaspoon dill weed
⅛ teaspoon ground hyssop
    or ¼ teaspoon hyssop tincture

4 drops myrrh oil
¼ teaspoon powdered galangal
2 drops anise oil

Cavern Treasures Bath Salts
—For Prosperity—

1 cup salt
8 drops myrrh oil
3 drops cinnamon oil

8 drops sandalwood oil
3 drops allspice oil

Gold Buddha Bath Salts
—For Prosperity—

1 cup salt
8 drops lotus oil
2 drops cinnamon oil

8 drops sandalwood oil
3 drops myrrh oil
2 drops allspice oil

Heart Sachet

Make a heart cut-out such as the one mentioned in the Heart Pincushion craft above. Instead of stuffing it with cotton or batting, fill it with the following mixture. Great for scenting stationery or drawers, or to hang in the closet. Unless otherwise stated, all flowers are dried.

Spicy Rose Sachet

2 ounces cornstarch
½ ounce powdered orris root
¼ teaspoon cinnamon

1 ounce talc
2 drops rose oil

Myths

Selene and Endymion

The Greek goddess Selene, sometimes called Mene, was the sister of Helios (the Sun) and Eos (the Dawn). She was one of the children of the Titans Hyperion and Theia (also called Tethys). Some sources list different parents. Although she began as a separate deity, Selene was later identified with Artemis and particularly the Roman Diana, who ruled over the Moon.

As a Moon Goddess, Selene was noted for her liaisons, with humans or gods, but she did not allow herself to become attached. When she became fascinated with the handsome shepherd Endymion, she began to shirk her nightly duty of guiding the Moon through the heavens. This came to the attention of the other gods, who became suspicious of Selene's unusual behavior. They noticed that Selene's chariot was often missing from its heavenly path. Night after night, the goddess sat beside the sleeping youth, gently kissing him and creeping into his dreams.

Finally Zeus decided that something had to be done. Selene was neglecting her duty and becoming excessively pale from her nightly rendezvous with the shepherd. Zeus called Endymion to him and gave the young man a choice: death in any manner he chose, or eternal sleep during which he would not age. Endymion chose to sleep.

It is said that in a Carian cave on Mount Latmos, Endymion still sleeps, and Selene still steals away from her nightly rounds to visit him. While Selene sits with her sleeping shepherd, the Moon begins to fade away until it is totally gone. When she returns to her duties, the Moon begins to grow again until it reaches Full. Even though Endymion sleeps and only sees the Moon Goddess in his dreams, tradition says she has borne him fifty daughters. The generic name of the bluebell, Endymion, shows its association with Selene's lover.

Endymion symbolizes the "sleeping" part of the human mind, the unidentifiable something that is influenced by the phases of the Moon, particularly in dreams. As Endymion created fifty daughters with Selene during his sleep, so we are fertilized with creative ideas during our receptive resting periods, whether this be in dreams, meditation, or daydreaming.

Diana the Huntress

The Roman Diana, similar in many ways to the Greek Artemis, was definitely a Moon Goddess, ruler of the wildwood and lady of beasts. She allowed no liberties with her person or favors. As the twin sister to Apollo (the Sun), she was a feminine balance to her brother. The twins were born on Mount Cynthus, on the island of Delos, to Latona by Jupiter.

Her ancient names in Crete and other surrounding countries were Britomartis and Dictynna. The herb dittany of Crete was sacred to her and was derived from the name

Diana as moon goddess from Jost Amman's
Kunstbüchlin, *published by Johann*
Feyerabend, Frankfurt, 1599

Dictynna. Other names under which she was known were Dione, Nemorensis, and Nemetona (Goddess of the Moon-grove). Before Zeus took over the oracle-shrine at Dodona, it belonged to Diana. At the woodland lake of Nemi in Italy there was a beautiful remote temple and sanctuary that were hers.

She was often pictured with a Crescent Moon on her forehead, clad in a short white tunic, armed with a bow, and surrounded by dogs and stags. The nymphs who ran at her side symbolized the carefree, eternally youthful part of the human mind and psyche.

When Diana showed her softer side by indulging in dancing and music, singing and playing the flute and lyre, she was accompanied by the Muses and Graces. At this time the goddess was a gentle healer and willing to aid those she considered deserving of her favors.

Diana, known as Artemis among the Greeks, was said to protect the pure and innocent when they called upon her. If she could not protect them because of the interference of other deities, she at least established their innocence.

When Iphigenia, daughter of Agamemnon and Clytemnestra, was to be sacrificed at the altar of this goddess, the girl called upon Artemis and was answered. Such a sacrifice would have been abhorrent to the goddess, as she did not accept human sacrifice. In a temple full of men, with the priest's hand raised to strike her dead, Iphigenia disappeared. A slain deer lay in her place.

In another legend, the Greek hero-king Theseus brought his Cretan wife Phaedra to his palace. His grown son Hippolytus, son of Theseus and an Amazon, lived there also. Phaedra developed a consuming, unhealthy lust for Hippolytus, causing him no end of embarrassment and unhappiness. At last, in disgust the young man left the palace, rather than let his father know what was going on. Afraid that someone would betray her lust of Theseus, Phaedra wrote a condemning letter and killed herself. He believed the lies, cursing his son and banishing him. As Hippolytus drove off in his chariot along the sea road, a monster came out of the water and fatally wounded the young man. Artemis appeared to Theseus and told him the truth, then disappeared, taking the soul of Hippolytus with her.

Faunus of the Woodlands

Faunus was a Roman deity of the fields, woodlands, shepherds, and prophecy. In general appearance he somewhat resembles the Greek Pan, with his short horns, pointed ears, and hooved feet. Ancient descriptions say that Faunus had the legs and tail of a deer and the smooth-skinned body, arms, and face of a handsome youth. He is said to have invented the shawm, a kind of flute.

His followers, the fauns, were beautiful young men with tiny horns and pointed ears, but not necessarily the hooved feet. Unlike Pan and his followers, the fauns and Faunus were gentle creatures who liked to dance with the woodland nymphs. They were no threat to human women. Faunus plays the pipes and fills the woodlands and fields with his haunting music. He was a grandson of Saturn.

Another of his names was Lupercus; he was honored at the Lupercalia celebration when his priests performed the rites naked. This joint Lupercalia celebration with an aspect of the goddess Juno shows his strong connection with fertility of the land, animals, and humans. He is the very ancient, primal force that is necessary to fertilize and balance the Great Goddess.

Faunus

We humans need to honor the Faunus-Pan forces of the Earth and within ourselves, instead of accepting the shame that is currently attached to it. However, there was always a purpose behind the actions of Faunus; he did not indulge in uncontrolled sexual exploits simply for the purpose of seeing how many partners he could have. He did not squander his powers, but used them wisely and to good advantage. At the same time, Faunus saw the joy to be experienced in life, not only through sex but through music. He expresses this joy when a prepared seeker enters the inner realms searching for a spiritual initiation.

There was another side of Faunus, as there was to Pan. He could fill humans and animals with the dark, terrifying emotions of mindless panic when they trespassed uninvited into his special areas. He often fulfills this role when a seeker pushes into Otherworld realms for which they are unprepared. The blind panic and fear such a person feels will cause them to swiftly withdraw. These impressed emotions are created to protect seekers who would not understand or benefit from the mystical experiences, or who seek such experiences for the wrong reasons.

Rituals

Return of the Kore

When the Kore, or Maiden, returned from the Underworld, she was no longer the innocent girl who had wandered through the fields of her mother Demeter, picking flowers. She had not only undergone a spiritual transformation, taking into her care the departed and confused souls of humans, but had assumed another name: Persephone. Her return also heralded the physical first signs of Spring, a promise that Winter would not last forever.

We each experience, at some point in our lives, a feeling that we have been plunged into the Underworld and darkness. If we undergo a spiritual transformation, we can come back stronger than before. True, we are not the same as before, but then would we want to be? With the transformation comes a new focus in life, often differ-

Demeter

ent goals and responsibilities. We relate to the "dark" side of life in a totally unique manner after such an experience, understanding its value in the cyclical rhythm of Nature.

All humans undergo times of darkness, of feeling buried and hopeless, uncertain whether they will emerge once more into the light and happier times. Sometimes this is precipitated by disastrous personal events, such as death of a loved one, a financial crisis, or illness. Other times it is brought on by negative periods whose cause is unknown. These times of depression and despair can be brief or longer lasting. Either way they can be very difficult to endure.

The following ritual helps to begin the subconscious changes necessary for dissolution of these dark, unhappy feelings. The worst thing about such times is the helpless, hopeless feelings that seem to fill the mind and spirit, dragging you down on all levels of your life. When you are experiencing such a dark spell, it is not important why, but how you can reverse it.

Set out everything you will need before you begin: a white candle in a holder, a bell, patchouli incense, a blanket. Light the candle and leave it in the bathroom while you take a bath with some salt in the water. Concentrate on washing all negative vibrations away. These vibrations aren't physical, so you don't need to scrub; just soak, rinse, and relax.

Put on a special robe, or at least something that isn't an everyday garment. Take the candle in one hand and the bell in the other. Go clockwise around each room in your house, ringing the bell as you go. Also hold up the candle before each window, door, and mirror, then ring the bell. Chant as you go:

Darkness, flee this bell and light.
Enter balance. Be gone, night.

Now set the candle in a safe place nearby where you will perform the ritual. Light the incense and gently wave the smoke over your body. Lie down in a comfortable position and wrap yourself completely with the blanket, leaving your nose and mouth uncovered for unrestricted breathing. Close your eyes.

Feel yourself sinking deep into the Earth. Relax and let yourself go. As you sink deeper and deeper, pour out your unhappiness and depressed feelings to the Earth

Mother and the Lord of the Forest. Don't be surprised if you find yourself curled in a fetal position. You may also do a lot of crying, which in itself is a cleansing mechanism.

Now listen with your feelings. Let those feelings go beyond control of your conscious mind and reach that inner place where there is no explanation for hearing what you hear, feeling what you feel. Don't try to hear or feel anything specific; just let it happen. You will feel yourself bathed in the love and warmth of the Earth Mother and the Lord of the Forest. The darkness and depression inside you will start to melt away. A deep peace will begin to penetrate your body, mind, and spirit.

As you feel yourself moving into a position of positive thoughts and budding hope, begin to wiggle free of the blanket. Don't unwrap it or thrust it aside as you ordinarily would. Just wiggle slowly out, as if you were a baby being born. It will be difficult getting out, but it is symbolic of your rebirth.

Once out, slowly stretch your arms and legs. It isn't unusual to find yourself laughing or crying for joy. Thank the Goddess and God for their help: past, present, and future. Look at your surroundings with new eyes. Welcome the budding changes beginning within and around you, even though you have no proof yet that they are occurring.

Now, go do something that makes you feel happy. Anticipate the positive changes, small and large, that daily will enter your life.

Averting Harmful Gossip

Each year in February the Romans celebrated the Day of Tacita, the silent goddess who averted harmful gossip. Since malicious, negative gossip can destroy careers, marriages, and lives, one should consider petitioning Tacita for protection from such harm and ask her to help you avoid causing such harm to others.

You will need three candles (a black, a magenta, and a green) and holders for your altar. Burn a success incense, or wisteria or heliotrope. Have ready a little patchouli, mint, and rose oils.

If you are dealing with a specific gossiping person, carve his or her name in the black candle with a knife. If you don't know a name, carve "all gossip." Anoint the black candle from the end to the wick with patchouli oil. While anointing it, concentrate on the removal of all damaging gossip from your life. Don't specify how this is to be done, but place your trust in the Goddess and God for the correct solution. Place the black candle in the holder in the center of your altar.

Anoint the magenta and green candles from the wick to the end with mint and/or rose oil. If you like, you could use rose on the magenta candle and mint on the green one. While anointing them, concentrate on positive energies coming into your life. Place these candles on your altar, the magenta to the left of the black candle, the green to the right.

Never spell or ask for removal of anything in your life without spelling or asking also for replacement by something positive. Nature abhors a vacuum and will fill it. Better you should have it filled with positives than for the negatives to return, usually stronger than before.

Spend a few moments breathing in white light and expelling darkness with each breath. Hold the palms of your hands toward the candles and chant:

> *Gossip does not harm or bind me.*
> *Evil words come not near me.*
> *I am light. I am truth. I am love.*

Repeat these words three, five, seven, or nine times. Feel their positive meaning sink into your subconscious mind. Know that you are building a shield of protection around you, a shield built out of positive energy so strong that negatives can't get through. Leave the candles in a safe place to burn out. Dispose of the wax.

Family Peace

The Carista was a day for family peace and accord in ancient Rome. In the beginning of their history, the Romans were strong supporters of the family life.

Today, when our own lives are hectic, just trying to keep afloat in a world full of problems and uncertainty, we need to have a day for family peace and accord. If you have no family with whom you can be at peace, celebrate with friends. After all, friends are often more of a family than blood relatives. And since all humans in the world are "family," as are animals for that matter, include all creatures in your wishes for peace.

If you have family or friends to join you, plan a dinner and invite them. It doesn't have to be elaborate. This is meant to be a time for building or strengthening peaceful ties, not wearing yourself out. If you have family with whom you are at odds and wouldn't feel comfortable with sharing a meal, at least keep them kindly in your thoughts during this time.

If you are alone, celebrate by yourself or with your pets. Celebrate as part of the Earth family: humans and animals. Make all the preparations as if you were having friends join you. The very act of this celebration will likely bring friends into your life in a short time.

Before you begin the meal, give a toast with your glass of juice, water, or cup of coffee.

May there be peace and harmony between all peoples and in all lives.
May we remember that all creation is part of the whole.
To peace and accord in the world!

Give your pets a special treat as part of the celebration. If you can, leave the wild birds an offering of bread and seeds.

Blessing the Boundaries

The Roman god Terminus was the deity of land boundaries, whether farm land or city villa. The Terminalia was a celebration in his honor.

Everyone has land boundaries, whether you live on a remote farm or in a city apartment. These boundaries need to be respected and protected. By blessing the boundaries of your private place of dwelling, you can strengthen your protection against intruders of all kinds: unwanted and unwelcome visitors, stalkers, burglars, noisy neighbors, intruding religious peddlers, and sales people.

If you can, or feel brave enough to, plan to walk the boundaries of your property. If you can't, such as living in an apartment or in an area where your activities would become the center of unwelcome attention, plan to walk through every room of your house.

OUTSIDE: If you can walk the boundaries outside, take a bowl of white cornmeal (a favorite of Native Americans). Hold it up to the Sun, or Moon if you do this at night. Ask the Gods to bless it for you. Cornmeal is a natural substance and will not pollute the ground. Begin to the left of your driveway or entrance and move clockwise, lightly sprinkling the cornmeal as you go. Chant:

Blessings and honor to all who guard my boundaries.
Blessings and thanks for your help and protection.
May my property and dwelling be safe under your care.
I offer you friendship and blessings.

When you come to the starting point, sprinkle the cornmeal once more across the drive or entrance path. This acts as a double seal in the most vulnerable area.

If possible, build a little special place in full view of the drive or entrance path. This will be a "home" or "altar" for your guardians. It can be a collection of rocks that you have picked up and admired. It could be a small patch of herbs or a tiny grove of flowering bushes.

INSIDE: Prepare a chalice or glass of pure water and a small plate of salt. If you have an altar, take these to the altar and ask for their blessing by the Gods. If not, hold them up toward the Sun or Moon for blessing. Sprinkle three pinches of salt into the water and swirl the chalice three times clockwise.

Begin near the front entrance of your dwelling. Lightly sprinkle the water-salt mixture across the door, moving clockwise. Chant while sprinkling:

> *Blessings and honor to all who guard my dwelling boundaries.*
> *Blessings and thanks for your help and protection.*
> *May my dwelling-place be safe under your care.*
> *I offer you friendship and blessings.*

Continue through each room in this manner until you have completely encircled the house or apartment. When you are once more at the front entrance, sprinkle the mixture across the threshold again.

Prepare some special "home" inside for your guardians. This should be in sight of the entrance. Such a "home" can be a bowl of tumbled stones, a vase of dried flowers, or a statue. As I've mentioned, we not only have two such statues in our home, but also a large old-fashioned mirror that directly faces the door. This reflector is an excellent boomerang for people trying to bring in negative attitudes.

Honoring Diana of the Woodlands
— Crescent Moon —

February 12 was a Festival of Diana, the Divine Huntress, in Rome. Diana/Artemis was Goddess of the Woodlands, a Nature deity who loved the forests and animals and sparkling water. She was also the protectress of all mothers and newborn creatures, including humans. She was depicted as a young, semi-nude woman with a Crescent Moon on her head; she carried a silver bow and a quiver of arrows. As Lady of the Wild Beasts, she had dominion over such animals as lions, tigers, panthers, cats, deer, and stags.

Honor Diana by setting aside time to help the immediate environment. I'm not talking about attending environmental meetings, but rather an actual personal activity. Choose a project in your neighborhood that could use your attention. Pick up litter in an abandoned lot. Help an older, handicapped, or ill person by cleaning up their yard. Carry a litter bag when you take a walk down the street. If there are abandoned domestic animals nearby, try to find them homes, or at least arrange for the Humane

Society to pick them up. There are numerous other ways of honoring Diana, not just at this Crescent Moon, but every day.

As a special ritual to animals of the Woodland Diana, hang apple slices, cups of peanut butter, and seed holders outside for the birds. Different types of birds have different needs. If you have squirrels, set out small holders of raw nuts in the shell (no salt, please!).

As a special tie between yourself and the Woodland Diana, find a statue or picture of an animal or bird that appeals to you and put it in a prominent place in your home. Each time that you look at it, think of the life-connection between you and every living creature.

There are now statues of the goddess Diana available at reasonable prices.[1] Having a statue of this goddess in your home place of worship is a reminder that you honor her each time you do something to honor the Earth and its creatures.

Whenever you go out into Nature, onto your patio, and into your special outdoor shrine, you can chant these words:

> *Goddess of the forests and the Moon,*
> *Diana of the Silver Crescent,*
> *I chant my praises to you.*
> *I lift my arms to your heavenly Crescent.*
> *My thanks to you for caring for the woodland creatures,*
> *For protecting the forests and meadow lands.*
> *Protect me and mine, for we are your spiritual children.*
> *Lovely Diana, I sing your praises.*

Celebrating Valentine's Day
— Full Moon —

On the Full Moon China and Taiwan celebrated the Lantern Festival; it was also a festival of the goddess Kuan Yin. The Greek day to honor Selene and other Moon goddesses (February 7) could also fall under this Full Moon ritual, as could Aphrodite's Roman Festival of Love (February 14-21). Our present Valentine's Day is a remainder of these ancient festivals.

A wonderful way of expressing the love of Kuan Yin, the goddess of children in particular, is to find out from the local hospital how many children (boys and girls) are there. Then buy or make valentine cards; don't sign your name or sign it "a friend." Deliver them to the nurses on the floor of the children's ward, and request that they give one to each child. The same anonymous good will gesture can be made to the mothers of newborns. And don't overlook the elders in hospitals or nursing homes. It's amazing how much joy such a card can bring.

The color red is connected with this holiday; it is also the color of the Mother aspect of the Triple Goddess and of the life blood itself. Wear something true red on this day, even if it is only an accent piece: jewelry, a flower, a hair ribbon, a tie, or a handkerchief tucked into a pocket. Send a card expressing your love to your mother or to the person you think of as your mother. Let her know how much her caring and concern mean to you. Do the same for other loved ones who mean a great deal to you. People need to be remembered and to feel that they are loved.

Treat yourself at this Full Moon too. Take a leisurely bath and splash on your favorite cologne or aftershave. Wrap yourself in a warm robe and curl up in your favorite chair with a hot drink. Burn a red candle. Read a romance story or book of poetry. Listen to romantic music.

If you have someone special to share this time with, enjoy a cozy evening together. If you don't have a special person at this time, the very act of immersing yourself in a romantic atmosphere may well open the door for such a person to enter your life. We draw whatever we put into our vibrations.

Feast of Ovens
— Dark Moon —

Although the Fornacalia, or Feast of Ovens, celebrated in Rome on February 20, was a happy time, there is every reason to place it at this time of the Moon. The Earth Goddess symbolized the planted grain which must first die in order to grow. The recycling cauldron of the Crone (the third aspect of the Triple Goddess) was often called an oven, symbolizing the forming of energy into matter, or rebirth after death.

Today's society as a whole is frightened of contemplating death and what happens afterward. Even though we may not remember, we all have been through it before, and will do so again. Death and rebirth should not be viewed in a morbid way, but with a sense of wonder and anticipation. Lest anyone misconstrue my intentions at this point, let me clarify that I do not place suicide in the category of wonder and anticipation; these people need special help, far beyond the scope of this ritual.

In preparation for this Dark Moon celebration of the Feast of Ovens, bake a loaf of bread or a batch of rolls. If you aren't a baking cook, you have the option of ready-to-bake grain products in the store. Just pop them in the oven or microwave, according to instructions. If at all possible, bake something rather than buying it already baked.

If you have an altar, do this ritual there. If not, use a cleared table or a tray. Arrange a roll or slice of bread on a plate in the center of your space. To the right of it put a small dish of salt. Place a chalice of juice or wine to the left. In the center, behind the plate of bread, set a black or very dark blue candle.

Light some myrrh incense. Begin by carrying the smoking incense to the East. Say:

East is the place of birth, the door to new life.

Move to the South and say:

South is the place of maturity, the gateway to responsibility.

Go to the West. Say:

West is the place of growing old, the beginning of the path leading into lands lost to memory.

Stand before the North and say:

North is the place of darkness and death, the final point in the spiraling path. But it is also the beginning of the spiral upward into a new life.

Place the incense back on the altar. Take a piece of the bread into your hand and think about the planted seed, the grain that died to be reborn into waving wheat. Let your thoughts move on to the cycle of human life: the birth, growth, death, and rebirth of your own body.

The Maiden Goddess and the Fertilizing God plant the seed of life. They are the planters, as the farmers planted the wheat that was the beginning of this bread. The Mother and the Lord of the Greenwood bring the life into existence, forming it into the required shape. They are the millers and bakers, like those who gave this bread its distinctive shape. At the proper time, when the life-seed is ripened, the Dark Lord and Lady cut it down. But that seed is not destroyed. Like the farmer who gathers the wheat seeds for the next planting, the Dark Lord and Lady gather the life-seeds within their hands and prepare them for the next planting—the next life.

Dip the piece of bread into the salt.

This salt represents the Earth and the waters of the Earth. All life must have food and water to grow and survive. My body was first nurtured in the womb of the Dark Mother and watered with spiritual love. I thank the Goddess and Her Lord for their care.

Eat the salted bread. Raise the chalice high.

As the fruit must be harvested and crushed before it can become a refreshing drink, so must each life be tempered by trials and experiences. Our life-essences are changed into new forms, flavored with the old yet sweetened by the new. May the Lady and Her Lord give me courage to undergo the process with dignity, and grant me understanding and guidance to make my journeys with ease.

Drink from the chalice. If you know how to use the tarot, runes, or other divinatory aids, now is the time to lay them out concerning your own future as it pertains to spiritual development and overall life paths. This is not a time to ask about love, money, etc. When you are finished, stand before the altar, arms raised, and say:

As I am part of the grain of wheat, so am I also part of the Lady and Her Lord. All creations and cycles of life are intertwined in an eternal cosmic dance. The doors to all Mysteries lie within me. Grant me the wisdom to open them at the proper time.

Leave the bread and chalice on the altar for a short time so that the Nature spirits can enjoy them. Then place the bread outside for the birds and animals, and dispose of the wine.

Endnotes

1. One place to order these, and many other deity statues, is JBL Statues, Crozet, VA 22932-0163. Their catalog is $3.00 and well worth it.

Chapter 6

STORM MOON

March

Also called: Seed Moon, Moon of Winds, Plow Moon, Worm Moon,
Hrethmonath (Hertha's Month), Lentzinmanoth (Renewal Month),
Lenting Moon, Sap Moon, Crow Moon, Moon of the Snowblind.

March 1: The Matronalia in Greece and Rome; a festival of Hera and Juno Lucina. Among the Celts, the Feast of Rhiannon was held.

March 4: In Greece, the Anthesteria, a festival of flowers; dedicated to Flora and Hecate.

March 5: Celebration of Isis as the ruler over safe navigation, boats, fishing, and the final journey of life.

March 14: The Diasia to ward off poverty in Greece.

March 17: Festival of Astarte in Canaan. The Liberalia in Rome, a women's festival of freedom.

March 18: Sheelah's Day in Ireland, honoring Sheelah-Na-Gig, the goddess of fertility.

March 19-23: The Lesser Panathenaea in Greece, honoring Athene.

March 20: In Egypt, the Spring harvest festival honoring Isis.

March 21: Spring Equinox. Festival of Kore and Demeter in Greece.
For five days over the Equinox in Rome, Minerva was honored.

March 22-27: The Hilaria, festivals honoring Cybele in Greece.

March 23: The Quinquatria, the birthday of Athene/Minerva in Rome.

March 29: The Delphinia, or Artemis Soteira, of Artemis in Greece.
Expulsion of the demons of bad luck in Tibet.

March 30: Feast of Eostre, the German goddess of Spring, rebirth,
fertility, and the Moon.

March 31: Roman Festival of Luna, the Moon goddess.

*T*his month was sacred to the Roman god Mars, hence the name March. Mars is similar to the Greek Ares, Tiu or Tiwaz of Central and Northern Europe, Teutates of the Celts, and Tyr of the Norse. The Roman goddess Bellona, goddess of war, had her special day during this month.

March is generally a blustery month weather-wise. The old weather saying "In like a lion, out like a lamb" is an apt description of March weather. For the Romans, it was the beginning of their year. The Spring Equinox, which falls around March 21 or 22, was a sacred and celebrated time in a great many world cultures. In the Southern Hemisphere, this would be equal to the Autumn Equinox, as the seasons are reversed. The Incas celebrated Pacha-puchy, or Earth Ripening, at this time.

The Roman Matronalia honored Juno Lucina, an aspect of the goddess Juno, who protected women, children, and the family. Statues of the goddess were decorated with flowers, and special temple fires were lit. Girls made offerings to Juno Lucina at this time of year for happy and prosperous marriages.

The statue of Isis suckling her child symbolizes this goddess's aspect as the Great Mother, the caretaker of the Earth and all life. Flowers were floated on the rivers and the boats blessed with incense.

In Canaan and other Semitic countries, the goddess Astarte was honored in a Spring celebration. Red eggs were given as gifts to family and friends, the beginning of our Easter egg tradition. Her sacred city of Byblos was noted for its extensive libraries before they were destroyed. As queen of heaven, Astarte wore crescent horns and was said to tirelessly create and destroy. The kings of Sidon ruled only with the goddess's permission and called themselves the Priest of Astarte. Other cultures in the Middle East knew Astarte as Asherat of the Sea and Ashtart, queen of heaven.

Athene/Minerva, the armed goddess of wisdom, reigned over the biggest social event in Greece—the five day Spring competition featuring events in athletics, music, poetry, and satire. Crowns of olive branches and flasks of olive oil were given to the winners of each event. On the final day, Athene's birth was celebrated by draping the goddess's statue in a new sacred garment.

This particular festival of Cybele, the Hilaria, was a happy time. Our word "hilarious" has similar word roots. The goddess Cybele can be compared to Demeter in many ways; Cybele represented the Earth as did Demeter and had a Spring resurrected son/lover Attis, who corresponded to Kore/Persephone. This happy festival celebrated the power of Cybele to overcome death.

Eostre was the German goddess of rebirth. Rabbits and colored eggs were fertility symbols connected with Her. Originally, Eostre was the goddess of the Spring Equinox whose name was changed to Easter by the Christians.

The Roman Luna, goddess of the Moon, was honored with the baking, exchanging, and eating of Moon cakes. Even the Chinese and Europeans knew of Moon cakes and some form of this goddess.

Correspondences

Nature Spirits: Mer-people, Air and Water beings who are connected with spring rains and storms

Herbs: broom, High John root, yellow dock, wood betony, Irish moss

Colors: pale green, red-violet

Flowers: jonquil, daffodil, violet

Scents: honeysuckle, apple blossom

Stones: aquamarine, bloodstone

Trees: alder, dogwood

Animals: cougar, hedgehog, boar

Birds: sea crow, sea eagle

Deities: Black Isis, the Morrigan, Hecate, Cybele, Astarte, Athene, Minerva, Artemis, Luna

Power Flow: energy breaks into the open; growing, prospering, exploring. New beginnings; balance of Light and Dark. Breaking illusions. Seeing the truth in your life however much it may hurt.

Old Sayings & Lore

- It is said of March weather that if it comes in like a lamb, it will go out like a lion.
- A verse:

New Moon, true Moon,
Star in the stream,
Pray tell my fortune
In my dream.

Pale Moon doth rain,
Red Moon doth blow,
White Moon doth neither rain nor snow.

- In South Africa, it is considered unlucky to start a journey or begin any important work during the last quarter of the Moon.
- After Christian influence began to be strongly felt, people became fearful of a Friday Full Moon. There was a saying:

Friday's Moon,
Come when it will,
It comes too soon.

- And if the Full Moon fell on a Friday that was also the thirteenth, it was considered to be the most unlucky day there could be.
- Almost every culture believed that if the New Moon came on Monday (Moon-day) it was a sign of good weather and good luck.
- Sailors believed that if a large star or planet was seen close to the Moon, there was wild weather coming. They called this star a "Moon dog."
- In Cornwall, they said that if a birth took place during the waxing Moon, the next child would be the same sex as the one just born.
- The Danes believed in a type of elves they called the Moon Folk. These were perfect in appearance when seen from the front, but were hollow when seen from the back. It was said that the Moon Folk caused sickness by blowing on humans.

Recipes

Mushroom Tidbits

This simplified recipe comes from an old Greek one for mushroom phyllo (Bourekakia me Manitaria). Few people today have the time to prepare it the original way. If, however, you want to be authentic, wrap the mixture in phyllo pastry sheets.

3 pounds fresh mushrooms	½ cup grated Parmesan cheese
½ cup minced onion	Salt and pepper to taste
1 stick margarine, plus melted margarine for brushing tops	¾ cup bread crumbs
	1 pound phyllo pastry or tubes of prepared dinner rolls

Clean mushrooms and chop fine. Saute onion in 1 stick margarine until soft and golden. Add mushrooms and cook until all liquid is gone. Remove from heat and add cheese, salt, pepper, and bread crumbs.

Separate dinner rolls. Roll each piece out into a very thin circular shape. Use about 1 teaspoon of filling in the center of each roll. Fold the edges over to make a half-circle and seal the edges with a fork. Place on a non-stick cookie sheet. Brush the tops with the melted margarine. Bake in 375° F oven for 15-20 minutes, or until golden. Best served warm. NOTE: If using phyllo sheets, carefully lay out one sheet at a time and fill; fold into a triangular shape.

Anise Seed Cookies

The Greeks have a wonderful anise and sesame seed cookie called Koulourakia me Glikaniso, but it uses a lot of olive oil and takes quite a lot of kneading and fussing. The easiest substitute is your own sugar cookie recipe or a box of cookie mix.

1 batch of sugar cookie dough or large box of cookie mix	1 teaspoon grated orange peel
	1 teaspoon grated lemon peel
1 tablespoon aniseed	1 tablespoon ground cinnamon
1 tablespoon sesame seed	

For the cinnamon sugar, mix the following thoroughly:

1 tablespoon ground cinnamon
2 tablespoons sugar

Prepare the dough or mix according to directions. Knead in the aniseed, sesame seed, lemon peel, orange peel, and cinnamon. Roll out on lightly floured board to ¼" thick. Cut with a cookie cutter (Moon circles or crescents are nice) and place on cookie sheets. Sprinkle with cinnamon sugar mixture. Bake according to the mix or recipe instructions.

Crafts

Herb Pillows

Herb pillows have been used for headaches, sleeping problems, and prophetic dreams for many, many years. They are also used to scent drawers and stationery. Choose a tightly woven fabric that will not allow the herbs to sift through. Cut into 3" squares for tiny pillows, 6" squares for slightly larger pillows, one foot square for large ones. Sew together three of the sides, leaving one end open for stuffing with the herb mixture.

- For prophetic dreams, stuff with dried mugwort. If you are very sensitive or dealing with many personal problems, you may not be able to use this often.
- A sleep mixture liked by men: 1 oz. lemon verbena; 1 oz. lavender flowers; a pinch each of thyme and mint.
- A good mixture for headaches and to guard against nightmares: 1 oz. lavender flowers; ½ oz. verbena; ½ oz. lemon thyme; ½ oz. woodruff; ¼ oz. rosemary.

Spanish Cologne

1 pint distilled water	1 ounce glycerin
4 ounces alcohol	2 drops orange oil
1 drop lemon oil	

Shake together and store out of the sunlight. To change the scent slightly, you might want to add one or two drops of bergamot oil.

Dragon Smoke Bath Salts
—For Prosperity—

1 cup salt	2 drops anise oil
5 drops cherry oil	

Merddin Bath Salts
—For Prophecy Spells—

1 cup salt	8 drops lilac oil
4 drops violet oil	8 drops narcissus oil
4 drops wisteria oil	4 drops synthetic ambergris oil

Sacred Light Bath Salts

1 cup salt	8 drops sandalwood oil
3 drops nutmeg oil	3 drops cinnamon oil

Aura of Venus Bath Salts

1 cup salt
4 drops lavender oil
4 drops frangipani oil

8 drops jasmine oil
4 drops rose oil
4 drops synthetic musk oil

Mystic Wand Bath Salts

1 cup salt
6 drops violet oil

8 drops heliotrope oil
4 drops sandalwood oil

Myths

The Birth of Athene

The story of Zeus and Athene may be a metaphorical way of explaining the take-over of a matriarchal society, one of whose goddesses simply would not go quietly into the background.

Zeus was king of the Greek gods who ruled Olympus with an iron hand. Fidelity and faithfulness were not in his vocabulary; he spent much time marrying, seducing, and raping a long list of goddesses and mortal women. He first married Metis, whose name means wisdom, but he promptly swallowed her and her unborn child as soon as he learned that the baby would be more powerful than he. He then went on to father many more children, both mortal and immortal.

In the midst of carousing, debauching, and creating children, Zeus developed a severe head-ache. It became so terrible he begged one of his sons, the god Hephaestus, for help. Hephaestus must have had an inkling of the real problem, for he split his father's skull with a bronze axe. Athene, who had been swallowed before her birth, sprang out. She was fully grown, armored, and shaking a javelin—enough to give any god a headache.

Athene was an absolutely chaste goddess, a rarity among the Olympians, and only gave her aid to those she considered deserving. Among her other attributes, Athene was the Greek goddess of weaving, a trait often connected with the Moon. Her companion animal was an owl, also a Moon creature.

Athene

Astarte

Astarte, Queen of Heaven, was known throughout the Middle East, even among the Hebrews. She was the chief local deity of the town of Sidon. Another of her many names was Ashtoreth. Like other lunar deities, this goddess often wore the horns of the Crescent Moon or a heifer's head with horns.

Astarte was not only a Moon goddess of love, but a deity of prosperity. Even the women of Israel were admonished for pouring out drink offerings, burning incense, and offering Moon cakes to Astarte. Her sacred groves, where love-priestesses lived, were frequented by the men. When the fire-and-brimstone prophets of Israel were trying to force the one-god worship on the people, they outwardly succeeded only after they destroyed the temples and cut down the groves of the Queen of Heaven. But the goddess went underground to remain a part of the new religion as the Shekinah. Christians still know her as Mary, the Queen of Heaven.

Cybele and Attis

In Greek and Roman times, Cybele was called the Mother of the Gods. The great Sophocles named her All-Mother. Her cult began in western Anatolia and Phrygia where she was "the Lady of Mt. Ida." Cybele was goddess of the dead, fertility, wildlife, agriculture, law, and the mystic Hunt. Tambourines, cymbals, and drums were sacred to her. Sometime during the fifth century, a statue of her seated on a throne and flanked by lions was placed in her temple in Athens. The Romans decorated her statues with roses. She had her own sacred, secret Mysteries where the rose became a symbol of reincarnation and the secret world of the goddess.

Cybele

There are several legends concerning the relationship of Cybele and Attis. Some stories tell of her finding the abandoned boy who grew up to become her lover; later he was accidently killed during a hunt. Another story says that the handsome Attis was the grandson/lover of Cybele. He had no trouble finding many females who succumbed to his charms. When Cybele found out, her jealous rage drove him mad; he cut off his genitals with a Moon sickle in a fit of remorse. All the legends end the same: Cybele mourned for him until he was reborn.

March was the time of the Cybele-Attis Mysteries. The death and rebirth of Attis formed the central portion of these sacred, secret ceremonies. During the march through the streets, it was not uncommon for devout young men, caught up in the ecstatic frenzy of the moment, to castrate themselves. All priests of Cybele were castrated in remembrance of Attis. Long before the advent of the Sun god Mithras, Cybele was honored by the sacrifice of bulls and the baptizing of her general followers in the blood.

When Attis was reborn, Cybele was happy again, shown by the joyful celebrations at the end of her Spring Mysteries. The name given to this joyful festival was the Hilaria.

Rituals

Warding off Poverty

The Greeks had a celebration called the Diasia to ward off poverty each year in March. In a time (and when isn't there such a time?) of economic uncertainty, it is up to each person to do what they can to keep his or her life in a positive, prosperous mode. Sometimes circumstances, for whatever reason, have landed us in financial straits. There are certain things we can do to improve the situation and eventually eliminate the lack in our lives.

The very first thing is to become financially responsible. Check your monthly expenses; eliminate the non-essentials. If you have a bad habit of charging purchases only to find yourself struggling to meet the payments, stop immediately! Don't carry the credit cards with you. If the situation has gotten really bad, see a credit counselor. Make a budget and stick to it. Begin tucking away a little cash each payday into a private "rainy day" fund: an envelope in the bottom of a drawer, the proverbial cookie jar, a box on the highest closet shelf. You want this cache available, not to spend, but to periodically count and prove to yourself that you are capable of self-restraint.

The second step to take is to begin the removal of programmed thoughts. You don't have to keep up with the neighbors, friends, family, or anyone else in the way of possessions or activities. Being thrifty isn't being miserly. Having a prosperous attitude toward life isn't sinful or wrong. Money isn't evil. Spending an occasional day doing nothing but relaxing isn't being lazy.

To do this ritual, purchase a green taper candle, mint or honeysuckle oil, and some play money. Choose the largest denomination of play money you can get.

Two days before the Full Moon, take the green candle to your altar or spiritual workplace. Carve several dollar signs into the candle, thinking of a more prosperous life as you do so. Anoint the candle with the essential oil by rubbing it from the wick down to the end. Place it in a fireproof holder and set it in the middle of your altar. Light the candle.

Spread out your "money" in front of the burning candle. Sort it out by denomination, or in piles for each bill or purchase you would like to take care of. Spend at least five to ten minutes thinking about how you would responsibly use this money. Then extinguish the candle.

The next night light the candle again and shuffle through the "money" again. After ten to fifteen minutes, extinguish the candle. The third night, the night of the Full Moon, go through the ritual another time, but this time let the candle burn completely out after you have finished sorting the "money."

Freedom Day
— Spring Equinox —

The Liberalia in Rome was a women's festival of freedom. This must have been an ancient festival remaining from a matriarchal society, for Roman women, although freer than the women of Greece, still were not free according to today's definition.

Today, this occasion can be used to petition for the freedom of women around the world who do not have control over their lives and destinies. In many countries, women are still bought and sold like cattle; when their dowry runs out, they can suffer death at the hands of their husbands. They are forced to bear child after child, even though they don't want any more children. In the so-called civilized countries, women are still discriminated against in ways ranging from blatant to extremely subtle. What many men refuse to see is that what harms women indirectly harms them. All humanity suffers.

Freedom Day can encompass much more than women's rights, however. It covers all people who are terrorized and abused by dictators, falsely imprisoned, locked by economics into jobs run by uncaring companies and bosses, or into living conditions that make them feel as if they are in prison; any circumstance where people simply cannot do much, if anything, to avoid or change the feeling of being without freedom.

Of course, this does not mean dropping responsibilities that are legitimately yours. It also does not absolve you of doing everything you can in a positive manner to remedy the situation. Ritual and magick do not drop results in your lap. They merely create opportunities.

If you are trapped in a situation with another person and wish to sever the relationship with the minimum amount of hassle, wait until the Dark Moon. You will need a black candle, a fireproof bowl, a pair of scissors, a pencil or pen, two small pieces of paper.

Light the black candle. Write your name on a small piece of paper and the other person's name on another piece. Tie the two papers together with a length of string or thread. Lay the papers on your altar with the edges touching each other. Visualize things as they are now between the two of you. Slowly move the papers apart as far as the string will go. Visualize a peaceful separation with the two of you turning your backs and walking away. Now cut the string in the middle with the scissors. Say:

I am free.
You are free.
We go our separate ways in peace.

Take the paper with the other person's name on it, light it in the candle flame, and drop it in the bowl to burn up. Dispose of the ashes when they are cool.

For peace in a world conflict, use this same ritual. An example would be the turmoil and war in Bosnia. This time use three pieces of paper: one for the Moslems, one for the Croats, and one for the Serbs. Tie the third paper's string to the center of the string binding the other papers. Visualize these factions peacefully resolving their problems. Then cut each string, separating the papers from each other. Say:

The Croats are free.
The Moslems are free.
The Serbs are free.

Burn all three papers.

Expelling Bad Luck Entities

Toward the end of March, the people of Tibet had a ceremony to expel the demons of bad luck from their homes, lives, and communities. The people of Bali, which is east of Java, also hold public expulsions of demons at least once a year, and on a New Moon. Each village sets food at the nearest crossroads and then goes to the local temple. Everyone prays and blows horns to summon the demons. Then people begin to bang on anything that will make a loud noise, thus frightening the entities which flee the area. The demons can't resist the food, pause at the crossroads, and are ambushed by a priest who curses them. This final ambush causes the evil demons to leave the area, and order is restored.

From time to time, we are likely to find ourselves the unwitting and unwilling hosts to bad luck entities. These entities can be sent to us by the jealousy and ill-will of others. Sometimes we pick up the negative vibrations when we are out in public; these entities will leap into our auras because we are depressed, angry, upset in any way, or ill. One must be really careful when going to a doctor's office, for example. Stores having big sales are another place where one inadvertently picks up such creatures. The last category of these bad luck entities consists of the ones we create ourselves through our own negativity.

However you became burdened with these bad luck entities, you want to get rid of them. The first thing to do is to clean the vibrations in your home. Take a small amount of salt in one hand; hold the other hand over it and asks the gods to bless this cleansing agent. Then go through every room and closet of the house, sprinkling a few grains of salt in every corner. When you are finished, take a bath with some salt stirred into the water. This helps to cleanse your aura, even though it is a physical action.

To help keep these creatures from returning, burn patchouli or frankincense incense for three days and ask that good luck enter your life; you never want to leave a vacuum, or you will get everything back you sent away.

As a last precaution, find a talisman to wear; run it through the incense smoke before wearing it. A talisman can be anything from a Thorr's hammer to a crystal. Periodically cleanse it in incense smoke to rid it of the negative vibrations it may have absorbed.

Loving the Child Within

It often seems that the hardest person to love unconditionally is yourself. We have been taught that any thought or action that does not put everyone else first in the priority list is selfish and wrong. Parents tend to fall into this trap with the excuse that their children should be treated better or have more than they did as children. Speaking as a mother, I can tell you that total devotion and giving up of your own dreams and hopes is not appreciated by children. Some of them grow up demanding that kind of "love" from everyone, as if it were their right. Doctors, psychiatrists, and the courts make a lot of money off this programmed attitude.

There is a definite line, however, between caring for and loving the self and being selfish and narcissistic. You must learn to follow through with responsibilities, make compromises when necessary, and still keep what is important to your inner child. This does not mean breaking the laws of the land, harming others, or living without morals.

The inner child is that part of us that carries our dreams and hopes, our unprotected emotions, our natural-born openness to everyone and all life. It is the deeply hidden piece of our personality that slips out to cry or laugh at a movie, enjoy the colors of autumn, lose all sense of linear time when involved in something we truly like to do. Unfortunately, we are taught early in life that such actions are undesirable and, therefore, must be squashed. The attitude of giving until it hurts, whether of your time, self, or money, has caused innumerable problems. I prefer the statement "Give until it feels good."

To re-acquaint yourself with your inner child, you will have to be patient. The "child" will be frightened of coming out into the open; after all, you might not approve of its behavior or thoughts. Allow yourself the luxury of watching a very humorous movie and laughing aloud. If you feel you can't do this in a theater, rent a video tape and watch it at home. It is an excellent way to let your "child" make its appearance. Laughter is also good for your health.

Listen to your inner child when it says it does or doesn't like certain colors or pieces of furniture, that it wants to be different today. Of course one must use common sense when reviewing inner child's suggestions. The "child" often has few morals and feels no obligation to be socially correct or live up to a social status. I've been known to jump rope or play hopscotch with neighborhood children. I once surprised my son and grandsons by ambushing them with a water-gun. Grandmothers aren't supposed to do things like that.

But I suppose the hardest thing is loving your inner child without restriction, which means loving yourself totally. Everyone has something, usually a lot of things, they don't like about themselves. The traits or habits we can change, and that we need to change, we should work on one at a time. Other traits are seen as really not that bad when we cease to be so condemning of ourselves.

If you've been told you cackle when you laugh, so what? Who wants to laugh like everyone else? If you don't like poodle perms, the latest fashions, sun tans, or every weekend filled with sports, cut them out of your life. Although you are a part of the life spark of the universe, you are still unique. Allow the intuition of your inner child to guide you. Life will be happier and a lot more comfortable.

We can also benefit from the inner child in different ways. If you are one of those people who always gives in to keep the peace, call upon the stubbornness of your inner child on occasion. If your inner child is uncomfortable in a situation or around a specific person, watch carefully what is going on: the choice of words, body language, tone of voice. You are being warned of a possibly unpleasant outcome.

Be tender with the inner child, but also firm when wrong or harmful suggestions are put forth. Although the inner child does indeed have little sense of morals at times, it is a forever part of you, a part you must love and seek to understand.

Artemis, Protectress of Women
— Crescent Moon —

This month saw the Delphinia, or Artemis Soteira, of Artemis, the Greek equivalent of the Roman Diana. Artemis was a Virgin Huntress; the Greeks called her the Huntress of Souls. She protected the wild places and animals; to her was known the deep places in Nature where one could rest and regain strength. Violence for itself was abhorrent to her, yet she was swift to deal out punishment to offenders, especially those who threatened or harassed women. Things sacred to her were the acorn, stag, bear, hound, the herb wormwood, and the Moon sickle. She was the deity of the Amazons.

The Cretan goddesses Britomartis and Dictynna were very similar to Artemis/Diana. Mt. Dikte in Crete was Dictynna's mountain. On a peninsula to the West of Kydonia in Crete was the Diktynnaion, a great sacred temple and cave. The area was guarded by Dictynna's sacred dogs, as related in the story of Apollonius of Tyana. Both goddesses were known as the Mistress of Animals. However, only Britomartis was linked with a male, a son/lover/consort who was called the Master of Animals.

Artemis

In praying to most gods, the Greeks stood holding the arms upward. When praying to a sea god, the arms were hold forward; to an Earth or underworld deity, the arms were held down toward the ground, at the same time stamping on the Earth to attract the deity's attention. In all ritual positions, they faced East. When praying in temples, they faced the altar and the deity's statue.

An ancient Greek custom of honoring Artemis' birthday with a Full Moon cake is still seen today in our birthday cakes. The Greeks even put lighted candles on the Moon cake.

To honor the birthday of the goddess Artemis, and your own unbirthday (like *Alice in Wonderland*), bake or buy a small cake or cupcake. On the night of the Crescent Moon, dress in nice clothes as if you were entertaining a friend. Cover your altar or spiritual place with a nice cloth. Put the cake with a small candle on it in the middle of altar. Set pictures or statues of animals around it for decoration. Artemis loves cats of all kinds, deer, and all wild animals. Set a glass of juice or wine next to the cake.

Take a sip of juice and light the candle. Sing "Happy Birthday" to the goddess if you wish. Then say:

> *Lady of Wild Things, Moon Huntress,*
> *Mistress of magick and enchantment,*
> *I chant your lovely name for protection.*
> *Artemis! Artemis! Artemis!*
> *I whisper your praises to the Full Moon.*
> *Cradle my restless, worn spirit*
> *In the secret places of your deep woodlands.*
> *Renew my life, swift Artemis.*

Cut yourself a piece of the cake and eat it. Drink the juice. Tell the goddess why you need protection. When you are finished, thank her for the help that will come. Put the remainder of the cake outside as a feast for the birds and animals.

Festival of Flowers
— Full Moon —

March 20 was the Egyptian Spring harvest festival of Isis. March 31 was the Roman festival of Luna, the Moon goddess. Both of these deities were Full Moon and Mother goddesses who ruled over fertility and growth. March 4 was the Greek festival of the Anthesteria, which was a celebration of flowers and dedicated to Flora.

To celebrate this Spring festival of flowers, buy fresh flowers for your home. If you have house plants, repot and fertilize them. Burn a flowery incense, such as jasmine, rose, or honeysuckle. Wear pastel colors to represent the delicate shades of the new Spring blossoms. Place a pretty bowl of fresh water on your altar and float a light flower in it.

When the Full Moon is up, go to your altar and light a white candle. Sit in the darkness with only the candlelight. Look at the floating flower and think about the wonderful powers of Nature that bring the flowers back year after year. Contemplate the way this power touches your own life.

Feel your "roots" sinking deep down into the Earth, from which you can draw sustaining energy. Feel the energy being fed back to you. Now, reach your arms upward toward the Moon. Feel its energies adding to those of the Earth. Let these energies swirl around and through you, cleansing, healing, balancing. To break the flow, place both hands on the floor. Let the energies sink back into the Earth.

Cybele, Queen of the Night
—Dark Moon—

March 15 and March 22-27 were festivals honoring the Underworld goddess Cybele in Anatolia, Greece, and Rome.

From the very earliest times and well into the patriarchal religions, the Dark Moon symbolized divination, illumination, sacred mysteries, and many of the powers of healing. This Moon phase was also linked to the Underworld and serpents. Serpents tend to live in dark holes, and many ancient cultures thought their homes were linked to the Underworld, thus making serpents sacred animals.

Cybele was known as the Mother of the Gods, the All-Mother. Her worship spread from western Anatolia and Phrygia to Greece and Rome. She was goddess of the dead, fertility, wildlife, agriculture, law, and the mystical Hunt. Tambourines, cymbals, and drums were used in her rituals. A Greek statue of her shows the goddess seated on a throne and flanked by lions. The Romans decorated her statues with roses.

Cybele had her own sacred, secret Mysteries, much like the goddesses Demeter and Persephone. Her ceremonies were held at night, since the goddess was Queen of the Night. She was also known to have deep wisdom that she shared only with true seekers.

To have a question answered, or to ask about your life in general, perform this ritual on the Dark Moon night.

Take a ritual cleansing bath and dress in a dark robe or go naked. Cast your circle as usual, or at least bless salt and sprinkle it around your working area. Light a black candle on each side of the altar. Have ready an appropriate incense. Place your tarot cards or runes in the center of the altar. Lay your wand beside the cards. Stand with your arms outstretched and say:

The cycle of the Moon has turned once more.
The Moon hides her light from the uninitiated.
Those who follow the Ancient Paths know that her power is not gone,
is not diminished.
The wisdom of the Dark Mother is there for all who truly seek her.

Tap the altar three times with your wand:

Hear me, O Carrier of Wisdom.
My voice flies through the night to you.
Show me new pathways I must tread
To change my life and make it new.

Light the incense and life it high over the altar:

I bring an offering, fine and fair.
The scent will rise upon the air
To reach your realms. Bless me soon,
O Lady of the Darkened Moon.

Tap the cards or rune bag three times with the wand, then circle them clockwise three times with the wand. Tap them three more times, to equal the number nine, a Moon number. Lay the wand aside and shuffle the cards or stir the runes.

Divide the cards into three piles, moving from left to right; or lay out three runes in the same pattern. The left pile is the past; the middle the present; the right the future.

Turn up the top card on each pile and contemplate what you see. Be open even if you don't understand the message. It will become clear later. Turn up a second card on each pile and think about what you see. Then do this a third time. What was not clear with the first card will probably be clarified with the others.

If you want to use both tarot and runes, turn up the first round of the cards. Then choose a rune stone and lay that next to each upturned card. Finally turn up the second round of cards.

This also works with more than one tarot deck or type of card deck. For example, you might use a standard tarot deck, the Medicine cards, and Star-Gate cards.

Write down what has been revealed to you. In this way you will be better able to remember and understand when things begin to happen at a later date.

Chapter 7
GROWING MOON
April

Also called: Hare Moon, Seed or Planting Moon, Planter's Moon, Budding Trees Moon, Eastermonath (Eostre Month), Ostarmanoth, Pink Moon, Green Grass Moon.

Full Moon is the Dragon Boat Festival in China.

April 1: Festival of Kali in India. The Fortuna Virilis of Venus in Rome. Day of Hathor in Egypt.

April 4: The Megalesia of Cybele, or Magna Mater, in Phrygia and Rome, commemorating the arrival of the goddess to her Roman temple. A seven-day festival.

April 5: Festival for Good Luck in Rome; the goddess Fortuna.

April 8: The Hana Matsuri, the Flower Festival, in Japan; honor of the ancestors and decoration of shrines. The Mounichia of Artemis in Greece; a day of Moon cakes.

April 11: In Armenia, the Day of Anahit, goddess of love and the Moon.

April 12-19: The Cerealia, or Return of Persephone, in Rome, honoring Ceres and her daughter.

April 15: Festival of Bast in Egypt.

April 22: Festival of Ishtar in Babylon.

April 28-May 3: The three-day Festival of Flora and Venus, or the Floralia, in Rome; goddess of sexuality and Spring flowers.

The name April comes from the Greek goddess Aphrodite, who is identified with the Roman Venus. Because the Christian holiday of Easter sometimes falls in this month, the Anglo-Saxons and Franks called it Easter Month; of course, the word Easter comes originally from the name of the Pagan goddess Eostre, deity of Spring, fertility, and new life. The Romans called this month Aprilis, a time of unfolding leaves and flowers.

The Megalesia of Cybele, who was also known as Magna Mater (Great Mother) in both Phrygia and Rome, celebrated the arrival of this goddess in Rome. In 204 BCE, Rome was in the midst of a great war with Hannibal. Things were going very badly for the Roman legions. Finally, the Romans sent a delegation to the Delphi oracle for an interpretation of their sacred Sibylline Books. This passage said that foreign invaders could only be driven away when the Mother of Mount Ida was transferred from Pessinus to Rome. The oracle sent the delegation to the king of Pergamum in Asia Minor, where they were told that a black meteorite embodying the spirit of Cybele was. Pine trees from Mt. Ida, sacred to the goddess, were made into a ship, and the stone was transported from one sanctuary to another until it reached Rome. In about a year, Hannibal left Italy forever.

The Japanese Flower Festival has now become a celebration of Buddha's birth. In the older celebration, however, the people gathered wildflowers for the family shrine. Those in the Shinto faith placed wooden markers on the graves and said prayers.

The Roman festival of Cerealia celebrated the return of Proserpina to the Earth goddess Ceres. Our word "cereal" comes from the name Ceres. It was the time of planting grain. Ceres was the Roman equivalent to the Greek goddess Demeter.

Anahit of Phoenicia, Canaan, and Ur was portrayed as carrying an ankh and wearing horns and a Moon disk. She was known by many other names, among them Anat, Qadesh, Anait, Anahita, and Anatu.

The Egyptians called their land Khemennu, or Land of the Moon. Plutarch wrote that they believed the Moon to be the Mother of the Universe. Although the goddess Bast was primarily considered to be a deity of the gentle Sun, she was also connected with the Moon.

The Floralia is still celebrated in many Central and Eastern European countries. It is a time to honor the goddess of flowers. People dress in gaily decorated costumes and wear flowers in their hair. Secretly delivering baskets of flowers on May Day is a remnant of this old festival. Although I did it as a child, I haven't seen this custom for years. This is such a shame, as children love to make the little paper baskets, choose the flowers, and leave them on a doorstep.

During this month was also the Incan Ayrihua or Camay Inca Raymi, the Festival of the Inca.

Correspondences

Nature Spirits: plant faeries

Herbs: basil, chives, dragons blood, geranium, thistle

Colors: crimson red, gold

Flowers: daisy, sweetpea

Scents: pine, bay, bergamot, patchouli

Stones: ruby, garnet, sard

Trees: pine, bay, hazel

Animals: bear, wolf

Birds: hawk, magpie

Deities: Kali, Hathor, Anahita, Ceres, Ishtar, Venus, Bast

Power Flow: energy into creating and producing; return balance to the nerves. Change, self-confidence, self-reliance, take advantage of opportunities. Work on temper and emotional flare-ups and selfishness.

Old Sayings & Lore

- Two New Moons in one month were said to predict a month's bad weather.
- Any New Moon on a Saturday or Sunday was said to predict rain and general bad luck.
- Good luck will come your way if you first see the New Moon outside and over your right shoulder. You can also make a wish that will be granted. The best luck came from looking at the Moon straight on.
- A ring around the Moon means rain or snow.

- If you move to a new house or location during a waning Moon, it will ensure you never go hungry.

- In medieval Europe and England, "Moon's men" were thieves and highwaymen who plied their trade by night. The current term "moonlighting" is similar, meaning to hold down an additional night job.

- In certain parts of England, the term "Moonrakers" eventually came to mean simple-minded people. The factual story behind this, though, reveals some pretty fast thinking by local smugglers. The English excise men (a combination of border patrol, ATF, and IRS) were out at night, trying to catch the smugglers red-handed. Hearing the excise men coming, the smugglers sank their loot in a lake and pretended to be fishing for the Moon reflected in the water. When the excise men asked what they were doing, the smugglers innocently replied they were raking for the Moon. The excise men went away shaking their heads over the stupidity of the local folk, while the smugglers fished up their goods and went on with their business.

Recipes

Herb-Frosted Currant Rolls

These are much like Hot Cross Buns, which date further back than the Christian tradition that has popularized them. Makes six dozen.

1	13¾-ounce package hot roll mix	¾	cup confectioners sugar
6	tablespoons sugar	½	teaspoon aniseed
½	cup currants or raisins	1	tablespoon lemon juice
1	egg, well beaten		

Prepare the roll mix according to the directions on the package, but add the sugar, currants, and egg. Cover with a dish towel or cheesecloth and let rise in a warm place until light and double in size, about 30–45 minutes.

Roll out the dough to a 1" thickness on a floured board. Cut with a floured biscuit cutter or the rim of a large glass. Place the rolls on a well-greased baking sheet. Cover again and let rise again until doubled in size.

Bake at 375° F for 20–30 minutes. Combine the confectioners sugar, aniseed, and lemon juice. Beat until smooth. Spread on warm rolls.

Deviled Eggs With Smoked Salmon

(Russia)

1 dozen hard-cooked eggs	1 8-ounce package cream cheese
1 teaspoon dry mustard	¼ cup mayonnaise
Pepper to taste	½ cup chopped smoked salmon

Cool and peel cooked eggs. Slice lengthwise and carefully remove yolks. Mash yolks and add mustard, cream cheese, mayonnaise, and salmon. Fill each egg-white half with the mixture. Cover and refrigerate.

Russian Tea

1 pot hot tea	Rum or vodka (optional)
⅛ teaspoon each cloves and nutmeg	Sprigs of mint
1 whole cinnamon stick	

Steep cloves, nutmeg, and cinnamon in the tea for several minutes. When ready to serve, add rum or vodka to each cup with a sprig of mint.

Crafts

Sixteenth Century Potpourri Mix

1 pint peppermint leaves, cut	1 tablespoon crushed cloves and coriander
1 pint lavender flowers	
1 tablespoon well-crushed caraway seeds	1 tablespoon crushed gum benzoin or orris root.
1 pint thyme	

Lightly mix together all of the ingredients. Put into a potpourri jar with a few dried rose and marigold petals on the top for color.

Equinox (Easter) Eggs

Decorated eggs at the Spring Equinox are nothing new. They were in use long before any connection with the Christian Easter. Red eggs in particular were given by many cultures as gifts at this season, in remembrance of the Great Goddess and Her life-renewing abilities. The ancient Romans celebrated the season by running races on an oval track and giving eggs as prizes.

Easter Egg

If you aren't fond of left-over hard-cooked eggs, and plan to use the eggs only as decorations, consider using just the empty shells. With a needle, make a small hole at the top and a slightly larger hole at the bottom of a raw egg. Be sure the needle or ice pick punctures the membrane inside. Hold the egg over a bowl and blow into the top hole until all the contents flow out the bottom. You now have an empty shell that can be decorated, and the insides can be scrambled or used for cooking. Be sure to gently wash the shell out before you decorate it.

Polish peasants used to decorate their eggs with elaborate cut-paper designs. Sometimes they colored the shells first, covering them with colored paper. Sometimes they left them white, using white paper. To cut a repeating design, fold a piece of paper into as many layers as needed to repeat a motif. Make a sketch of the design on the top layer. Cut around the design with scissors, being sure to cut through all the layers at the same time. Unfold the paper and paste the little cut-outs on the egg. Eggs can also be decorated with colored paper to resemble animals and birds, by attaching wings, ears, etc.

Spell Weaver Bath Salts

| 1 | cup salt | ¼ | teaspoon powdered dragons blood |
| 8 | drops myrrh oil | 2 | drops pine oil |

Cauldron Bath Salts
— For use During the Waning Moon —

| 1 | cup salt | 3 | drops synthetic musk oil |
| 3 | drops vervain oil | 6 | drops cypress oil |

Fantasy Bath Salts
— For Love —

| 1 | cup salt | 8 | drops rose oil |
| 8 | drops honeysuckle oil | 4 | drops patchouli oil |

Cerridwen Bath Salts

1 cup salt	8 drops jasmine oil
8 drops lotus oil	

Dark Huntress Bath Salts
—For Use During the Waning Moon—

1 cup salt	2 drops pine oil
3 drops rose geranium oil	8 drops magnolia oil
4 drops synthetic ambergris oil	

Myths

The Birth of Aphrodite/Venus

The Romans borrowed many of the Greek deities and their legends, changing the names but very few of the story details. One such deity was Aphrodite, who became the Roman Venus. In the beginning of the world and the deities, Rhea (the Earth) gave birth to several children by her son Uranus (the sky). But when Uranus started imprisoning her offspring, Rhea made a Moon sickle and talked her youngest son Cronus into castrating his father. When Cronus dropped the severed genitals into the ocean, a great mass of foam arose. Out of this foam stepped the beautiful goddess Aphrodite/Venus.

Venus

Actually, Aphrodite, like Athene, was of a much older origin than the usurping patriarchal pantheon. This tale of her "birth" was a way of granting an older powerful goddess a position of importance once again. In her Middle East aspect as Asherah or Astarte, this goddess had the oldest continuously-operated temple in the world.

Under the Roman name of Venus, this deity fell in love with a mortal man and gave birth to Aeneas. The Romans considered Venus their ancestral mother, since legend says that Aeneas founded the Roman civilization. The city of Venice is named after her.

Venus/Aphrodite is a Full Moon deity, one who sustains and nourishes life. Her powers are ripe, full-blooded, and powerful, but she also fiercely protects all that she creates. As a symbol of love and fertility, her symbols were cows, goats, sheep, doves, and bees.

Hathor, the Bright/Dark Mother

One of the Mother goddesses of Egypt was Hathor, often called mother of all deities and goddess of the Moon. Originally, she was called Het-Hert or Hat-Hor, meaning the House or Womb of Horus. Hathor was self-created, a strong hint that her worship

was in place when the male-dominating deities took over. The Egyptians called her the Heavenly Cow who made the Milky Way from her life-giving fluids. She was also identified with the legendary Nile goose who laid the Golden Egg of the Sun. She was queen of the West (the dead), but also the protectress of women and motherhood.

Hathor also had a darker side. In the beginning, when humankind was new upon the Earth, the Sun god Ra decided to punish humans because they became wicked and very disrespectful to the gods. He ordered Hathor to carry out his vengeance. The goddess slew humans until blood ran in rivers. Ra began to feel sorry for humans and called for Hathor to stop, but, being filled with anger, she refused. Finally Ra set out 7,000 jars of beer spiked with mandrake to resemble blood. Hathor drank them all, became very drunk, and forgot her blood-lust.

Hathor

The Cat-Goddess Bast

Although Bast was mostly identified with the gentle, creating power of the Sun, she was also identified with cats and the Moon. Herodotus said that the great sacred shrine in Bubastis was built in her honor. The cat was Egypt's most sacred animal, and the black cat was especially sacred to Bast. To kill a cat was an automatic death penalty. When the cats in the temple of Bast died, they were embalmed and buried with great ceremony. Bast's statues portray her with a cat-head.

A huge annual fair was held in her honor in Egypt. Thousands of worshippers journeyed up and down the Nile, accompanied by flutes, castanets, and lots of wine. Splendid processions went through the streets to her temples.

Bast also had a dark side which was known as Pasht, the Tearer. Pasht was an aspect of the Dark Moon, a goddess of retribution, revenge, and terror who could and would follow a human wherever he/she went in order to exact the punishment Pasht felt was due. Death was no deterrent to the Dark Moon goddess Pasht, for her powers extended beyond death and into the next reincarnation.

Rituals

Boat Blessing

The Chinese Dragon Boat Festival was held on the Full Moon in April. There was a procession of decorated boats up and down the rivers and lakes in the moonlight. Everyone participated, for they believed that this pleased the dragons who brought life-energies to the community. They would throw flowers into the water to carry their blessings and wishes.

To the Chinese, dragons were not loathsome creatures to be avoided, but rather wise, powerful beings who could help in many ways. Dragon-lovers of today realize the same thing and court their friendship. Dragons are powerful allies.

This is an excellent time to bless boats, whether or not they are decorated as dragons. The ancients said that each boat had a spirit built into it, and if that spirit were dissatisfied or angry, the boat would not handle properly in the wind and waves.

If you have a boat, large or small, consider using this ritual to improve its safety and performance. If you don't have a boat, this ritual can be used to bless cars, bikes, motorcycles, or whatever you use for transportation.

Walk around the boat clockwise and sprinkle it with a mixture of water and a bit of blessed salt. If the boat is in the water, walk around the deck, or as much of it as possible.

When you have finished, stand on the prow of the boat, or in front of it, and say:

> *Spirits of this boat* (call the boat by name if it has one),
> *I ask the blessings of the gods upon you.*
> *May you guide this vessel safely in calm or in storm.*
> *Use your powers to protect both this vessel and those who journey in it.*
> *I thank you for your efforts in our behalf.*

Hang a garland of flowers on the boat as an offering.

If you don't personally own a boat, but want to send your blessings of safety to all boats everywhere, choose a river that runs into the sea. Select flowers that are light enough to float on water. Go to the river bank or a dock and gently breathe your good wishes on each flower-head before dropping them one by one into the water. Say:

Spirits of all boats everywhere,
I ask the blessings of the gods upon you.
I ask that you bless and guide all vessels and mariners who
journey upon water,
Those that sail for pleasure,
Those that ply their trades upon the waves, bringing food
and supplies to needy people.
Let neither wind nor wave harm them.
Help them to avoid any disaster that threatens.
I thank you for your efforts.

It doesn't matter whether or not the flowers actually reach the ocean. Any vessel that passes these blessing-flowers will carry the message to other boats. The effect will ripple outward, like a stone dropped into a pond.

New Beginnings

There are innumerable times in each life when you are faced with the necessity of beginning anew. Too many times we do not give these beginnings the attention and consideration they deserve. Without planning and consideration, they can go off in directions other than positive. Some new beginnings might be: graduating from high school or college; new relationships; marriage; the birth of a child; a new job; the end of relationships or marriage; a death of someone close to you; an illness, or the aftermath of such an illness.

In order to open a new door we must close an old one. Often we know this must be done, but are at a loss as to how to do it. This ritual will set the stage. Be prepared to take advantage of the opportunities that will present themselves.

To help yourself prepare or deal with new beginnings, the following ritual can be of help. Set up an altar with a central lighted white candle. Cut a five-point star out of paper, or have a drawing of one. Have lotus oil ready beside the candle. Burn carnation incense to provide energy to tackle your new life. Dress in a white or pale lavender robe. If you wish to cast a circle, you can do so and include this ritual as part of your regular ceremony. However, it is not necessary to perform it within a cast circle.

Stand for a few moments before the altar. Breathe out all negative vibrations and breathe in only positive ones.

Holding the star in one hand, take your ritual dagger or sword in your power hand. Go to the East and hold the weapon's point outward, saying:

Be gone, all problems of thought and mind.
Be blown away by the winds of heaven.

Move to the South. Hold out the sword, say:

Be gone, all fears and harmful angers.
Be burned away by the fires of Spirit.

Go to the West. Hold out the sword, say:

Be gone, all insecurity and uncontrolled emotions.
Be washed clean by the sacred waters of the Great Mother.

Finish by going to the North. Hold out the sword, say:

Be gone, all stubbornness and rigidity.
Be buried deep in the cleansing, renewing Earth.

Return to the altar and hold the sword upright in salute. Say:

All negative influences and habits are cleansed by the gods.
I stand at my altar, renewed in spirit and strength.

Put a drop of lotus oil on the forefinger of your power hand. Visualize each chakra color as you touch that chakra. Begin by touching the top of the pubic hair triangle at the root chakra area. Say:

May the Kundalini rise in its proper time.
Grant me balance in my physical life.

Touch the spleen chakra (midway between the navel and the genitals). Say:

Open my mind like a flower to the wisdom you give.
Grant me balance of the mental powers.

Touch the navel at the solar plexus chakra. Say:

Guide my steps in my search for the truth.
Grant me balance and control of my emotions.

Touch the heart chakra in the center of the chest. Say:

Give me insight into the mysteries of the Cave of the Universal Heart.
Show me the spiritual path I must take.

Touch the base of your throat. Say:

Prepare my spiritual being to hear the voices of the gods.
Teach me the way of constructive creation.

Touch between the eyes and a little above the brows. Say:

Open my inner eyes to the psychic gifts.
Grant me correct usage of will power.

Touch the top of the head for the crown chakra. Say:

Unfold the thousand-petalled lotus blossom
That I may give and receive blessings.
Bless me, O Eternal and Ancient Ones,
So I may grow beyond the wheel of karma.

Bast, The Cat Goddess

The cat in Egypt was associated with both Bast and Pasht (the Moon). Pasht was the dark aspect of Bast. She was the Lady of the East, the mother of all cats, and wife of the god Ptah. Although she was said to be the embodiment of the living power and gentle heat of the Sun, through her sacred cats she was also connected with the Moon.

The cat was Egypt's most sacred animal. The temple of Bast kept especially sacred cats and embalmed them with great ceremony when they died. To kill a cat in Egypt meant a death sentence. Black cats were especially sacred to Bast; the black cat symbol was used by Egyptian physicians to advertise their healing.

The cat decorated the sistrum and sometimes Hathor's mirror. This animal represented the Moon. Mau was the Egyptian name for cat. The cat was domesticated very early and was valued as a snake-destroyer. The lynx (a type of wild cat with tufted ears) was known to the Egyptians as Maftet, and was considered benevolent and protecting. It was also a destroyer of serpents.

Bast was portrayed with a cat-head, carrying a sistrum in her right hand and a basket in her left. Usually she was draped in a green robe.

She was the goddess of fire, the Moon, childbirth, fertility, pleasure, benevolence, joy, sexual rites, music, dance,

Bast holding sistrum

protection against disease and evil spirits, intuition, healing, marriage, and all animals (especially cats).

Bast can be honored by establishing a woodland or garden shrine to the Nature spirits and wild animals. Put a statue of a cat in this sacred space to represent the goddess.

For blessing by the goddess Bast, of yourself and your cat pets, set up an altar with cat pictures and/or statues. These pictures and statues can be of any kind of cat, domestic or wild. Place a picture of yourself, your family, and some of your cats there also. Have two green candles on the altar. This ritual can be performed by itself or as part of a cast circle ritual.

Take the sistrum and slowly dance or walk around the ritual area, shaking the sistrum as you go. Begin and end in the East and move clockwise. Chant as you go:

> *Joy comes from Bast, the Lady of Cats.*
> *The goddess loves and protects all animals.*
> *As a daughter/son of Bast, I call upon her*
> *To pour out her blessings.*

Return to the altar and shake the sistrum while you say:

> *Hail, Bast, Lady of Cats.*
> *Hail, Goddess of earthly delights.*
> *Teach me to rejoice in the being that I am.*
> *Teach me to love and be happy.*

If you have pictures of your cats, look at them now with love and happiness. If you don't have pictures, call up their images mentally. Call each cat by name as if presenting her/him to the goddess. Be alert to the atmosphere around you, for you will very likely experience the presence of the goddess in some manner.

When you have finished, take the sistrum and go to the East. Shake the sistrum five times. Say:

> *The ears of Bast are sensitive to every word of harm sent*
> *against me and my pets.*
> *My cats and I are protected.*

Go to the South, shake the sistrum five times, and say:

> *The claws of Bast are sharp in my defense.*
> *My cats and I are protected.*

Move to the West. Shake the sistrum five times. Say:

> *The teeth of Bast are bared to evil-doers.*
> *My cats and I are protected.*

Finally, go to the North and shake the sistrum five times. Say:

> *The eyes of Bast can see through darkness.*
> *Nothing escapes her notice.*
> *My cats and I are protected.*

Return to the altar. Shake the sistrum three times. Say:

> *Listen well, all those who would harm me and mine.*
> *Here is erected a mighty fortress, an unbreakable shield.*
> *You cannot enter here. Your evil thoughts return to you.*
> *The gate is locked against you.*

Visualize a green light filling the room, caressing you and the pictures of your cats. Don't be surprised if your cats themselves enter the room to soak up this blessing.

> *Lovely Cat-Goddess, I thank you for your blessings.*
> *Keep us in safety, good health, and happiness.*
> *Protect my little ones wherever they may roam.*

Blow a kiss to the goddess and extinguish the candles. As a special treat, both to Bast and to your cats, present your pets with a catnip toy to play with.

To petition Bast for healing of cats, chant the following before her picture/statue, while holding an actual picture or mental image of the sick animal:

> *Lift the hand of disease.*
> *Restore health!*
> *Cast out all illness.*
> *Restore health!*
> *Pour your healing powers through* (name of the cat).
> *Bast! Restore health!*

If your cats are really in physical danger, call upon the dark aspect of Bast—the goddess Pasht.

Neith of the Veil
— Crescent Moon —

Neith (pronounced Night) was the Opener of the Ways, the Huntress, Lady of the West, warrior-goddess and protectress. Her name means "I have come from myself," or self-begotten. The Greeks identified her with Pallas Athene.

Egyptian records show Neith's cult to be an ancient one, with two queens of the First Dynasty named after her. She wore the red crown of Lower Egypt, and in her hands she held a bow and two arrows. The vulture was sacred to Neith and other goddesses. The hieroglyphic sign for "mother" was a vulture.

Plutarch visited the great temple of Neith in Sais and read there the inscription: "I am all that has been, that is, and that will be. No mortal has yet been able to lift the veil that covers me." Part of this sanctuary was a school of medicine called the House of Life. This school was run by the priests of Neith.

Neith was the deity of herbs, magick, healing, mystical knowledge, rituals, and meditation. She was patroness of the domestic arts, weaving, hunting, medicine, war, and weapons. She was also called the protectress of women and marriage.

Stand before the altar. Raise your arms in greeting as you say:

Dark Huntress, Opener of the Way, Lady of the West,
I call upon you.
You who are all that has been, that is, and that will be,
Teach me the Dark and sacred Mysteries.
For without understanding the dreams that lead to the inner door,
I am not complete.
Dreams are the night-teachers of the Ancient Ones.
Teach me, great Neith.

Cross your hands on your breast and await Neith's blessings. Raise your arms in greeting once more and say:

Silver Huntress, riding the pale clouds of midnight,
I greet your celestial light with gladness.
Beauteous Lady of the Night, I await the dreams you send,
Visions and magick lie within your realms of power.
Teach me the Mysteries of the Threefold Goddess
Symbolized by the turning Moon on high.
Mother of healing and ancient wisdom, bless me.

Petitioning the Love Goddess
—Full Moon—

Venus was a Moon goddess, the patroness of flowers and vegetation, as seen in her participation in the Floralia. Although she was sometimes called virginal, this meant independent, not the physical sexual state. The heron and dove were her sacred birds. Although Aphrodite and Venus were similar in nature, Venus was definitely a goddess of sexual activity, not necessarily having anything to do with marriage. Her temples housed sacred prostitutes, and her priestesses were not required to be physical virgins. She was the deity of love, beauty, the joy of physical love, fertility, continued creation, renewal, and herbal magick.

This ritual is best performed during or on the Full Moon. Burn a love incense, such as rose. Have roses or rose petals on the altar, along with a pink cord or thread long enough to go around your waist. A little statue of Venus or a dove can be used to strengthen your connection with the goddess. You also need a pink candle in a holder and a metal bowl.

Write on a small piece of paper "Someone to truly love me." If you are spelling a specific person, think carefully about the karmic repercussions before you proceed. This is trying to control another person, something which you would not like done to you. Besides, if you magickally force another person to "love" you, there will always be a feeling of resentment, even if they never know what you did. And most of the time, these "lovers" will create a situation that will allow them to get away from you. Those who do stay you can count on being the kind that you will have to work hard to get rid of at a later date. Don't play Russian roulette with your love life. The goddess of love is far wiser than you. Let her choose the perfect companion.

When you are ready, stand at your altar quietly for a few minutes to relax. Then light the pink candle. Say:

> *My heart is empty.*
> *Send one who will fill it with love.*
> *My soul is longing.*
> *Lead me to spiritual harmony.*
> *My mind lies dormant.*
> *Fill it with fertility.*

Pass the thread or cord through the incense smoke. Then pass the paper through the smoke, saying:

> *Let there be a bond of love*
> *That holds us fast through time and space,*

And draws us onward till we stand
Heart to heart and face to face.

Bind the paper to your waist by the cord. Stand silently for several moments, thanking Venus for her help. Listen to her advice; she may speak to you later in dreams or through friends. Then lay the paper on your altar tied up with the cord. Leave the paper and cord there overnight. Extinguish the candle.

The next evening, go back to the altar. Light some love incense and the pink candle. Talk to Venus in your own words, telling her what characteristics you most desire in a companion. Then light the paper from the candle flame and drop it to burn in a metal bowl. Dispose of the ashes when they are cool.

Lady of the Sycamore
— Dark Moon —

The Egyptian goddess Hathor was known as the Lady of the Sycamore, Queen of the West (or the Dead), House of the Womb of Horus, Queen of Heaven, and "the golden." Seven aspects of her, called the seven Hathors, were said by the Egyptians to be the Holy Midwives and associated with the seven planets. It was her duty to carry the Sacred Eye of Ra. The mirror, tambourine, and sistrum were sacred to her. Hathor's appearance could be as a cow-headed woman or one with a human head and horns. It was said that this goddess embodied herself in the sistrum to drive away evil spirits.

Her main sanctuary was at Dendera where she was worshipped with her infant son Ihi, "the Sistrum Player." She was also worshipped at Edfu along with her husband Horus. The Egyptians said she carried the dead to the afterworld.

Hathor was another protectress of women, marriage, the family, and motherhood. She had power over love, pleasure, flowers, the sky, the Moon, tombs, the arts, wine and beer, music, the dance, physical comfort, astrology, prosperity, and protection.

Cast your circle as usual. Besides your regular ritual tools, you will need: an ankh and lotus incense. After casting the circle and setting the direction guardians, stand before the altar. Chant:

The Moon is dark, and the goddess is near.
Hail, Hathor, Lady of the Sycamore, Queen of the West!
The time of magick is high, and I ask your presence here.

Reach out over the altar and, as if parting a veil, move your hands away from each other. Say:

Behold, the goddess comes!
See her beauty in the star-filled sky.
Hear her whispers within this sacred place,
Whispers of magick and instruction.
Hear the mighty voice of Hathor in the evening winds.
Her words of wisdom and prophecy are whispers,
Whispers within this sacred place.

Bow your head for a few moments to the approaching goddess. Take up the ankh and press it briefly against your breast. Then go to the East. Hold up the ankh, say:

From the East and the dawn skies come words of magick and power.
Great Hathor, I listen for your teachings.

Move to the South. Hold up the ankh, say:

From the South and the noonday come action and purpose.
Great Hathor, I listen for your teachings.

Go to the West, hold up the ankh, say:

From the West and the twilight comes emotional power.
Great Hathor, I listen for your teachings.

Finish by going to the North. Hold up the ankh, say:

From the North and the night skies comes the grounding to Earth,
necessary in all magick.
Great Hathor, I listen for your teachings.

Return to the altar and lay aside the ankh. Say:

O Great Hathor, I listen and take into myself your offered
words of magick and power.

Place your power hand on the altar and chant:

I return through the temple Veil of Mysteries
To stand once more within my own place and time.
Praise be to Hathor.

Reach out your hands and bring them together as if closing a curtain. Close the circle as usual.

Chapter 8

HARE MOON

May

Also called: Merry or Dyad Moon, Bright Moon, Flower Moon,
Frogs Return Moon, Thrimilcmonath (Thrice-Milk Month),
Sproutkale, Winnemanoth (Joy Month), Planting Moon,
Moon When the Ponies Shed.

Fifth day of the New Moon is the Mugwort Festival in China.

Full Moon is also known as the Pestilent Moon in China; Chung K'uei, the
great spiritual chaser of demons, is honored.

May 1: Rowan Witch Day for the Finnish goddess Rauni.

May 4: Sacred Thorn (Moon) Tree Day in Ireland; the Hawthorn
Month begins.

May 5: Feast of the Dragon in China.

May 9: Feast of Artemis in Greece.

May 9, 11, and 13: The Lemuria in Rome, when the wandering spirits
of family members were acknowledged.

May 12: Festival of Shashti in India; Aranya Shashti is a Forest god similar to Pan.

May 15: Day of Maia, a Full Moon goddess, in Greece.

May 16: The Savitu-Vrata in India, honoring Sarasvati, Queen of Heaven.

May 19-28: The Kallyntaria and Plynteria: a festival of Spring cleaning and purification in Greece and Rome.

May 23: The Rosalia in Rome, the Rose Festival of Flora and Venus.

May 24: Birth of Artemis/Diana; called the Thargelia; usually on the New Crescent Moon. An older Greek celebration on this day was to honor the Horae. Also the celebration of the Three Mothers of the Celtic countries, who brought prosperity and a good harvest.

May 26: The Day of Chin-hua-fu-jen in China, an Amazon goddess similar to Diana.

May 26-31: Festival of Diana as goddess of the wildwood in Rome.

May 30-31: Feast of the Queen of the Underworld in Rome.

The Greek goddess Maia, the most important of the Seven Sisters (the Pleiades) and said to be the mother of Hermes, gave the name to this month. Some form of this goddess's name was known to people from Ireland to as far away as India. The Romans called her Maius, goddess of Summer and honored her at the Ambarvalia, a family festival for purification and protection of farm land.

In the Celtic cultures, May was called Mai or Maj, a month of sexual freedom. Green was worn during this month to honor the Earth Mother. May 1 was the Celtic festival of Beltane, a festival celebrating fertility of all things. Cattle were driven through the Beltane bonfires for purification and fertility. In Wales, Creiddylad was connected with this festival and often called the May Queen. The maypole and its dance is a remnant of these old festivities.

The Sheila Na Gig is still seen carved in the decorations of many Irish churches. This goddess figure is a grotesque, often emaciated, woman shown squatting and holding wide her private parts. Many Irish still know her as the protector of the poor and hang old clothes on hawthorn bushes on May 4; this is believed to avert poverty. It is possible that the Australian term "Sheila," used as a name for any woman, refers to this ancient deity and her carvings.

Bona Dea, the Roman Good Goddess, had her festival on the night between May 2 and 3. No men were allowed to attend.

The Roman festival of Lemuria was to placate and remember the Lemures, or the wandering spirits of the dead. Each family performed its own private ceremonies, which ended with taking gifts to the graves. For those who had died and had no graves, the head of the household walked barefoot through the house, casting nine black beans behind him.

The Greeks had a special festival for the god Pan during May. Pan was a wild-looking deity, half man, half goat. As a token of his frequent sexual adventures, he was shown with an erect penis. Pan invented the syrinx, or pan-pipes, made out of reeds. Originally, he was not an oppressor of women, but their loving companion.

May 19-28 was the solemn Greek festival called Kallyntaria and Plynteria. This was devoted to the cleaning and freshening of sacred statues and temples. The statues, small enough to be moved, were taken to a nearby river or lake and washed until clean. This was serious business with no singing or merry-making.

At the end of the month was a Roman celebration honoring the Underworld Queen Prosperina and her consort Pluto. Proserpina ruled over the resting place of the shades (souls), but her kingdom was connected with more than death. Pluto was also known as the deity of hidden wealth.

In Finland, May 1 was celebrated as Rowan Witch Day, a time of honoring the goddess Rauni, who was associated with the mountain ash or rowan. Twigs and branches of the rowan were, and still are, used as protection against evil in this part of the world. Some sources list Rauni as a god.

The Slavonic-Russian cultures had a similar, but longer, festival celebrating merriment, rivers, and well-being. This occurred between May 25 and June 25. Originally, it honored the goddess Lada, who later was changed to the god Lado.

Mugwort was a sacred herb in China and Europe. As part of the celebration on May 5, the Chinese made dolls out of the leaves. They hung these dolls above gates and doors to repel negative influences and entities.

In Tibet, an old Nature festival for the beginning of Summer and the rain deities became a celebration of Buddha's death and his attainment of Buddha-hood. The attainment festival occurred on May 8, while celebration of Buddha's death was on May 15. Deceased relatives were prayed for at this time.

The Incas held Aymoray Quilla or Hatun Cuzqui, which was the Great Cultivation.

Correspondences

Nature Spirits: faeries, elves
Herbs: dittany of Crete, elder, mint, rose, mugwort, thyme, yarrow
Colors: green, brown, pink
Flowers: lily of the valley, foxglove, rose, broom
Scents: rose, sandalwood

Stones: emerald, malachite, amber, carnelian

Trees: hawthorn

Animals: cats, lynx, leopard

Birds: swallow, dove, swan

Deities: Bast, Venus, Aphrodite, Maia, Diana, Artemis, Pan, Horned God

Power Flow: full creating energy; propagation. Intuition, contact with faeries and other supernatural beings. Strengthen connection with supernatural protectors and beings around you. Power flowing from the Greenwood Gods and trees.

Old Sayings & Lore

- To dream of a future husband, go out into the light of the first Full Moon of the new year. Say:

  Moon, Moon, tell unto me
  When my true love I shall see.
  What fine clothes am I to wear?
  How many children shall I bear?
  For if my love comes not to me
  Dark and dismal my life will be.

- The Irish say that to see the future, for good or ill, take a mirror outside. Let the light of the Moon fall on the surface and stare into it. Any face that appears will be connected with your future.

- In some parts of Ireland, upon seeing the New Moon, people bowed or knelt, saying:

  O Moon, leave us as well as you found us.

- Some farmers still believe that crops sown near a Full Moon will be ready for harvest a month earlier than crops sown during a waxing Moon.

- Cornish tin miners had some very interesting ideas about the Moon. One of these said that if you put a piece of tin in an ant hill near a certain phase of the Moon (unspecified), it would turn into silver.

- Upon seeing the New Moon, bow to her and turn over the silver or coins in your pocket. This will bring you luck in all your affairs.

Recipes

Yogurt Drink

The people of the Far East, particularly India, use yogurt in much of their cooking. This drink is rather like an exotic milkshake and so much more healthy. Serves six.

1	quart plain low-fat yogurt	6	tablespoons honey
2	tablespoons rose water or		or light brown sugar
	4 drops of rose essence	6	ice cubes

Put the yogurt, rose water, and honey in a blender and puree. Add the ice cubes and blend until the yogurt is whipped. Serve in tall glasses.

Herbed Sour Cream Dip

This garnish is good with sticks of celery, carrots, or zucchini, or cherry tomatoes. It makes good finger-food for children or adults. Makes ¾ cup.

½	cup plain yogurt or	⅟₁₆	teaspoon ground red pepper
	dairy sour cream	¼	teaspoon dried basil leaves,
¼	cup mayonnaise		crumbled
⅛	teaspoon garlic powder	¼	teaspoon salt
⅛	teaspoon onion salt		Paprika
⅟₁₆	teaspoon pepper		

Combine the yogurt, mayonnaise, garlic powder, onion salt, pepper, red pepper, basil and salt; mix thoroughly. Chill. Just before serving, garnish with a sprinkle of paprika.

Crafts

Perfumed Bags

As recently as the early 1900s, perfumed bags for drawers were used to impart a pleasant odor to clothing, stationery, and the room itself. Houses tended to get damp and musty smelling, and this was one of the methods housewives used to overcome the problem. The following has been modified from a nineteenth century recipe.

2 ounces yellow sandalwood
2 ounces orris root
2 ounces cloves
2 ounces dried rose petals
1 pound oak shavings

2 ounces coriander seeds
2 ounces calamus aromaticus
2 ounces cinnamon bark
2 ounces lavender flowers

Cut and slice the ingredients into a coarse powder and mix well together. Essential oils of rose and lavender may be discreetly added to intensify the scents. Put the mixture into small draw-string bags and place in clothing drawers.

Hollyhock Dolls

This pastime was taught to me by my grandmother, who said she and her sisters made these dolls when they were small. It is still a fascinating pursuit for little girls. Take a fully-opened blossom with a short piece of the stem still attached. Turn it upside-down; this will be the skirt. Pick a tight bud for the head. With a toothpick make a hole in the "neck" at the bottom of the bud. Insert the stem tip of the skirt portion. These dolls make unusual and delightful table decorations as well as toys. There was a rhyme about hollyhock dolls:

Hollyhock, hollyhock, bend for me.
Give me some cheese (pollen) for my dolly's tea.

Lavender Hot Pot Potpourri

2 ounces lavender flowers
1 broken stick cinnamon
1 ounce granular myrrh gum

1 ounce rose petals
2 ounces damiana leaves

Mystery of India Cologne

1 pint distilled water
1 ounce glycerin
1 ounce powdered frankincense
1 drop lemon oil

¼ pint alcohol
1 teaspoon nutmeg
1 teaspoon cinnamon
1 drop tonka bean extract

Mysterious Orient Cologne

¼ pint alcohol	1 pint distilled water
1 ounce glycerin	1 drop wisteria oil
1 drop rose oil	1 drop lemon oil
1 teaspoon vanilla	

Great Goddess Bath Salts

I've been told this smells like White Shoulders perfume.

1 cup salt	4 drops myrrh oil
8 drops magnolia oil	8 drops lily oil

Circle of Flame Bath Salts
—For Love—

1 cup salt	8 drops violet oil
4 drops synthetic musk oil	4 drops rose oil

Oak Leaf Hat

The Oak King, the Green Man, and the Lord of the Forest (Cernunnos) were probably aspects of one deity. To honor this god of Nature, children (and adults) can make and wear an oak leaf hat. Collect a number of large oak leaves. Using either short pieces of tender twigs or toothpicks, begin by pinning two leaves together in two different places.

Cernunnos

Place the first twig near the stem and the other near the lobe. Arrange the leaves so they meet at the top. Continue adding and pinning the leaves together. Shape to the head, being careful not to make the hat too flat. These hats remind me of the woodland faeries one sees peeking from behind trees.

Myths

The Birth of Artemis/Diana

The Greek god Zeus was always involved in some affair with either a goddess or some hapless mortal woman. Leto, also called Latona, was a daughter of Titans and so beautiful that the king of the gods fell in love with her. Soon she was pregnant with twins. To avoid the wrath and revenge of Hera, Leto fled to the island of Delos, originally called Ortygia, where she gave birth to her children in a cave. The Moon goddess Artemis/Diana was born a full day before her brother, the Sun god Apollo.

Artemis/Diana

Hera was furious. She sent the great serpent Python after Leto, but the sea god Poseidon hid her. The young Apollo, extremely strong and handsome, fortified himself with nectar and ambrosia. Taking the arrows forged for him by the smith-god Hephaestus, he sought out the monster in Parnassus and killed it.

Artemis was as beautiful as her brother was handsome, but unlike Apollo, this goddess did not partake of sexual pleasures. She was the Virgin Huntress, the Hunter of Souls. As soon as she was born, Artemis went directly to her father Zeus and begged for a short tunic, hunting boots, a silver bow, and a quiver full of arrows.

The Amazons were loyal to her under her New Moon phase. Her favorite places were the woodlands and mountains of Arcadia, where she roamed accompanied by sixty Oceanids, twenty nymphs, and a pack of hounds called the Alani. She became the defender of women who were harassed or threatened by men. Although she had nothing to do with men and did not allow her nymphs to become involved either, Artemis was the patroness of women's fertility and childbirth.

The Horae

The Horae (the Hours or Seasons) were the guardian goddesses of the cycles of Nature and law and order. They were Eunomia (wise legislation), Dike (justice), and Irene/Eirene (peace). They were the daughters of Zeus and the Titaness Themis. The Greeks considered only Spring, Summer, and Autumn as seasons, looking upon Winter as a time of sleep and death. But most of Greece honored the Horae as deities of order, propriety, and morality in human life.

Eunomia was especially honored by the Senate since she dealt primarily with political life and the making of just laws. Dike was said to report directly to her father Zeus of every injustice to any human. Eirene was honored by songs and festivities; she was also considered to be the mother of Plutos, the god of riches, who accompanied Dionysus.

Maia & the Pleiades

Maia, for whom the month of May was named, was one of the Seven Sisters of Roman-Greek mythology; these sisters were later called the Pleiades. They were born in Arcadia to the giant Atlas and an unnamed mother. Their names are given as Alcyone, Calaeno, Electra, Maia, Merope, Asterope, and Taygete. Although these sisters originally accompanied Artemis, they later were involved with men. Electra had a son, Dardanus, who was said to have founded the city of Troy.

The giant Orion saw them once as they danced in an Arcadian meadow and decided he wanted all seven of the sisters. They refused and he gave chase. They cried out to Zeus who changed them into a constellation; he also placed Orion and his dog Sirius in the heavens. Legend says that only six of the sister-stars are visible because Electra hid to avoid seeing the destruction of Troy. Later Electra was transformed into a comet, ranging the heavens in her grief.

Pan

The woodland god Pan was an amorous deity who liked nothing better than to chase down and seduce females. One day Syrinx, the daughter of the river god Ladon, walked along the riverbank near Pan's woodland domain. When Pan spied her, he set out in pursuit, chasing the frightened nymph for some time. At last he was close enough to reach out for her. As Syrinx felt his rough hand and heard his heavy breathing near her ear, she screamed out to her father Ladon to protect her. The river god changed the nymph into a clump of reeds along the bank near the water's edge.

Unwilling to concede defeat, Pan waited for a long time for Syrinx to change back, but she never did. Finally, the woodland god plucked some of the reeds and fastened them together in a horizontal line with stopped ends. When he blew across the open upper end, he found he made beautiful music. Thus the syrinx, or pan-pipes, were invented.

Although Pan came to be portrayed as a lecherous being under patriarchal rule, originally he simply represented the male forces of Nature. He was a son of the Earth, a fertility deity, the Little God. The Christians made him into their main devil.

Rituals

Feast of the Dragon

In China, the Feast of the Dragon was held during this month. To the Chinese, dragons were not evil creatures, but helpful ones. They were said to bring rain and prosperity, rule all water, be healing, and chase away evil. Most people are familiar with the dragon images paraded during the Chinese New Year celebrations, but few understand that China had many other dragon festivals.[1] Dragons are fascinating, but wily, creatures who have great power and magickal knowledge.

Boats decorated as dragons were sailed on rivers and lakes in the moonlight to entice the dragon-energies to come into the community. The people floated flowers on the waters to carry their messages to the dragons.

Dragons are wonderful supernatural beings. They have had bad experiences with human adults, though, and tend to be wary about making themselves known. If you are patient and persistent, you can entice dragons to be friends. The easiest to encounter are the guardian dragons, the "baby" of the species.

Personal guardian dragons come in various shapes and sizes, and are usually quite small in comparison with the adults. They come in all colors, pastel or light shades with belly scales of a multitude of hues. The little guardian dragons are almost always supervised by one or more adult dragons, which you may or may not see.

The little dragons are not as powerful as the larger ones, but they can help with protection, friendship, love, divination (such as tarot, runes, crystal reading), the development of psychic abilities, dancing, music, and general rituals. Their most important task, however, is protection of you, your family, and your home. They are more or less astral watch-dogs.

These little personal dragons are the most friendly of their species and the most fun-loving. They enjoy impromptu rituals that include dancing, singing, and fun in general. They like ginger and sweet smelling or spicy incenses. They are likely to hang

Dragon Motif

over your shoulder while you read cards or look into a crystal. If you have trouble visualizing your dragons, try putting a piece of crystal to your third eye on your forehead.

If you want to make friends with your guardian dragons, and let them know you are aware of their existence, do this simple welcoming ritual. Burn a candle, any color except black; this color is predominantly that of the huge Chaos Dragons. Burn a spicy or sweet incense. Set out a few crystals to draw their attention. Then chant:

> *Little dragons, rainbow bright,*
> *Good friends of this family,*
> *Send good wishes to us all.*
> *Join our rituals merrily.*
> *Protect us through each day and night,*
> *While awake or while asleep.*
> *Through your love and vigilance*
> *Do this family safely keep.*

Day of Remembrance

The ancient Romans celebrated the Lemuria on May 9, 11, and 13; why they split the days this way, no one knows. During these times they honored the wandering ancestral and family spirits. Many modern people still make the trip to the cemetery during the Memorial Day weekend for the purpose of putting flowers on graves, a way of acknowledging and remembering deceased family members. However, it is not necessary to go to cemeteries to honor your ancestors. In your long lineage, most of your ancestors will not have been buried near you, and some will have been cremated and their ashes scattered or their physical bodies lost. This day of remembrance is not to honor a decayed physical body, but to honor the bloodlines that led to your existence.

Set up a spot within your home as a temporary ancestor altar; choose a setting that will not be disturbed for at least a week. On this altar place what pictures you have of deceased family members. If you have no pictures, print out their names on a nice piece of paper. Arrange a small vase of fresh flowers near the pictures. Burn lavender or rose incense daily near this area.

Sometime during each day of this week, go to your remembrance altar and talk with your ancestors. Don't forget to call upon the ones so far back in your lineage that you never met them. Burn a white candle there for at least an hour each day.

Perhaps you have a few immediately deceased family members with whom you didn't get along. Most people do. If you find their spirit energies causing problems (and some will do this), simply remove their pictures until they can behave themselves. This may sound silly, but it works on most spirits. They want to be remembered and acknowledged, not put out of mind and sight. However, a very few will be incorrigible and will have to be denied admittance to your home.

Each day, ask your ancestors for advice and help. If you meditate near this altar, you may well find yourself visiting with loved ones. And remember to think about and call upon them throughout the rest of the year, especially at important occasions. The Irish side of my family always lit a white candle during the Winter Solstice-Christmas season and set an extra place at the table. I was told this would help the loved ones find their way back so they could join in the festivities.

Festival of Cleaning & Purification

On May 19-28, the Greeks and Romans celebrated two festivals: the Kallyntaria and the Plynteria. This was a ceremony of Spring cleaning and purification which extended all the way from the temples to individual homes.

In Greece, the Full Moon goddess Maia was honored during May, to which she gave her name. But ancient China called this the Pestilent Moon, a time of being invaded by demons and other supernatural troublemakers. They called upon Chung K'uei, who was known as the great spiritual chaser of demons, to clear out those entities intent on causing problems.

Whether you live a fast-paced existence or a laid-back lifestyle, personal environments tend to get cluttered. One needs to have a repeating cycle of cleaning and purification. It is easy to extend this train of thought to the personal life. We have a habit of holding on to old friendships or relationships that should have been allowed to cease existence. We hold on to old emotions, good and bad. By locking ourselves into dying and dysfunctional habits, we limit our forward progress.

This is an excellent time to recycle clothing that you haven't worn for the past two years. Donate it to an organization that helps those in need. Take a look at your kitchen cupboards; if you have unused or duplicate utensils, recycle them too. Some people like to have yard sales. I would rather donate my clean-outs to an organization such as Good Will or the Salvation Army.

This cleaning, followed by a purification of yourself and your home, is an excellent preparation for the ritual of the Three Mothers of prosperity. After all, Nature abhors a vacuum and will fill it. Why not set up your vacuum to be filled with prosperity?

Although this ritual is given as a part of cleansing and purification, it is also valuable if you are feeling under attack, either from others or from life itself. This ritual is actually to strengthen the psychic shield around your body and aura.

Begin on the night before the Full Moon. Set your altar in place where it will not be disturbed for at least twenty-four hours. Place a cauldron in the center of the altar with a red candle on the right, a black one on the left, and a white directly behind the cauldron. Do not light the candles at this time.

Sprinkle a mixture of equal parts of elder blossoms, marjoram, mint, and rue in an unbroken circle around the cauldron. Into a tiny vial, put equal drops of oils of clove, frankincense, jasmine, and lavender. Set the sealed bottle into the cauldron and leave it until the night of the Full Moon.

On Full Moon night, take a cleansing bath and either dress in white or go nude. Burn a good protective and/or purification incense, and carry it through every room in the house. Make certain that the smoke drifts into closets.

Return to the altar and light the candles. Take up your ritual knife or sword, face the East, and raise the knife in salute. Say:

> *By the power of the rising Sun,*
> *All evil in my life is done.*

Turn to the South and say:

> *By the power of the noonday blast,*
> *All control is mine at last.*

Turn to the West and say:

> *By the power of the darkening night,*
> *My shield is strong, my armor tight.*

Turn to the North and say:

> *By Full Moon in blackened sky,*
> *I am not alone. My help is nigh.*
> *The Goddess's hands around me stay,*
> *To keep me safe by night and day.*
> *Begone, foul spirits, unbidden here!*
> *I send you out. I do not fear,*
> *For I have won. I am set free!*
> *You have no further power o'er me.*

Take up the vial of oil. Put a drop of oil on your forefinger and anoint your forehead, heart, solar plexus, wrists, and tops of your feet. As you do this, visualize a shining blue suit of armor slowly descending over your body until you are entirely protected. Cap the bottle and store it in a safe place. Thank the Goddess for her help and extinguish the candles.

Apply the oil and repeat the chants whenever you feel the armor is slipping.

Mugwort Festival

Mugwort is a very magickal herb, especially when gathered at the Summer Solstice or Full Moon. It was sacred to the Druids and many other ancient cultures for ritual workings. The Chinese considered it so important that they gave mugwort its own festival.

Mugwort can be rubbed on crystal balls and magick mirrors to increase their strength. To create a clairvoyant drink, soak ¼ ounce of mugwort in a bottle of light wine for nine days (a Moon number), beginning on the New Moon. At the end of that time, strain out the mugwort. Use several layers of fine cloth as mugwort has a lot of fuzz. Replace the wine in the bottle and cap tightly. Drink a small amount to aid clairvoyance, divination, and crystal reading.

This ritual is for use with a crystal ball, magick mirror, or piece of crystal. Even a cup of water can act as a scrying device. A fancy, expensive crystal ball is not a prerequisite to reading the future. Whatever you decide to use (crystal ball, mirror, or sliver of crystal), keep it covered when not in use. People are fascinated by such things and like to handle them. This overlays your vibrations with those of someone else, thus making it more difficult to use the device. Some cats can become absolutely engrossed in looking at crystal balls. I've never found a cat to leave vibrations, though.

Scrying requires a tremendous amount of patience. Seldom do the pictures, in the ball or within the mind, come at once. Relax; don't strain to get something. You don't have to stare at the crystal until you get eye strain or a headache either. Let your vision go slightly out of focus and try to be a spectator. Watch and listen within your mind to what may surface. Some people actually see pictures within the crystal. My experience is that the device seems to clarify and strengthen my psychic powers, providing me with mental images and messages.

Place your scrying aid on your pentacle[2] and circle it five times with your wand while saying:

> *One for the Maiden, shining bright.*
> *One for the Lady of the night.*
> *One for the Old One, all-knowing and wise.*
> *One for the God of the Sun-washed skies.*
> *One for the gift of prophecy.*
> *I ask you now, show the future to me.*

Proceed with your scrying.

Honoring the Three Mothers

The Three Mothers, or Triple Goddess, were known around the world. The Triple Goddess represented the three stages of human life: youth and puberty, parenthood and maturity, old age and wisdom; or body, mind, and spirit. This triad symbolized the three phases of the Moon: Crescent, Full, and Dark. The goddesses were most often known by the titles of Maid, Mother, and Crone. The ancient Mystery schools, which were originally centers of Goddess knowledge, had three main steps or degrees.

The number three was a sacred number from the time of the ancient Babylonians on. Pythagoras wrote that the Uni-

Celtic Knotwork

versal Order had to manifest itself in threes. The ancient Chinese thought that three engendered all things. Even today, in numerology the number three stands for activity, creativity, talent, and knowledge.

The Celtic countries, in particular, honored this triad as the bringer of prosperity and a good harvest. The Celts considered the Horned God of the Forests to be Her consort and help-mate. During the month of May, especially at the ceremony of Beltane, wearing of the color green and freely expressing themselves sexually was widely practiced by the Celts. This practice became a real headache for the Christians when they took over. They tried to curb this custom by declaring that the color green was unlucky and that sex was sinful and dirty.

Today, we realize that sexual freedom must be used with discretion. Unplanned pregnancies can create emotional havoc in all lives, including that of the child. Over-population is also the biggest pollution of the Earth. With population sky-rocketing, sexual diseases on the increase, and AIDS a constant danger, all people, young and old, must act responsibly.

We can look at the Three Mothers as more than sexual activity. They are symbols of the cycles of growth upon the Earth, the phases we physically go through in our present life, cycles of events within our lives.

Sometimes we are uncertain as to where we actually are in a cycle of events. This can be frustrating and depressing. We may have to endure until the completion of the cycle, but it's comforting to have some idea how much longer we must grin and bear it. This divination ritual can give you some idea of where you are in that cycle. If you are observant, wise enough to seek guidance, and willing to make changes, however painful, you can often shorten the cycle.

This is best done during the waxing or Full Moon, but in a pinch can be performed any time. If performed during a Crescent Moon, it will predominantly point out the root beginnings of the cycle, possibly what started the events in motion. The Full Moon will tell you how the events went, or will go, during the height of the happenings. The Dark Moon reveals the outcome or ending of the cycle.

Spread a nice cloth on a table where you can sit and spread out the tarot cards. Light a white candle on each side of your working area. Burn a good divination incense. If you use charcoal and a burner, add mugwort to the incense. Sit for a few moments with the tarot cards in your hands. Breathe out all negatives, and breathe in positive energies.

Shuffle the cards three, six, or nine times, while thinking strongly about the cycle of events you wish clarified. Six and nine are multiples of three and therefore powerful. Divide the deck into three piles from left to right. Tap each pile three times with your fingers and chant:

> *One for the Maiden, free as the air;*
> *One for the Mother, lovely and fair;*
> *One for the Wise One, in her dark hall;*
> *Harken, Great Ladies! List' to my call.*

Turn up the top card on the left-hand pile. Think carefully about it, as this card represents what set the cycle in motion. Turn up the top card on the center pile; this symbolizes the full-blown activity of the cycle. Turn up the top card on the right-hand pile; this is the ending, the winding down of the cycle. From these three cards you should be able to determine where you are in the cycle of events.

If you feel you can endure through the rest of the cycle, you need do nothing further. If, however, you wish to change or end the cycle, you will need spiritual guidance as to which steps to take. In this case, turn up another card on each pile, moving from the left to the right. These revealed cards should give you clues as to what action, if any, to take.

It is a good idea to make a note of the cards you turned up, in their proper order. In this way you can think about the things you need to do or change. We have a tendency to block out what we don't like about a reading.

Vesta of the Hearth-Flame
—Crescent Moon—

The Roman goddess Vesta (Greek Hestia) was an ever-virgin who was known as the "one of Light." Her priestesses were the Vestal Virgins who kept the sacred fire of Rome always burning. Six Vestals of good family background served her for thirty years, coming into her service when they were seven to ten years old. These priestesses offered no blood sacrifices. If a Vestal chanced to meet a condemned man, he was set free. She was the deity of both domestic and ceremonial fires. No temple or home was considered complete until Vesta's fire was lit in it.

As the deity of purity and purification, Vesta helps when we need spiritual purification in our lives. Plan this ritual for the Crescent Moon or waxing Moon.

You will need purification incense, a cauldron, a wand, and a red candle. Many people do not associate the color red with purification, but red is the color of fire, Vesta's symbol. Cast your circle as usual.

Kneel on the floor before the altar until you feel recognized by the goddess. Say:

> *May I be cleansed outwardly and inwardly, body and soul,*
> *That all things in my life may be made new.*

Light the candle in the cauldron. Touch the candle lightly with your wand; say:

> *Vesta of the Sacred Flame,*
> *Goddess of purification and renewal,*
> *Lady who sets the imprisoned free,*
> *Pour your cleansing fires upon my heart and soul*
> *That my life may be made new, my spirit receptive.*
> *Awaken my mind to new opportunities.*
> *Call my soul to greater spiritual knowledge.*
> *Reveal to me your Inner Mysteries*
> *That I may experience initiation anew.*
> *Purify and bless me, O Vesta.*

Remain kneeling as you wait for purification. You may feel either very warm or very cold. You may experience a sensation like cobwebs brushing over your face and arms. One can never be certain how the goddess will announce her presence.

The purification process, which generally occurs within days of this ritual, may be as minor as a sense that you should change your eating habits. Or it may be as severe as to mimic the symptoms of a cold or flu. Remember, you asked for purification, so accept it with grace and learn from it.

Inanna, Lady of Prosperity
— Full Moon —

This goddess was called by the name Inanna in Sumeria, but was known as Ishtar in Babylon. She was a deity of light, life, love, death, and the evening star. She had great power over the destinies of cities and lovers. She personally overcame great adversity and helps her worshippers do the same.

If you are faced with difficult decisions or adversities that you can't seem to solve, call upon Inanna. You must have done everything you can do before this goddess will work with you. She has no time for those who won't take responsibility, try to shift the blame, won't make decisions, or want everything dropped in their lap.

This ritual can be performed with or without casting a circle. Decorate an altar space with flowers. Also have a new indoor or outdoor plant as an offering to the goddess. Burn cinnamon incense. Stand at the altar and say:

> *Lady of the fullness of life,*
> *Show me the best of all your ways*
> *That I may know the joy of all,*
> *And praise and bless you all my days.*

Go to the East; say:

> *Inanna, goddess of flowers and vegetation,*
> *I call to you for aid.*
> *Bless me with your presence.*

Move to the South; say:

> *Inanna, goddess of all the joys of love,*
> *I ask for love and happiness to fill my life.*
> *Bless me with your presence.*

Go to the West. Say:

> *Inanna, goddess of creativity and spiritual growth,*
> *I ask for wisdom and guidance to do my best.*
> *Bless me with your presence.*

Finish by going to the North; say:

> *Inanna, goddess who descended into the Underworld and came*
> *forth again in glory,*
> *Let the old that is useless in my life drop away, the new come in.*
> *Bless me with your presence.*

Light the pink candle. Meditate or lay out tarot cards, or do both. When you are finished, stand again at the altar.

> *Great Mother of deep caverns and tall pines,*
> *I await your wisdom.*
> *Lady of the Full Moon and wild beasts,*
> *I seek your guidance.*
> *Your silver orb is in the sky.*
> *I salute you, Mother of Birth and Rebirth.*

Be alert to dreams and things that happen around you until the next Moon phase. The goddess often brings her wisdom through others or books.

Ishtar of Battles
—Dark Moon—

For two days at the end of May, the Romans held the Feast of the Queen of the Under-world, a celebration honoring Underworld goddesses such as Hecate, Cybele, and in later times Black Isis.

Although Ishtar of the Middle East was known as the goddess of love, she was also known for her ferocity in battle and protection of her worshippers. In this aspect, Ishtar rode in a chariot drawn by seven lions, or sat on a lion throne, holding a double serpent scepter and with dragons by her side. She was called Possessor of the Tablets of Life's Records, Guardian of Law and Order, and Lady of Battles and Victory. Her symbols were the eight-point star, pentagram, dove, serpents, and the labyrs. She was the goddess of the positive and negative sides of all she ruled, a patroness of priestesses. She could be stern, cruel, and bad tempered. Her powers extended over many areas, including the overcoming of obstacles.

This ritual of banishing and release is best done during the Dark Moon or waning Moon. It can be done for a specific person or problem that is troubling you. It is also good when you know you need to break off a relationship.

You will need a banishing incense, a small piece of paper, pencil, patchouli or camphor oil, a sword or dagger, a bowl of small amounts of crushed laurel and powdered frankincense, and a metal cauldron.

Burn the banishing incense. Write the name of the problem or person on the small piece of paper, and place it on the altar along with the patchouli or camphor oil. In a small bowl have ready the bay laurel and frankincense.

Hold your sword or ritual dagger straight out before you, resting the edge of it on the cauldron. Stamp your foot and say:

> *Hear me, O mighty Ishtar.*
> *This is a time of releasing, of sending away.*
> *I sever all ties with* (name of person or problem).
> *Send your great powers to sweep it* (him/her) *out of my life.*

Continue holding the sword outstretched while mentally visualizing the person or problem quickly moving away from the tip of the sword. See it (him/her) fall into the cauldron to disappear. Try to see it (him/her) vanish completely. Don't specify how you want this to occur, just that the problem will no longer be in your life.

Take the paper and impale it on the tip of the blade, saying:

> *All ties between us are severed.*
> *Nothing binds me to thee.*
> *You are blown away on the winds of the Lady of Battles.*

Remove the paper from the blade. Dot it with patchouli or camphor oil on all four corners and in the center. Burn it in the cauldron.

> *Queen of Heaven, Moon Goddess,*
> *Cast your powerful rays upon my enemies.*
> *Let them be thrown down in defeat.*
> *Defend me, Lady of Battles and Victory!*

Sprinkle some of the crushed herbs onto the burning paper, or if the paper is out, make a little pile of the herbs and set them on fire. Say:

> *Renewal comes from the cauldron of the Underworld.*
> *As Ishtar ascended victorious from her journey to that land,*
> *So am I renewed through her love and wisdom.*

Dispose of the burned paper and herbs by flushing them down the toilet, an apt symbol of getting rid of the trouble.

Endnotes

1. For those interested in further information on dragons and using their help in rituals, there are a few books on the market, including my own *Dancing with Dragons,* published by Llewellyn Publications in 1994.
2. A pentacle is usually a wooden disk engraved with a five-point star, one point upward. The pentagram (star) is a symbol of the Element of Spirit.

Chapter 9

MEAD MOON

June

Also called: Moon of Horses, Lovers' Moon, Strong Sun Moon,
Honey Moon, Aerra Litha (Before Lithia),
Brachmanoth (Break Month), Strawberry Moon,
Rose Moon, Moon of Making Fat.

Full Moon was the Festival of Edfu for Hathor in Egypt; on the New Moon her image began its journey by boat to Edfu.

June 1-2: In Rome, the Day of Carna, goddess of physical survival, doors and locks. Syn, the Norse goddess of inclusion and exclusion, is similar.

June 2: The Shapatu, or Sabbat, of Ishtar in Babylon.

June 6: The Bendidia of Bendis, the Moon goddess of Thrace. In Greece, cakes were set out at crossroads for Artemis.

June 14: Birthday of the Muses.

June 16: Night of the Teardrop, Feast of the Waters of the Nile, in Egypt, celebrating the goddess Isis and her sorrows.

June 17: In Rome, the Ludi Piscatari, or festival of fishermen.

June 21: Summer Solstice. In England, the Day of Cerridwen and her cauldron. In Ireland, dedicated to the faery goddess Aine of Knockaine. Day of All Heras, or Wisewomen. Day of the Green Man in Northern Europe.

June 24: Burning of the Lamps in Egypt at Sais, a celebration of Isis and Neith.

June 25: In India, Teej, a festival for women and girls in praise of Parvati.

June 27: In Greece, the Arretophoria, a nymph festival honoring the Maiden and Amazon goddesses.

The original Roman name for this month was Junonius, after the Great Mother Goddess Juno; her counterpart among the Greeks was Hera. The Summer Solstice has been and still is important to many religions and cultures around the world. Not only was it sacred to goddesses of fertility, marriage, and love, but it was considered to be a time when faeries, elves, and many other supernatural beings were abroad in great numbers.

This Moon has enormous energies for calling upon and working with elementals of all types. Tides of psychic energy flow freely, enabling even the most staid of people to experience unusual happenings.

The Summer Solstice festival in Slavonic-Russian cultures was called Kupalo and Jarilo. Other names were Kostroma, Sobotka, Kresnice, and Vajano. Kupalo/Kupala was the name of an ancient Slavic deity, originally a goddess, later a god. Special features of this festival were the lighting of fires, the sprinkling of water, and foretelling the future.

The Full Moon festival of Edfu in Egypt honored the goddess Hathor. The cow horns on her head represented the Crescent Moon. Every year at the New Moon the statue of Hathor was taken from her temple at Dendera and transported by boat to the temple of the god Horus at Edfu, arriving on the Full Moon. This festival celebrated the frank sexual union of the two deities. It was a time of great festivities and very likely human marriages, since it was considered a period of good luck.

The Egyptian festival called the Burning of the Lamps took place in Sais in the temple of Isis. There, in an underground chapel beneath the main temple, was a wooden coffin for the god Osiris. Priestesses, priests, and initiates gathered in this hidden place carrying lamps. Then they marched in a procession around the coffin. The

Egyptians said that it was the light of the Moon that Isis called upon to bring Osiris back to life. Myth says that when Osiris ascended to the heavens, he went to the Moon.

In Rome, the month of June was sacred to the goddess Juno and therefore a lucky month in which to be married. It was also a time for the Vestal Virgins to cleanse the penus (a sacred vessel) in the Temple of Vesta.

The Roman celebration of the Ludi Piscatari, or festival of fishermen, was really a blessing of boats. They believed that every boat had a personal spiritual entity. If the powers that went into the boat during its building were not in harmony with the entity, the boat would never ride easily on the water; it would always fight with the wind and waves. The ritual of blessing the boat harmonized the energies imbued in the vessel, making it lively, willing, and enduring.

The Celtic Day of Cerridwen and her cauldron may have originally been associated with the Summer Solstice. Cerridwen of Wales was a Dark Moon goddess; her symbols were the cauldron, grain, and the Moon. The white, corpse-eating sow, representing the Moon, was one of her animal emblems.

In Tibet, this was a time of masked sacred dances and mystery plays. They had celebrations of the Medical Buddhas and of the Birth of Padmasambhava, who was considered to be a great spiritual teacher.

To the Incas in the Southern Hemisphere, this was the season of the Winter Solstice, since seasons are reversed. They had the Feast of the Sun, or the Inti Raymi, to celebrate the maize harvest. Chanting would last from sunrise to sunset. Inti was the Sun god of the ruling dynasty, represented by a great golden disk with a human face.

Correspondences

Nature Spirits: sylphs, zephyrs

Herbs: skullcap, meadowsweet, vervain, tansy, dog grass, parsley, mosses

Colors: orange, golden-green

Flowers: lavender, orchid, yarrow

Scents: lily of the valley, lavender

Stones: topaz, agate, alexandrite, fluorite

Trees: oak

Animals: monkey, butterfly, frog, toad

Birds: wren, peacock

Deities: Aine of Knockaine, Isis, Neith, Green Man, Cerridwen, Bendis, Ishtar

Power Flow: full but restful energy; protect, strengthen, and prevent.
A time of Light; Earth tides are turning. Decision-making, taking responsibility for present happenings. Work on personal inconsistencies. Strengthen and reward yourself for your positive traits.

Old Sayings & Lore

- When the Moon is New, braid your hair or some kind of string while saying:

  I braid this knot, this knot I braid,
  To know the thing I know not yet,
  That while I sleep I plain may see
  The man (woman) that shall husband (wife) be,
  Not in his (her) best but worst array,
  Just what he (she) weareth every day,
  That I tomorrow may him (her) ken
  From among all other men.

- Pick some yarrow at the time of the New Moon. Put it under your pillow and say before going to sleep:

  Good night, fair yarrow,
  Thrice good night to thee.
  I hope before tomorrow's dawn
  My true love I shall see.

  Look at a New Moon and say:

  New Moon, New Moon, do tell me
  Who my own true lover is to be.
  The color of his (her) hair,
  The clothes that he (she) will wear,
  And on what day he (she) shall appear.

- To remove a wart, find an ash tree and go there under a Full Moon. Rub the wart lightly against the ash and say:

  Ash tree, ash tree,
  Pray buy this wart of me.

  Leave a gift, such as a little ginger or milk, at the base of the tree.

- A verse:

  If the Moon shows a silver shield (ring)
  Be not afraid to reap your field.

- A verse:

  I see the Moon,
  And the Moon sees me.
  Goddess bless the Moon,
  And Goddess bless me.

Recipes

Tea Sandwich Spread

An excellent, but different, egg spread that is delicious in sandwiches, on toast squares or English muffins. A good, but quick, luncheon served with salads. Makes about 1¼ cups.

4 hard-cooked eggs, finely chopped	1 tablespoon Herb Mustard
8 pimento-stuffed olives, chopped	¼ cup mayonnaise

Mash together the eggs and olives. Mix with the Herb Mustard and mayonnaise until well blended. Chill.

Sharbatee Gulab

This drink is from India and June is an excellent time to make it since the roses will be in bloom. Serves six to eight.

5 large fragrant roses in full bloom	3 cups crushed pineapple,
2 quarts cold water	fresh or canned
1⅓ cups sugar	Finely crushed ice
¼ cup lemon juice	Extra rose petals

Choose only roses not sprayed with pesticides. Wash the roses and shake off the excess water. Carefully take off the petals and put them in a large bowl. Pour the cold water over them and let stand in a dark, but not refrigerated, place for about 4 hours. Strain out the petals, saving the water. Dissolve the sugar in the lemon juice and add this to the rose water. Stir in the pineapple. When ready to serve, pour over crushed ice and top with a rose petal in each glass.

Crafts

Tussie Mussie

Tussie mussies are hand-held bouquets and were at one time a regular feature of women's outfits. Like hand-held pomanders, the tussie mussie was made of aromatic herbs and flowers, whose scents would help combat the odors of poor personal hygiene and bad sanitation. The wearing of corsages is a remnant of the use of tussie mussies.

Tussie Mussie

Women do not carry pomanders or tussie mussies any longer. The modern woman has a need to have her hands unencumbered, for every reason from carrying groceries to holding on to a child to decking a would-be purse-snatcher. But she can enjoy the old-fashioned scent by making a very tiny tussie mussie to wear in her lapel or pinned to her dress.

Start in the center with a small but perfect bud, such as a rose. Using floral tape, build tight circles around this bud with tiny flowers, such as baby's breath, alternated with little sprigs of aromatic herbs. Keep it simple and small. It can be finished by tying a colored ribbon around it. If you do not want to use fresh flowers, make a tussie mussie out of dried sprigs of flowers and herbs.

German Witch's Potpourri

2 ounces witch hazel	1 ounce rosemary
1 ounce rue	1 ounce powdered myrrh gum
1 ounce sweet woodruff	1 teaspoon lemon or orange peel
¼ teaspoon ginger	2 teaspoons vanilla
2 drops pine oil	

Place in a small jar with a lid. Remove the lid when you want to perfume the room.

Victorian Pincushion Potpourri

4 ounces rose petals	1 ounce granular frankincense
2 ounces lavender flowers	2 ounces rosemary
1 broken cinnamon stick	

Use dried flowers. Many Victorian pincushions were stuffed with rough-cut potpourri; sometimes the mixture was wrapped in cotton to make it easier to insert the pins.

Wheels of Fortune

In Sweden and Norway at the Summer Solstice, people made wheels of fortune. Some of the wheels were wrapped in straw, set on fire, and rolled down hill, not a safe or legal thing to do. Other wheels were decorated and kept. These were used in two ways: one, the wheel was rolled away from a person to take away misfortunes; two, it was rolled toward a person to bring all kinds of good fortune.

To make a good fortune wheel, use a piece of wire that has been fastened in a circle. An embroidery hoop will work also. Wrap yarn or ribbon around the hoop until it is completely covered. To this wheel, tie dried or artificial flowers, good luck tokens, and streaming ribbons. These wheels can be hung as wall decorations or twirled so they spin toward you during spellwork.

Wheel of Fortune

Perfumed Inks

Perfumed inks have been used since Babylonian and Egyptian times for magickal spells. These were used to draw sigils or write out spells on paper. They can be used whenever you want to intensify a spell. If burning a candle, write out your objective on a small piece of paper and place it under the burning candle. If doing a spell that calls for burning the paper, this ink will strengthen what you are writing. Some magicians use a magickal alphabet instead of the everyday one.[1]

The making of perfumed ink is quite easy. Simply purchase a bottle of ink, either black or colored, and add two or three drops of the appropriate essential oil to the bottle. Let the bottle of ink sit on your altar overnight. This is best done on the Full Moon for positively-charged inks, on the Dark Moon for negatively-charged inks.

There are several good books written by Scott Cunningham and published by Llewellyn which will help you decide on the appropriate color and essential oil to use. Any of Scott Cunningham's books are good source material.

Myths

Ishtar of Babylon

Some legends say that Ishtar was the daughter of the Great God Anu, while others list her as the child of the Moon god Sinn. She was the sister of the Sun god Shamash. She called herself the goddess of the morning and evening; this associates her with the planet Venus. She was both a goddess of love and war. But her love proved fatal on more than one occasion to humans to whom she gave her favors.

Ishtar

When Ishtar fell in love with the harvest god Tammuz, her love literally killed him. The goddess mourned his death so much that she decided to go into the underworld to bring him back. Down Ishtar went into the darkness. To be able to pass each of seven gates, she had to leave behind one piece of adornment—jewelry or clothing. When she finally reached the underworld palace of Ereshkigal, Ishtar was naked and defenseless. Ereshkigal imprisoned and tortured her.

It took the powerful magick words of Asushu-Namir, the messenger from the great Ea, to free Ishtar. Ea was touched by Ishtar's tears for her lover and decreed that Tammuz could spend part of the year with the goddess, but had to return to the land of the dead the rest of the time. He sprinkled Ishtar with the water of life to revive her. As the goddess ascended to the surface, she retrieved each piece of jewelry and clothing at the seven gates, thus regaining her powers.

The Sorrows of Isis

The Great Goddess of the Egyptians was Isis, sister/wife to Osiris. Like her brother/husband, she was associated with the Moon. Among many other titles, she was called the Creatress and the Giver of Life. According to legend, she and Osiris were married while still in the womb of their mother Nut. She was born in the swamps of the Nile Delta.

She and Osiris taught humans all the arts of civilization. Then while Osiris wandered the world, teaching other cultures besides the Egyptians, Isis ruled in his place. Their brother, the evil Set, was jealous of Osiris' power and position. When Osiris returned home, Set and his followers gave a feast for him. At the feast was a beautifully decorated box that Set said would belong to whomever fitted inside it. Osiris climbed in; Set and his followers sealed the box with lead and threw it into the Nile. The box washed out to sea, then ashore in a foreign land where a tree grew around it.

When Osiris disappeared, Isis was heart-broken. She searched long and finally, following a sweet odor, found the box inside a pillar in a king's house. She revealed her identity to the queen and recovered her husband's body. Back in Egypt, Isis, with the help of her sister Nephthys, reanimated the body long enough for Isis to conceive a child. They hid the coffined body deep in the swamps of the Delta but Set found it while hunting. Set cut up the body in several pieces and scattered them throughout Egypt. The sisters searched until they found all the parts, except the phallus. Together with Thoth, they fastened the parts back together and embalmed Osiris.

The Egyptians still have a festival called the Night of the Teardrop. This festival has been preserved by the Arabs as their June festival Lelat al-Nuktah.

The Green Man

There is a fascinating carving among the antiquities of the English: a face peering out from among leaves and vines. This is the Green Man, a mysterious woodland deity who cares for the forests and especially all kinds of trees. He is said to be of a man-form, green in color, and dressed in leaves and bark. To those who are indiscriminately destructive of the woodlands and trees, the Green Man is a malevolent spirit. To those who love and wisely use trees, he is a timid entity who encourages the trees to grow. Legend also says that he hides treasure under his fruit trees, but disappears with it if farmers uproot their orchards to search for it.

Cerridwen and Her Cauldron

The goddess Cerridwen was the great Crone of Wales. She was connected with the Moon, the magick cauldron, and grain. All true Celtic Bards claimed to have been born of her; in fact, the Welsh Bards as a group called themselves the Cerddorion (sons of Cerridwen). Drinking from her magick cauldron was said to confer the greatest inspiration and talents for poets and musicians. The journey to the cauldron was part of a Bard's initiation, and was a dangerous journey, as seen in the tale of Taliesin.

Taliesin began life as Gwion Bach. As a young man, Gwion Bach wandered through northern Wales. Suddenly he found himself at the bottom of Lake Bala where the giant Tegid and his wife Cerridwen lived. The goddess had two children, a

Cerridwen's Shape-shifting

boy and a girl. The girl was very beautiful, but the boy was extremely ugly. So Cerridwen was brewing a potion for her son that would make him very wise. She set Gwion to stirring a cauldron containing this potion. He stirred for a year and a day until there were only three drops left. The drops flew out onto his finger; he thrust the burnt finger into his mouth and instantly realized the terrible power of Cerridwen. He fled the lake in terror.

Furious, Cerridwen went after him. In an attempt to escape the goddess, Gwion changed himself into a series of shapes. Cerridwen changed along with him, finally eating him when he changed into a grain of wheat. Nine months later she gave birth to a baby boy, whom she cast into the sea in a little boat.

Elphin, son of a wealthy landowner, rescued the baby and named him Taliesin (radiant brow). The child remembered all the knowledge he had gained from the potion and grew up to be a talented, important Bard.

Rituals

Physical Survival

On June 1-2 was the Roman festival of the Day of Carna, a goddess of both physical survival and doors and locks. Today when crime rates are soaring, especially burglaries and assaults, locked doors and physical survival often become one and the same. The Norse goddess Syn, who was a deity of inclusion and exclusion, is very similar to Carna. We have the right to include or exclude anyone from our homes or even our immediate surroundings if we do not wish their presence.

This spellworking is very simple, but requires full concentration. Use a short length of black thread. Tie a knot in one end of the thread, saying:

> *One to seek him/her/them.*
> (Tie knot in middle) *One to find him/her/them.*
> (Tie knot in other end) *One to bring him/her/them.*
> (Tie ends together) *One to bind him/her/them.*
> *Stone to stone, forever one.*
> *So say I. This spell is done.*

Bury the knotted thread off your property. If you can't do that, drop it in a river or along the highway.

Faery Queen & The Green Man
— Summer Solstice —

In Ireland, the Summer Solstice was dedicated to the faery goddess Aine of Knockaine. In Wales and Britain, this was a time of Cerridwen and her magickal cauldron. However, it was said in a great many places that this was a powerful time for faeries, elves, and other supernatural beings.

Today, Pagans believe that all the Little People are abroad in great numbers during this balance of Light and Dark. If you are on good terms with them, it is said that standing within a faery ring will help you to see them. It is an excellent time of the year to become friends with faeries and other such beings.

June and the Summer Solstice was considered the time of the Green Man and the Faery Queen in Northern Europe in particular. It is certainly a powerful Moon month for you to work on and strengthen your psychic abilities and contacts with other realms of being.

In the Mediterranean areas, this was a time of the god Pan and the Forest Goddess. Pan, with his pipes, enticed nymphs and maidens to rendezvous with him in the green woods for love and pleasures. The Green Man and the horned god Cernunnos may well be the Celtic version of the very ancient Pan.

If possible, hold this ceremony outside at night. If you don't have a secure place, or have nosey neighbors, hold it inside in a darkened room lit only by candles. Have ready fruit and flowers as offerings. You will also need a green cord long enough to go comfortably around your waist. Have a few cookies to share with the faeries and elves. Dress in a comfortable robe. A garland of flowers is nice to wear on your head. At least have a vase of flowers nearby.

Either play a tape of flute or pan-pipe music or make the music yourself. Have beside you a chalice of juice or wine; each time you drink from it, raise the chalice first in an offering to Pan and the Lady of the Greenwood. Be happy and enjoy yourself, for Pan and the Lady of the Greenwood don't like long faces and negative vibrations.

Raise the chalice in offering, then take a drink. Chant:

> *Strange music floats within the glade*
> *From reedy pipes that Pan has made.*
> *The woodland god of Nature old*
> *Has come back as the tales foretold.*
> *With horned head and tapping feet,*
> *I shall not fear him when we meet.*
> *Great Pan is Nature at her best.*
> *His soaring notes can give us rest*

From care and worries, synchronize
Us with the water, Earth, and skies.

Take some fruit and flowers to an eastern point. Lay them there and say:

Great Pan and Lady of the Greenwood,
Release your pleasant breezes to blow sweet and fresh upon the land.

Take fruit and flowers to the South. Lay them there.

Great Pan and Lady of the Greenwood,
Let the tender sunbeams warm the Earth and bring continued life.

Do the same in the West:

Great Pan and Lady of the Greenwood,
Bless us with refreshing, renewing rains.

Finish by laying fruit and flowers in the North:

Great Pan and Lady of the Greenwood,
Let the seasons come in the proper times,
Both on the Earth and in my life.
Bless me with good things.
Let life's lessons not be harsh and cruel.
All hail Pan and the Lady of the Greenwood!

Raise one end of the green cord and kiss it.

The Lady of the Greenwood is love and happiness.
Her consort bows to her will this night.
Great Lady, bless me with all good things
And make my life fulfilled and bright.

(Save the green cord to wear on other occasions when you contact Pan and the Lady of the Greenwood.)

Lay an offering of cookies at each circle-point beside the flowers, always moving clockwise, and saying at each point:

All you Nature spirits and faeries,
I welcome your presence and aid.

Relax and let yourself be open to communication with the Little Ones and the woodland deities. If you do a meditation, invite them to make an appearance during your quiet time. Ask their aid in protecting your property, home, and pets. Some of the Nature spirits and faeries will stay in your home year round if they are made welcome. End your ritual by thanking them for joining your celebration.

Day of Wisdom

All of us need wise guidance from time to time. When we have done everything we know to solve a problem and are still faced with bewilderment, then it is time to consult with higher powers. In ancient Greece, they celebrated the Day of All Heras (Wisewomen). There is evidence to indicate that most oracles, at least in the beginning, were dedicated to an aspect of the Great Goddess, one of whose later names was Hera.

However, the Greek goddess Athene was also considered to be the goddess of wisdom. She was called Bright-Eyed and the All-Wise. Although this deity wore a helmet and breastplate and carried a spear and shield, she was primarily a goddess of the arts and crafts, writing, science, protection, renewal, wise counsel, peace, and battle strategy. She was known as the goddess of freedom and women's rights, the patroness of soldiers, and protectress of cities. Legend says Athene invented the plow, bridle, rake, ox yoke, and flute. She also taught humankind to breed and break horses. The owl, olive, oak, and intertwined snakes were sacred to her.

In this ritual for receiving wisdom, you will need a small statue of an owl and a blue candle in a fireproof holder. Anoint the candle from the wick to the end with lotus oil.

Set the owl beside the candle. Spend as long as necessary talking with the goddess about the specific wisdom you wish to obtain, especially that needed to solve problems. If you have no particular problems that need immediate answers, ask for wisdom that will better your life.

After lighting the candle, say:

> *Wise Athene, great counselor,*
> *Teach me waking and sleeping.*
> *Send me omens true and dreams wise.*
> *Instruct me in your great wisdom.*
> *I open my heart and mind to you, Wise One.*
> *I ask for your all-knowing counsel and guidance*
> *That my good may come quickly!*

If you use tarot cards or other divinatory aids, lay them out now. Write down the answers and study them thoroughly in the days to come. When you are finished, say:

> *Grant skills of the hands and justice.*
> *Great Athene, make me wise.*
> *Protection, all of the wonderful arts,*
> *Are yours to bestow, Bright-Eyes.*
> *You who are both skillful and strong.*
> *Guide my steps. Keep me from wrong.*

Leave the candle to burn out completely.

Parvati, the Faithful
— Crescent Moon —

The month of June had two festivals to goddesses of the Crescent Moon: the Bendidia of Bendis from Thrace, and the Arretophoria, a Greek nymph festival honoring the

Parvati and Shiva

Maiden. Moon cakes were set out at crossroads in Greece to honor the Virgin Huntress Artemis. In India, the Teej was held, a festival for women and girls in honor of the goddess Parvati. Parvati seduced Shiva, but was considered to be the Maiden aspect of the goddess Kali.

Parvati was the consort of the god Shiva. She seduced him when she tired of his asceticism; she represents the union of god and goddess, or positive and negative energies. Shiva was considered to be the creating god of sexual ecstacy, who shows the Tantric method of raising the Kundalini through ritual. Although this Hindu festival is primarily a fertility ritual, and is excellent for those who want to conceive a child, there is no reason that creating energy cannot be transformed into higher uses than the purely physical.

Burn jasmine and/or sandalwood incense. Have a small dish of salt and a chalice of water on the altar.

Stand before your altar with your palms pressed together in prayer. Say:

> *May my body be cleansed, my mind be cleansed, my spirit be cleansed.*
> *I now enter the magickal realms of the gods.*
> *Prepare me to receive creating power.*

Hold your hands over the salt and chalice of water. Say:

> *Agni, god of fire and purity,*
> *Bless and purify this water and salt.*
> *Fill them with divine cleansing*
> *That what I bless in the outer world may be blessed in the inner.*

Sprinkle a small amount of salt into the water. Swirl the chalice three times clockwise to mix. Hold the chalice high for a few moments. Sprinkle yourself with the consecrated water and replace the chalice on the altar.

Press your hands together again and bow to the deity statues, or at least to the altar. Say:

> *Lord of the Dance, God with the Moon in your hair,*
> *I hear your drumbeat in the Cave of my heart.*
> *Your eternal Dance of Life in the Center of the Universe*
> *Is repeated within me.*
> *I feel your dancing feet treading the eternal pattern*
> *In my own sacred Center.*
> *Sky-clad King of the Dance, you who give and take away,*
> *Help me to dance the joyous Dance of Life.*
> *Lead me to spiritual understanding*
> *Of the rhythm of the Universe.*

Spend a few moments meditating on your own heart beat and its connection to the universal rhythm of life. Press your hands together and bow again.

> *Lovely Parvati, faithful consort of Shiva,*
> *Teach me balance between the physical and spiritual.*
> *As the union between you and your lord brings harmony,*
> *So I ask for harmony of spirit, of life itself.*

Stand quietly as the goddess blesses you. You may feel as if feathery hands are brushing over your face and body. You may feel a warmth spreading through you. The goddess makes herself known in many ways.

Press your hands together, fingertips touching your forehead. Say:

Beautiful Parvati, I thank you for your presence here.
Lift my heart in joy, my mind in wisdom.
Bless this house with harmony and balance
That my life may be an example of love to others.

Taking the consecrated water, go through each room of your home, always moving clockwise. Lightly sprinkle the corners of each room. Unless you have someone within the home working actively against you, this should create a harmony and balance in the atmosphere.

Ishtar, Goddess of Love
—Full Moon—

At the Full Moon, the Egyptian Hathor had a festival called the Festival of Edfu. On the following Crescent New Moon Hathor's image started on its watery journey by boat to the temple in Edfu.

Eight-point star of Ishtar

June 2 was one of the holy days of Ishtar of Babylon; it was called the Shapatu, or Sabbat, of Ishtar. Ishtar, Lady of heaven, goddess of the Moon, the Great Mother, was a goddess of both positive and negative qualities. The Babylonians knew this deity as the Light of the World, Opener of the Womb, Lawgiver, Lady of Victory, etc. She was the sister of Ereshkigal, queen of the underworld.

Ishtar had a lion throne and double serpent scepter; sometimes she was pictured accompanied by dragons. Like the Norse Freyja, Ishtar had a rainbow necklace and was associated with sexual love, but not necessarily marriage.

This is a ritual for companionship and love. You will need a lavender candle, a fire-proof candle holder, jasmine oil, and jasmine incense.

Set up a small altar with the candle in the center. If you like, place a small lion statue beside it. Stand quietly for a few moments, visualizing the room filled with swirling golden light. You must know what you want in a companion, not necessarily in looks, but most definitely in character. Otherwise you are apt to draw those who are fascinated with you, but totally unsuited.

If you desire, you can make this part of a regular ritual, casting the circle as usual and setting the guardians of the four directions.

Raise your arms in greeting as you stand facing East. Say:

Within this secret place, hidden from the world,
Outside of time and free of control by man,
I worship in this sacred center.
I greet the Old Gods once again.

Anoint the lavender candle with jasmine oil from the wick to the bottom. Place it in the holder.

Love in all its many forms,
Sweetness, joy, delight,
Bless me with, sweet Ishtar.
Brighten each new night.

Think happy, loving thoughts; dance and sing; play music. Do this until you feel more positive about your love life. Once more stand before your altar facing East. Say:

The Full Moon rises o'er the hill.
Mother, hear me!
Lead me with your loving will.
Mother, hear me!
Grant me joy, my wishes fill.
Mother, hear me!

Light the candle. Leave it to burn out completely. Close the circle as usual.

Nephthys, Beloved of the Night
—Dark Moon—

June was also the month of two festivals of the Egyptian Isis. First came the Night of the Teardrop, or Feast of the Waters of the Nile, when Isis mourned for her lost husband. Later came the Burning of the Lamps, a celebration at Sais which honored both Isis and Neith.

The Egyptian Nephthys is called Mistress of the Palace, Lady of the House, and the Revealer. She was an Underworld goddess who represented life and death. Although she was portrayed as fair with green eyes, she was called the dark sister of Isis. By her brother Osiris, she was the mother of Anubis, who guided the dead. Sometimes Nephthys was pictured with long winged arms stretched in protection; other times she carried a basket on her head.

As a Dark Moon goddess, Nephthys is compassionate and understanding of frail human nature. Her counsel is wise and just. She rules over the magickal arts, secret knowledge, and oracles and prophecy. Animals such as snakes, white/black horses and dogs, and dragons belong to her, as do the birds the owl, raven, and crow. In Egypt, the pentacle (five-point star) was called the star of Isis and Nephthys.

This goddess ruled over death and dark magick, hidden things, mystical knowledge, protection, invisibility or anonymity, intuition, dreams, and peace.

Nephthys can introduce us to our shadow self, that part of our psyche which is always with us and influencing us. The shadow self contains what we find threatening, shameful, inadequate, or just plain don't like about ourselves. We try to repress and disown it, not realizing that by making a truce and using its strengths we become more powerful and whole people.

The shadow self can also be the messenger of the subconscious and the gods. Using dreams and vision-images, it can reveal what is necessary for protection, knowledge, and expansion of both our physical and spiritual lives.

For this ritual, in addition to your regular ritual tools, you will need lotus incense, a single-sided mirror, a sistrum, a picture of yourself and/or family and pets, lapis lazuli or moonstone for Isis, crystal or onyx for Nephthys. Pictures or statues of Isis and Nephthys are optional and can be substituted for the stones. Cast your circle as usual and set up the guardians of the four directions.

Place the stone and/or image of Isis to the left of a small bowl of water, the stone and/or image of Nephthys to the right. Say:

I call upon Isis and Nephthys for protection and instruction.

Burn the lotus or protection incense. Take the sistrum in your power hand and shake it three times. Say:

Great Isis, you come to protect me with the north wind.
You strengthen me against all adversity.
You defend me against all my enemies.
You are Isis, the Divine One, Lady of Heaven, Queen of all Gods.
Your magick and words of power guard me.

Take the wand in your other hand and hold it upright before the altar. Say:

Nephthys, Lady of Life, Mistress of the Gods, Dark Goddess
of mighty words of power,
I ask your presence here.
Let your eternal strength always be behind me, before me,
under me, over me,
Protect me, Dark Mother!

Beginning in the East and moving clockwise around the circle, hold the wand upright while shaking the sistrum three times at each Element direction. Go back to the altar and set aside the tools.

Take up the mirror in your power hand with the reflecting side outward. Hold your picture behind the mirror as you slowly turn clockwise, beginning in the East, so that the mirror with the hidden picture is presented to all the Elements. Lay the picture on the altar with the mirror over it, reflecting side upward. (Leave the mirror and picture in their positions on the altar overnight.) Say:

I am hidden under the protecting wings of Isis!
The shadowy wings of Nephthys cover me.
I am hidden from the eyes of my enemies.
Their spells and thoughts have no power over me.
All negativity must return to the senders,
For Isis and Nephthys protect me.

Take the sistrum in your power hand, wand in your other, and visualize yourself covered with the wings of the goddesses. When you feel their protection, shake the sistrum three times and silently thank Isis and Nephthys.

Touch the stone/image of Nephthys gently. Feel the power of the goddess pouring through it into your hand. Say:

Ancient Mother, Holy One of many names,
Show to me the secrets of dreams.
Teach me Moon magick and the lore of herbs.
Give me the wisdom to deal with my shadow self,
Using its strengths and overcoming its weaknesses.
I do thank you, Great Lady.

Now is the time to read the tarot cards or runes for immediate hints at what you can do. When you are finished, close your circle as usual.

Be prepared to write down all dreams until the next Moon phase, for Nephthys speaks primarily through dreams, using the power of the Moon. You will soon see a pattern in your dreaming. Dreams under the influence of the Full Moon may deal with physical events, while those under the Dark Moon are on a more spiritual level.

Endnotes

1. In my book *Ancient & Shining Ones,* I give several examples of magickal alphabets.

Chapter 10

HAY MOON

July

Also called: Wort Moon, Moon of Claiming,
Moon of Blood (because of mosquitoes), Blessing Moon,
Maedmonat (Meadow Month), Hewimanoth (Hay Month),
Fallow Moon, Buck Moon, Thunder Moon.

End of July in Greece: the Panathenaea to honor Pallas Athene.

July 4: Day of Pax, goddess of peace, and Concordia in Rome.

July 7-8: In Rome, the oldest of women's festivals, the Nonae Caprotinae, dedicated to Juno the Great Mother.

July 10: Day of Hel, or Holde, (Anglo-Saxon and Norse goddess) and Cerridwen (Celtic goddess).

July 14: O-Bon, or Festival of Lanterns in Japan; dedicated to the spirits of the ancestors.

July 15: Chung Yuan, or Festival of the Dead, in China.

July 17: Birthday of Isis in Egypt.

July 18: Birthday of Nephthys in Egypt.

July 19: The Egyptian New Year. The Opet Festival, or Marriage of Isis and Osiris in Egypt. Also a celebration of Venus and Adonis in Rome.

July 23: In Rome, the Neptunalia to honor Neptune, god of earthquakes.

July 27: Procession of the Witches in Belgium.

*A*t first the Romans called this month Quintilis, but later renamed it Julius after Julius Caesar. The Greek Olympian was held for about a week in July. This festival in honor of Zeus consisted of competitions in athletics, drama, music, and other activities. During the time of the Olympian, all participants were given safe-conduct to and from the games. The constant petty Greek squabbles were put aside. A victory in the Olympian was a great achievement, both for the individual and for their city.

Two of the Roman holidays held during this month were July 7-8 when the goddess Juno was honored and the Neptunalia on July 23, when Neptune, the god of the seas and earthquakes, was placated.

In Japan, the Full Moon of July saw the O-Bon, or Festival of Lanterns. This was a combination of Buddhist and Shinto beliefs that honored the dead. Homes, tombs, and ancestral tablets were thoroughly cleaned. Altars and shrines were decorated. The gardens were hung with lanterns to light the way of the dead so that they could join with their families for the three-day ceremony.

The Egyptian New Year fell in July, as did the Opet Festival, which commemorated the marriage of Isis and Osiris. Their sexual union was said to bring good luck to all people. About the same time in Rome, the love of Venus and Adonis was celebrated. The Egyptian year was measured against the Nile and its yearly fertile floods. This was also the time of the birth of Isis and Nephthys, Osiris, Set, and Haroeris. These days were the ones won by Thoth for these deities' births; in other words, they were the necessary days to make the solar and lunar calendars match.

The Incas had a ceremony called Chahua-huarquiz, Chacra Ricuichi, or Chacra Cona, which meant Plowing Month. While the Northern Hemisphere was beginning its agricultural harvests with the reaping of the corn crop, the Southern Hemisphere was just beginning to break ground for planting.

Buddha's Birth and Preaching, also called the Picture Feast, was celebrated in Tibet.

Correspondences

Nature Spirits: hobgoblins (small, grotesque but friendly brownie-type creatures), faeries of harvested crops

Herbs: honeysuckle, agrimony, lemon balm, hyssop

Colors: silver, blue-gray

Flowers: lotus, water lily, jasmine

Scents: orris, frankincense

Stones: pearl, moonstone, white agate

Trees: oak, acacia, ash

Animals: crab, turtle, dolphin, whale

Birds: starling, ibis, swallow

Deities: Khepera, Athene, Juno, Hel, Holda, Cerridwen, Nephthys, Venus

Power Flow: relaxed energy; preparing; succeeding. Dream-work, divination, and meditation on goals and plans, especially spiritual ones

Old Sayings & Lore

- If the New Moon is seen for the first time straight ahead, it predicts good fortune until the next New Moon.

- If there are two Moons (two New or two Full) in the same month, the weather will be unfavorable and unsettled until the next New Moon.

- If you suffer from corns, cut them during the waning Moon and they will disappear for good.

- Wood cut at the New Moon is hard to split. If it is cut at the Full Moon it is easy to split.

- Grass crops should be sown at the Full Moon. Then the hay will dry quickly.

- In Wales, fishermen avoid the Moon line, or the moonlight showing on the water, when setting out to sea; they consider crossing this bad luck. However, in other areas they say to make a wish when crossing the Moon line.

Recipes

Deviled Tuna Spread

Some people just don't care for the taste of fish. This recipe gives tuna a whole new flavor. Makes about 2½ cups filling.

1	13-ounce can water-pack tuna, drained and crumbled	1	tablespoon parsley flakes, flaked
2	tablespoons pickle relish	½	teaspoon curry powder
¼	cup finely chopped walnuts	½	cup mayonnaise

Mix the tuna and pickle relish, then blend in the walnuts, parsley, and curry powder. Add the mayonnaise and mix thoroughly.

Marinated Mushrooms

(Russia)

2½	pounds fresh mushrooms	2	small minced onions
4	minced shallots		Chopped parsley to garnish
4	tablespoons minced chives		

Marinade:

1⅓	cups olive oil	2	tablespoons grated lemon rind
½	cup white wine	2	cloves garlic, crushed
½	cup tarragon vinegar		

Trim the mushrooms and slice thin. Put in a bowl with the shallots, chives, and onions. In a small bowl combine the olive oil, wine, and vinegar. Add the garlic and lemon rind. Blend well. Pour the marinade over the mushrooms and chill. Toss gently at intervals over one hour. Keep in the refrigerator. When ready to serve, sprinkle with parsley.

Honey Zucchini Bread

3	eggs, beaten	1	teaspoon baking soda
1	cup honey	½	teaspoon baking powder
2	cups grated zucchini	3	teaspoons cinnamon
3	teaspoons vanilla	1	teaspoon salt
1	cup vegetable oil	1	cup finely chopped nuts
3	cups all-purpose flour		

Mix the beaten eggs, honey, zucchini, vanilla, and oil. In a separate bowl, mix the flour, baking soda, baking powder, cinnamon, and salt. Add the egg mixture to the dry mixture, stirring only enough to moisten. Add the nuts, and pour into two well-greased loaf pans. Bake at 325° F for one hour or until bread tests done.

Crafts

Floral Mix for Sachets

½ ounce mignonette or other sweet-smelling flowers
½ ounce dried roses and/or peony petals

½ ounce lavender
1 tablespoon orris powder
5 drops of rose geranium oil

Lightly mix together the mignonette, dried roses, and lavender. Sprinkle with orris powder and geranium oil. Toss lightly and fill small sachet bags.

Men's Sachet

Men usually don't care for sweet sachets or pillows. This mixture generally meets with their approval. Little sachets of this also make good shoe deodorizers.

Dry and grind the peel of one orange into coarse pieces. Don't let orange rind dry too hard, or it's like trying to grind rocks! Mix this with 1 tablespoon orris powder and ½ ounce lemon verbena. Fill small sachet bags.

Tibetan Cologne

¼ pint alcohol
1 ounce glycerin
1 drop bergamot oil

1 pint distilled water
1 drop patchouli oil
1 drop synthetic musk oil

Myths

Athene and Pallas

The goddess Athene, who was born from the head of Zeus after he swallowed her pregnant mother, was an all-powerful and wise warrior deity. The Parthenon (Virgin Temple) was her shrine in Athens. Athene wore a helmet and aegis (breastplate) and carried a shield and spear. However, this goddess abhorred senseless violence. Perhaps this was because of the tragic accident that happened to her closest friend.

Athene had a female human friend and lover whose name was Pallas. Pallas enjoyed hunting and sports, much as did Athene. They would debate issues, the goddess giving the gods' side, Pallas defending the humans. Athene never felt threatened by the abilities of this human companion but loved her dearly. Then one day, while out taking part in the Amazon games, Pallas fell from a steep cliff and was killed. Athene's sorrow for her lost friend was so great that the goddess adopted the name Pallas as part of her own name.

Athene became the deity of women's rights and freedom, as well as patroness of all crafts, soldiers, wisdom, and the horse. She was celebrated especially at the Lesser Panathenaea in March and again on the Day of the Geniae on December 25.

The Birth of Isis and Nephthys

When the Great God Ra abdicated his throne, he left it to his son Shu, who in turn yielded the throne to his children, Seb and Nut. Now these two children married,

Isis

although they had been forbidden by Ra to do so; they spent so much time copulating that Ra finally ordered Shu to forcefully separate them. Ra also declared that the pregnant sky goddess Nut could not give birth in any month of the year.

The great and wise god Thoth felt sorry for Nut and decided to help her. He played draughts with Selene the Moon and won enough light to make five extra days for each year. Since these days did not belong to the regular Egyptian calendar of 360, Nut was able to give birth. Her five children were born in five different parts of Egypt. These children were: Osiris, Haroeris, Set, Isis, and Nephthys.[1] These holy five days of birth became the in-between times: the time when the old year ended and the new year began for the Egyptians.

Isis and Nephthys were opposite aspects of the same power. Isis was the Queen of the Living, the wife of Osiris and mother of Horus, the goddess of the Full Moon. Nephthys was the Dark Mother, Queen of the Dead, mistress of Osiris and mother of Anubis, the goddess of the Dark Moon. Both had great magickal powers which complimented each other.

Thoth, who was considered self-begotten and self-produced, was honored at his chief festival a few days after the Full Moon at the beginning of the Egyptian year.

Neptune/Poseidon

The Titan Cronus and his sister Rhea had six children: Hestia, Demeter, Hera, Hades, Poseidon, and Zeus. After Zeus liberated his swallowed siblings, he divided the kingdom with his brothers. Zeus took the heavens and Olympus, Hades the Underworld.

Poseidon chose to make his realm in the Earth's oceans and seas. Poseidon, however, always desired to expand his kingdom and was often in contention with Zeus over land. He never completely won and had to settle for only part of what he wanted.

His wife was the nereid Amphitrite, daughter of the Titan Oceanus. He drove a chariot pulled by Tritans blowing conch horns; tridents, bulls, and horses were his symbols. He had the power to summon monsters from the depths of the ocean to avenge himself on humans, and did so on several occasions. Poseidon was also called Earth-Shaker, a reference to his power to produce earthquakes. A turbulent and independent god, he used his trident

Neptune

to stir the seas into terrible storms. Since earthquakes were a frequent part of Mediterranean life, Poseidon/Neptune was honored with special festivals.

Rituals

Request for Peace in the World

This can be done at any time. There is so much unrest and civil strife in the world that humans need to remember to ask for peace. Burn jasmine incense and light a blue candle. Chant:

> *We strive toward Spirit again and again,*
> *With faltering steps, unsure of the way.*
> *Open the gates of enlightenment.*
> *Make for us a new day*
> *Of karmic purpose and goal,*
> *A path to a new Earth soul.*

Sit quietly visualizing a blue cloud of healing and peace slowly but surely covering the entire Earth. If you have a specific area in mind, work on mentally permeating that area with the blue cloud. Send out vibrations of love, understanding, cooperation, and peace. Don't visualize how this is to come about, just that it will. Follow the blue cloud of peace with a pink fog of universal love. Say:

Let there be peace among all lands.
Let there be harmony among all peoples.
Cosmic love enters every heart and mind.
All strife is replaced by peace.
By the power of the Supreme Creator within me,
It is so!

Request for Religious Freedom

Often individuals and/or groups become persecuted for their religious beliefs and their choice of spiritual paths. This persecution can range from subtle hurtful remarks to outright physical assaults and discrimination. Hate mail and harassing phone calls (all anonymous, of course) can make you feel miserable and fearful. Probably the most difficult to handle, though, is when the trouble comes from within your own circle of family and friends.

The first step is to do a banishing of negative vibrations that have been sent to you; also, build up a wall of protection that not only protects you, your family and pets, but moves with you through your day, wherever you may be. At the same time, don't be naive. Take measures to protect yourself physically. Notify the proper authorities and insist that they uphold the law. Freedom of religion is a constitutional right.

Secondly, ask the gods for religious freedom to be recognized and accepted throughout the world. A multitude of spiritual paths are necessary, for all humans do not have the same needs. Burn jasmine incense and light a blue candle. Say:

Problems have come, not all of my making,
Enemies gather to bring my downfall.
Great Ones, protect me. Grant me courage.
Build up a powerful wall.
Teach me self-discipline. Help me clean out my life.
Rid me of negatives, problems, and strife.

Sit quietly and visualize yourself clothed in an impenetrable blue armor. From this armor radiates a pink glow that touches the hearts and minds of prejudiced people, making them realize that you have a right to your spiritual path. (By the same token, don't go around shoving your spiritual opinions on everyone else.) Keep moving the pink glow out farther and farther until it encircles the world. Say:

Every person is different. Their needs are unique.
Each spiritual pathway meets a need of a soul.
Each one travels alone to seek for their God.
Merging with One is the ultimate goal.
Send spiritual freedom for all.
Great Ones, answer my call.

Call for Rain

The Norse god Thorr, known as the Thunderer and the High Thunderer, was considered to be a champion of the Gods and an enemy of the Giants and Trolls. He was very popular among the people as a protector and friend; symbols of his magick hammer Mjollnir are still worn today. He drove a chariot pulled by two giant male goats. His wife Sif, with her golden hair, was a grain and harvest goddess. Although he was known to be hasty sometimes in judgment, Thorr was always a reliable friend and battle-companion. He was pictured with wild red hair and beard and dressed in battle clothes.

Thorr's Hammer

Thorr ruled over strength, law and order, defense, oaks, goats, thunder, lightning, storms, weather, crops, trading voyages, water, courage, trust, revenge, protection, and battle. Legends say that he struck the clouds to release the rains needed for crops.

If you have a Thorr's hammer pendant, wear it for this ritual. Have a sword or spear at hand; if you don't have these, use your ritual dagger. Give yourself plenty of room if you do this inside. If you want, you can go outside. However, don't go outdoors carrying any metal tool during a thunderstorm. Lightning is attracted by metal! Take with you a bucket or pitcher of water.

Decide upon the center point of your working area. Move to the East with your sword in one hand, the pitcher of water in the other. Stab toward the sky with your sword. You have to put a lot of emotion into this ritual.

> *Thorr of the Mighty Hammer, send the moisture ladened winds over this land.*
> (Pour out a little water) *Release their waters gently.*

Move to the South and stab with the sword.

> *Thorr of the Battle Chariot, withhold the celestial fire.*
> (Pour out a little water) *Keep back the lightning from the dry and parched Earth.*

Go to the West and stab with the sword.

Thorr, whose beard is the red of the evening sunset,
awaken the Water Elementals.
(Pour out a little water) *Ride before them in your goat drawn chariot.*

Finally, go to the North and stab with the sword.

Mighty Thorr, friend of all humans,
crack the storm clouds with your hammer.
(Pour out a little water) *Let the rumbling thunder*
open the water-filled clouds.

Stand again in the center of your working area. Lay aside the sword and begin slowly turning clockwise. At the same time, throw handfuls of the remaining water out of the pitcher into the air. Pour the last drops onto the ground. Set aside the pitcher, and jump or dance around the area, singing "Thorr and rain, comes again!" Imagine yourself dancing in the rain. When you feel pleasantly exhausted, give thanks to Thorr and the Water Elementals for hearing you.

Earthquake Protection

The Greek god Poseidon, known as the Earthshaker, was petitioned for protection from earthquakes. This deity's power over earth tremors was known from the very earliest of Mediterranean culture and continued as long as he was worshipped. In later times, Poseidon was called the Supreme Lord of the Inner and Outer Seas, the god of everything that swam in or on water. Although his sea-wife was the nereid Amphitrite, Poseidon had a mortal wife at one time. She was Cleito by whom he had ten sons who ruled Atlantis.

Horses and bulls were sacred to Poseidon. He used his trident to stir the seas into wild storms and to spear the clouds to release the rains and floods. He was considered to be both turbulent and independent. He ruled over storms, all marine life, intuition, human emotions, sailors, ships, hurricanes, rain, weather, and revenge.

Set out a glass or chalice of water. Place a small statue of a horse or a bull beside it. Light a blue or blue-green candle. Add a pinch of salt to the water and gently swirl it three times clockwise. Stand with your arms stretched out before you as the Greeks did when addressing Poseidon. Say:

Earth Shaker! The seas and land tremble before you.
Quake Maker! The deep ocean opens before you.
Sea-Rider! Hold back your hand.

Trident Bearer! Vent not your anger on the Earth.
Let the Earth Mother rest in peace, Poseidon.
Spare the humans living upon Her.
Do not shake or crack the land.
I recognize your existence and honor your power.
Spare us, Earth Shaker!

Take the water outside and pour it very gently onto the ground.

Marriage of the God & Goddess

The sacred marriage of the God and Goddess was celebrated by almost every culture in the world in one form or another. This marriage has been honored at various times, from the Spring Equinox to the Hay Moon celebration of the Egyptians for Isis and Osiris. It was symbolic of the necessary union of the positive and negative forces that keep the universe and everything in it in balance.

Set red-colored eggs around the cauldron to symbolize the divine source of renewing life. Place a picture of the magick Buckle of Isis and tat (sometimes called a tet or djed) of Osiris side by side before the cauldron. Cast your circle as usual.

Light the golden candle in the cauldron and say:

The Goddess has entered the Sacred Marriage with her consort
That all beings may be blessed.

Take the Buckle and tat in your hands and, beginning in the East and moving clockwise, retrace the circle outline with them. Return to the altar. Hold the Buckle and tat to your heart and say:

Isis, Giver of Life, lies upon the marriage bed with Osiris,
Osiris, Lord of Lords, the Everlasting,
Osiris of renewing life, of death and reincarnation.
The union of Isis and her virile lover
Quickens the life-forces working within the world.
I feel their power fermenting within me,
Working, growing, re-creating.
From out of this thrice-sealed circle
Creating power of love goes forth
To bless all forms of creation
Of mind and on the Earth.

Continue to hold the Buckle and tat to your heart. Think deeply upon new beginnings you desire to enter your own life. Place the Buckle and tat before the cauldron. Now is the time for meditation and spellworking.

If you want to empower a new talisman, or an old one that needs new energy, place it on the altar and hold your wand over it. Say:

> *Might into magick, power into spell,*
> *Empower this* (name of object). *Heed me well.*

Maat, Goddess of Truth & Justice
— Crescent Moon —

Maat of Egypt was known as the Lady of the Judgment Hall and the Virgin. She was the cherished daughter of Ra and the wife of Thoth. Her laws governed the three worlds; even the gods had to obey her rulings. In the Hall of Double Justice where the souls of the dead were weighed for truthfulness, Maat stood in one pan of the balance scale opposite the heart of the deceased. Sometimes her image was symbolized by a feather.

Maat wore an ostrich feather on her head while standing, or sitting on her heels. She held a scepter and an ankh. Maat was the deity of truth, right, justice, law, final judgment of the soul, order, and reincarnation.

For this ritual, the extra tools you will need are wisteria or sandalwood oil, a white candle, an ankh, purification incense, a small bowl of water, and a sistrum.

Stand at the altar facing East. Light the white candle and set it behind the bowl of water. Say:

> *This is a time of cleansing, a time of spiritual growth and renewal.*
> *Maat, the self-begotten, is renewed by each truth that is*
> *spoken into the world.*
> *She judges each soul against her feather-light wisdom.*

Carry the incense clockwise slowly around the ritual area. Return it to the altar. Place the oil on the pentacle disk. Take up the ankh and say:

> *The Maiden comes to test the hearts of all believers.*
> *O, Maat, let my heart be purified*
> *That the scales of Justice may balance my life.*

Hold the ankh against your heart and continue:

> *Your spiritual feather of Truth lies upon the scales*
> *in the Hall of Judgment.*
> *Show me the true way, Lady of Justice,*
> *That I may walk the path of enlightenment.*
> *Lead my feet to the still waters of Truth.*
> *Reveal to me green pastures of silence*
> *Where I can find renewed purpose in life.*[2]

Kneel before the altar. Anoint your forehead with oil, saying:

> *Open my mind and inner eye to greater truths.*

Anoint your heart, and say:

> *Cleanse my heart of all impurities.*

Anoint the palms of your hands, saying:

> *Let my hands be lifted up in true worship of the Gods.*

Anoint the tops of your feet. Say:

> *Guide my feet into paths of growth and enlightenment.*

Hold the ankh to your heart again and say:

> *Hear me, O Maat.*
> *Teach me the way I must go,*
> *That, when I appear before you in the Hall of Judgment,*
> *The scales of Life may be balanced.*

If you have any spiritual spellworking, now is the time to do it. This is also a good time for meditation for guidance and spiritual growth. If you plan to do scrying, set the crystal ball or bowl of water on the altar. Anoint your third eye with wisteria oil. Tap the ball or bowl lightly seven times with the ankh. Say:

> *Into the paths of time I cast my mind*
> *To see the paths that yet may be.*
> *O Lady of Truth and Wisdom,*
> *Give me the gift of prophecy.*

Answers may come in images, pictures or thoughts in the mind, or later in dreams.

When finished, stand before the altar with the ankh in your right hand, sistrum in your left. Say:

> *Mistress of the Judgment Hall, Lady of Truth,*
> *Bring me to wisdom and knowledge.*
> *I need your guidance in this life,*
> *That my spiritual growth may increase.*
> *Look upon me with compassion and love, Lady.*

The Incan Mothers
— Full Moon —

Mama Quilla was the Incan Moon goddess. Her image was a huge silver disk with a human face; this disk hung in her chapel, nearly covering an entire wall. This chapel was part of the Temple of the Sun. Mama Quilla the Moon was next in reverence to the Sun God. She married the Sun Inti and gave birth to Mama Ogllo ("Egg"), the Moon maiden and her brother the Sun man. It was from these two that the Inca royal line was said to evolve. Mama Quilla was also connected with the calendar and the timing of festivals. When an eclipse of the Moon occurred, it was said that a snake or puma was trying to eat the goddess. She was the protectress of women, and ruled over the calendar and religious festivals.

Mama Cocha was Mother Sea. She was worshipped especially along the Peruvian coast where fishing was essential to life. She also protected against tidal waves and marine disasters. Pachamama was Earth Mother. She presided over agriculture and was invoked in all daily rites.

This chant can be included as part of regular ritual or chanted while spellworking. It can also be used just before meditation when you are seeking aid in strengthening your knowledge of magick.

> *Great Incan Mothers, Ladies of words of power,*
> *Teach me the works of magick and of initiation.*
> *Triple Mothers, come to me in my time of need.*
> *Let my spells have strength.*

Whenever you do a divination, call upon the Incan Mothers to help by chanting:

> *Grant me balance and inspiration.*
> *Grant me the key to manifestation.*
> *Creative force direct toward me*
> *That a stronger person I may be.*

Arianrhod, Lady of the Silver Wheel
—Dark Moon—

Arianrhod of Wales was a Dark Moon goddess. Her symbols, like those of Cerridwen, were the cauldron and the white sow. Her Silver Wheel, sometimes portrayed as a paddle-wheeled boat which carried souls to their starry home, may have been symbolic of the zodiac and its signs (the wheel-spokes).

Arianrhod was called Silver Wheel, High Fruitful Mother, Star Goddess, Sky Goddess, and Goddess of Reincarnation. Her palace was called Caer Arianrhod (Aurora Borealis). She was the keeper of the circle Silver Wheel of Stars, a symbol of time and karma. This wheel was also known as the Oar Wheel, a ship which carried dead warriors to the Moon-land (Emania). Her original consort was Nwyvre (Sky or Firmament). She was also the mother of Lleu Llaw Gyffes and Dylan by her brother Gwydion. Arianrhod had power over beauty, fertility, karma, and reincarnation.

You will need a green candle on your altar; a wand; the pentacle; a metal bowl large enough to burn papers; several small pieces of paper, and a pencil. This ritual can be part of your regular ritual or performed by itself.

Write your dreams and desires on the papers, one desire to a small sheet. Lay the papers on the pentacle with the wand on top of them. Take the ritual dagger in your power hand. Go to the East; say:

> *Awake, O Gods of Air!*
> *Blow out the old!*
> *Bring in the new on your winds of change.*

Go to the South; say:

> *Awake, O Gods of Fire!*
> *Burn away the endings that hold me back.*
> *Shine your gentle rays upon new goals.*

Move to the West; say:

> *Awake, O Gods of Water!*
> *Cleanse my life of unnecessary and harmful habits.*
> *Drop your spring rains upon me for growth.*

Finish by going to the North. Say:

Awake, O Gods of Earth!
Let your renewing magick bury old ways,
And open new paths before me.

Take up the wand and lightly tap the papers seven times.

Pick up one paper and hold the end of the wand against it. Visualize a stream of brilliant white light emanating from the wand and penetrating the paper. If the light does not stay white, reread the desire and decide if it is really good for you. If it isn't, discard the paper, reword the desire, or perhaps save it for another time. If the light stays a pure white, light the paper from the candle and drop it carefully into the metal bowl. For each burned paper, say:

To the winds of heaven and to the Gods,
I give these thought-desires for manifestation.

Let the ashes cool overnight. The next morning carefully discard them. If possible, bury them or cast them into flowing water. A good flush down the toilet counts.

Now is an excellent time to do a meditation in which you ask to be shown past lives, particularly ones which have a bearing on your present life. Prepare for a past life meditation by chanting:

Ancient One of reincarnation and rebirth,
Open the doors to my past lives.
I would correct all errors and relearn all skills,
That I may walk a free pathway.
Starry Arianrhod, show the proper way to go.

Endnotes

1. This list of names often varies.
2. Lest anyone think I'm copying from the Christians here, these words and expressions were recorded in ancient Egyptian writings long before the Christians decided to call them their own.

Chapter 11

CORN MOON

August

Also called: Barley Moon, Dispute Moon,
Weodmonath (Vegetation Month), Harvest Moon,
Moon When Cherries Turn Black.

Month of the Hindu festival for Ganesha; called the Ganesha Chaturthi, or
Chauti.

Aug. 1: Festival of New Bread among the Celtic countries. Among the
Aztecs, the festival of Xiuhtecuhtli, god of the calendar and spiritual fire.

Aug. 1-3: Festival of the Dryads in Macedonia, honoring the maiden spirits
of the water and woodlands.

Aug. 6: A festival of Thoth in Egypt. Beginning of the Month of Ghosts in
China and Singapore.

Aug. 7: In Egypt, the Breaking of the Nile, dedicated to Hathor.

Aug. 12: The Egyptian Blessing of the Boats.

Aug. 13 & 15: Diana of the Wildwood and Hecate, the Dark Mother of the
Moon in very early Greece and Rome; Full Moon.

Aug. 17: Full Moon feast of Diana in Rome.

Aug. 23: Nemesea, the festival of Nemesis (goddess of Fate) in Greece. In Rome, the Volcanalia, a festival for the god Vulcan to ward off accidental fires. In Rome, the Vertumnalia, honoring Vertumnus, god of the changing seasons.

Aug. 25: In Rome, the Opseconsiva, a harvest festival for the goddess Ops.

Aug. 26: Feast Day of Ilmatar or Luonnotar, Finnish goddess.

Aug. 29: Birthday of Hathor and New Year's Day in Egypt.

Aug. 30: Roman festival of thanksgiving, called the Charisteria.

Aug. 31: Hindu festival of Anant Chaturdasi, women's purification, honoring the goddess Ananta.

August, originally called Sextilis by the Romans, was later named Augustus in honor of Augustus Caesar. Gathered harvests were celebrated in many lands during this month.

August 1 was a Celtic feast called Lunasa or Lughnassadh, meaning the celebration of harvest and new grain for bread. In Old English this became Lammas, or "Loaf Mass." The Romans also had a harvest festival during this month, that of the Consualia when sacrifices to Consus were made. Consus was the god of the underground storehouse where the grain was kept.

They also celebrated the Opseconsiva, a harvest festival for the goddess Ops. Wine and freshly baked bread were placed on her altars. Near the end of the month they had a thanksgiving feast called the Charisteria.

At three times during August, the Romans honored the god Vulcan: on August 17 at the Portunalia; on August 27 at the Volturnalia; and again on August 23 at the Volcanalia. This last festival was held outside the city boundaries and was to ward off accidental fires, a real threat in such closely-packed and fire-prone towns. Vulcan was not the only deity honored during these festivals. The goddesses Juturna (deity of fountains) and Stata Mater (who put out fires) were invoked as a counterbalance to Vulcan's fires—volcanoes or otherwise.

The very early Greeks had a holy day for Hecate the Dark Mother on August 13, and ten days later one for Nemesis, the goddess who balanced the scales of justice with rightful revenge and punishment. In Rome, women who had prayers answered by Diana and Hecate marched by torchlight to the temples of these goddesses. There they held a special ceremony for women only and gave thanks.

The Egyptian Blessing of the Boats is quite similar in nature to the Roman festival of the Ludi Piscatari in June during the Mead Moon. Each boat was considered to have its own personality and a need for protection and blessing. The same can apply today to cars, boats, bikes, motorcycles, and in fact to any form of transportation upon which one relies.

In India today, the Hindu people still honor the elephant-headed god Ganesha, the deity who removes obstacles and brings good luck. Flowers and dishes of rice were set before his statues. However, it is considered unlucky to look at the Moon during this festival.

Yapaquix (Sowing Month), also known as Chacra Ayapui or Capac Siquis, was celebrated by the Incas.

The people of Tibet had only one major holiday this month, the Sikhim festival of the birth of Padmasambhava.

Correspondences

Nature Spirits: dryads

Herbs: chamomile, St. Johns wort, bay, angelica, fennel, rue, orange

Colors: yellow, gold

Flowers: sunflower, marigold

Scents: frankincense, heliotrope

Stones: cat's eye, carnelian, jasper, fire agate

Trees: hazel, alder, cedar

Animals: lion, phoenix, sphinx, dragon

Birds: crane, falcon, eagle

Deities: Ganesha, Thoth, Hathor, Diana, Hecate, Nemesis

Power Flow: energy into harvesting; gathering, appreciating. Vitality, health. Friendships.

Old Sayings & Lore

- An old English harvest Moon ritual was to gather a key, a ring, a flower, a sprig of willow, a small piece of cake, a crust of bread, 10 of clubs, 9 of hearts, ace of spades, and ace of diamonds. Wrap these in a handkerchief and place it under your pillow. Say upon going to bed:

Luna, every woman's friend,
To me thy goodness condescend.
Let me this night in visions see
Emblems of my destiny.

If you dream of storms, it means coming trouble; if the storms end, a calm fate after strife. If you dream of a ring or the ace of diamonds, marriage; bread, a good job; cake, prosperity; flowers, joy; willow, treachery in love; spades, death; clubs, living in a foreign land; diamonds, money; keys, great power; birds, many children; and geese, more than one marriage.

- The English had a saying: that if a member of the family died at the time of the New Moon, three deaths would follow.

- The Fenland country of England is a very strange place and has kept its superstitions longer than other areas. They say that if public dinners are not held at a Full Moon, tragedy will follow. Since Fenland roads are built high above the marshy land and bordered on both sides by deep ditches, one can see why this is more sense than superstition.

- Many cultures felt that it was extremely unlucky to point at the Moon, and that curtseys to the Moon would bring a present before the next change of Moon.

- Originally, the term Moon-struck or Moon-touched meant chosen by the Goddess. These people were considered to be blessed.

- A Moon-calf now means someone who is absent-minded or not very bright. At one time it described a person who was so carried away by love of the Goddess that he/she was nearly oblivious to the world around them.

- It was often said that if a person was born at a Full Moon, he or she would have a lucky life.

Recipes

Sandalwood Drink

The people of India use quite a few essential oils and herbs in their drinks. The original recipe called for ½ teaspoon saffron threads (a very expensive item).

1½	quarts water	1	lemon, juiced
5	cloves	1	cup plain low-fat yogurt
5	green cardamom pods	1	quart tonic water or plain
1	cup honey		soda water
4	drops sandalwood, or 4 teaspoons sandalwood water		

Boil the water, cloves, and cardamom for 5-6 minutes. Add the honey and san-dalwood; boil until the syrup is thick. Remove from heat, stir in lemon juice, and let cool.

Put the yogurt and cooled syrup into a blender. Puree until liquid is frothy. Pour into a bowl and mix with soda water. Serve cold.

Toasted Pumpkin Seeds

This is eaten in Mexico like we eat popcorn. You will probably want to make more than one batch as they go fast. You may wish to experiment with other seasons than the garlic. Makes about 1½ cups.

1½	cups water	1 teaspoon salt
8	ounces raw pumpkin seeds, hulled	Several cloves of garlic,
1	teaspoon mild chili powder	finely chopped

Boil the water and pour over the seeds. Let them soak overnight at room temperature. Drain and spread evenly in a 10" or larger baking dish. Sprinkle on the chili powder, salt, and garlic. Bake at 350° F for 25-35 minutes or until the seeds are puffed up and dry. As they roast, they will sputter and pop a lot. Stir occasionally while cooling.

Other seasonings that are good alternatives for garlic and chili are cumin seeds, hot pepper, teriyaki and soy sauce. The toasted seeds are also excellent with only a little salt.

Salad With A Bite

Not everyone is fond of horseradish, but in this recipe it does not overpower the other flavors. It is excellent with sandwiches or meats.

1   8-ounce carton low-fat cottage cheese
1   small carton French onion dip
1   teaspoon horseradish, or to taste

Combine all ingredients thoroughly. Chill to blend the flavors.

Crafts

Cherokee Dream Pillow

The following mixture is stuffed into a small pillow that is placed under your regular pillow or next to your head while you sleep. It is said to bring good and prophetic dreams. Unless otherwise stated, all flowers are dried.

2	ounces lavender flowers	1	ounce cedar shavings
2	ounces sage	2	ounces coltsfoot herb
1	ounce ground orris root	2	ounces sweet fern
2	ounces deer's tongue herb	1	ounce violets

Arabian Nights Hot Pot Potpourri

2	ounces rose petals	2	ounces cedar shavings
1	ounce sandalwood shavings	1	ounce coffee blossoms
1	broken stick cinnamon		(optional)
1	drop lilac oil	1	drop jasmine oil

Rose Eau De Cologne

1	pint distilled water	4	ounces rubbing alcohol
1	ounce glycerin	1	drop rose geranium oil
1	drop rose oil	1	drop bergamot oil

Myths

Ganesha

The elephant-headed god Ganesha remains one of the most popular of Hindu deities. Legend says he was formed by the goddess Parvati from the sweat of her beautiful body mixed with dust. At the time of his creation, Ganesha had a face and form like the other gods. When Parvati was finished, she appointed Ganesha as guardian of the gate to her abode. Ganesha took his job very seriously, and when Parvati said she wished to see no one, he tried to turn away the god Shiva. Shiva was in no mood to be kept out and had Ganesha's head cut off.

Parvati was very upset and told Shiva she wanted nothing to do with him because of his actions against her special servant. Shiva relented; he said that Ganesha could have the head of the first animal to pass by. That animal happened to be an elephant.

The Hindu people love Ganesha. Little statues of him are everywhere: a short, pot-bellied man with yellow skin, four arms, and an elephant's head with one tusk. In his hands he holds a discus, shell, club, and water lily. He rides on a rat.

Ganesha

Hecate of the Dark Moon

Hecate was the oldest Greek form of the triform Goddess, who ruled heaven, the Underworld, and the Earth. She was known to the Amazons as the goddess of the Dark Moon, one of the three faces of the Moon, and ruler of the Underworld. In the beginning, Hecate was not a dread goddess. After the matriarchs fell, the Greeks worshipped her as one of the queens of the Underworld and ruler of three-way crossroads. As Hecate Trevia, Hecate of the Three Ways, her three-headed images stood at these crossroads, where she was worshipped on the Full Moon for positive magick and on the Dark Moon for dark magick.

Legend is not consistent as to the origins of Hecate. Some say she was the daughter of the Titans Tartaros and Night; other versions say of Perses and Asteria; still others, of Zeus and Hera. Tales of Hecate were told around the Mediterranean. She was connected with the cauldron, dogs, and keys.

Her festivals were all held at night by torchlight. Every year on the island of Aegina in the Saronic Gulf, a mysterious ritual was held in her honor. As Lady of the Wild Hunt and witchcraft, Hecate was primarily a woman's deity, both to worship and ask for help, and to fear if one did not have her spiritual life in order.

Ilmatar of Finland

Most of the Finno-Ugric legends are contained in the Kalevala. In the beginning, says this book, Ilmatar, who was the virgin daughter of Air, came down from the sky into the sea. Ilmater is also known as Luonnotar, Daughter of Nature. As she frolicked over the water, the East wind made her pregnant. The goddess floated on the water for seven centuries, unable to give birth because there was no land.

She prayed constantly to the god Ukko, the highest of gods, to help her. Ukko took pity upon her and sent a teal to build a nest on her knee. When the teal's eggs hatched, Ilmatar took the shells and with her magick created the Earth, sky, Sun, Moon, and clouds. Even though dry land was now available, Ilmatar continued to carry the child within her for thirty summers. Her son Vainamoinen had to struggle for another thirty-one years to reach the mainland and begin his life.

The Dryads

These supernatural creatures were part of the large family of nymphs, well known in Greece and the surrounding area, but they are also said to inhabit the entire world. The Dryads themselves are the nymphs of forests and trees. Their close relatives the Napaeae, the Auloniads, the Hylaeorae, and the Alsaeids lived in woods, glens, groves, and valleys, while the Oreads belonged to the mountains and grottoes. The Hamadryads protected and cherished specific individual trees. Close cousins to these Dryads were the Naiads of the brooks, the Crenae and Pegae of springs, and the Limnads of stagnant waters.

Sometimes these nymphs lived within the waters, sometimes in grottoes nearby. They were said to give the gift of prophecy and oracles, heal the sick, watch over the flowers of the area, and protect the fields and flocks. The relationship and powers of all the nymphs were so similar that often their duties and areas of influence overlapped. Dryads of the forests and trees sometimes watched over nearby pools and springs. Nymphs of the waters protected the surrounding woodlands.

The Greeks and Romans were careful not to antagonize these creatures. Grottoes, springs, groves, and all woodlands were treated with respect, for one never knew if the presiding nymph would be offended. Nymphs were companions of Faunus and Pan, both of which were capable of instilling panic and unnatural dread in any offender.

Rituals

Feast of New Bread

The original Feast of New Bread was a celebration of the harvesting of grain, a thanksgiving that there would be food for the Winter months. If you have a garden, this is still an appropriate celebration. If you don't garden, or haven't the space for one, you can still celebrate this old festival in a number of ways.

You can bake rolls or bread from scratch. The very act of mixing and kneading and shaping makes you aware of the Earth Mother's contribution to your life.

If you have a garden, supplement a meal with your harvested vegetables. Make a centerpiece out of a tray of sliced vegetables and Herb Dip.

Another way to celebrate the Feast of New Bread is to offer your services to a soup kitchen or other supplier of meals to the homeless and/or elderly. If you haven't the time for this, at least make a donation of food or money to such a place.

When you eat your bread, home-baked or otherwise, at this special meal, dip it in a little salt for the first bite. This is a very old custom still followed in many parts of the world today. Begin your meal with a few words of thanks to the Earth Mother who oversees the growth of the grain and all vegetables.

Celebration of the Dryads

The Dryads are the Nature spirits, or nymphs, of forests and trees. There are several divisions of Dryads, each of which have their special areas of expertise and magick. Some work only with groves, valleys, and trees. Others are found only around water. Still others belong to mountains and grottoes. Often their protective powers extend to the areas around their principal domain, such as those of water will protect and nurture the surrounding woods, while those of the woods will do the same for any nearby water.

The Greeks and Romans said the Dryads could give the gift of prophecy and oracles, heal the sick, watch over the flowers and wild animals of the area, and protect the fields and flocks.

Dryads were known in all the Celtic countries. The Celts believed them to be spirits who dwelt in trees, oaks in particular. The Druids contacted them for inspiration. Oak galls were known as Serpent Eggs by the Druids and were used in many of their charms.

The ancient people who knew about the Dryads were careful not to antagonize them. Grottoes, springs, groves, all woodlands were treated with respect, for they did not wish to offend the Dryads who lived there. Nymphs and Dryads were companions of Faunus and Pan; both of these forest deities were capable of causing panic and fear in any humans and animals. Our word "panic" comes from Pan's ability to incite panic.

Besides the obvious way of making friends with the Dryads—care of the woodlands and the creatures who live there—you can get to know the ones in the trees and shrubs on your property by enticing them with faery boat lights and tiny bells.

To make faery boat lights, use walnut shell halves. If you can't get walnut shells, use very small pieces of thin wood. Break birthday candles in half. Drip hot wax into the shell until you can anchor the tiny candle. Take a wide bowl of water outside and put it in a spot where you can sit comfortably and watch it. Light each candle, and float the faery boat in the bowl of water. Ring tiny bells to entice the Dryads closer; they will already be curious. Chant:

> *Come, Little Ones, join in my play*
> *And we'll be friends both night and day.*
> *Strange realms we'll seek; in fantasy*
> *Explore the Earth and sky and sea.*
> *Show me the powers of Elements,*
> *Knowledge old, ingredients*
> *Of spells and potions, magick true.*
> *And I shall be strong friends with you.*

Sit quietly and listen for strange rustlings in the leaves of the trees. Soon you should feel the presence of the Dryads. They like to play in your hair or brush against you. If you are having trouble with certain plants, inside or outside, ask for their help in healing and coaxing the plants to do better. Since the faery boat lights are in water, you can leave them to burn out if you wish.

Protection from Fire

The Roman god Vulcan, sometimes called Volcanus, was known as a tough, practical craftsman. Another of his titles was the Divine Smith. His forges were said to be under

Vulcan

either (or both) Mt. Etna or Mt. Vesuvius. As a smith, Vulcan was petitioned for protection from fire, something a smith must be able to control.

He was pictured as a bearded man with a short tunic and hat. He was the consort of Maia, mother of springs and an Earth goddess. Near him he kept a hammer, tongs, and anvil. Vulcan was a deity of the thunderbolt, fire, battles, blacksmiths, thunder, volcanoes, artisans, craftsmen, jewelry making, and mechanics. He was also a magician of metal and gems.

If you have had any personal problems with fire, no matter how small, you need to have a talk with Vulcan. This also applies if there is a fire-bug on the loose in the community. Include any neighborhood children who have a habit of playing with matches.

First, psychically cleanse your house by walking clockwise around each room, sprinkling a little blessed salt in each corner. To bless the salt, hold it in one hand and place the other hand over it. Ask the blessings of the Gods that your home may be made spiritually clean.

Light a red candle and lay beside it a hammer. You probably have a little hammer in your kitchen tool kit; this will do just fine. Face the South, the direction of the Fire

Elementals. Stamp three times on the floor and hold your hands down toward the Earth. The Greeks called all Underworld gods in this manner. Say:

Vulcan, god of forge and flame,
Hear me when I call your name.
Hold back the fire, destruction.
Keep me safe from this disruption.

Pick up the hammer and strike it sharply three times on the table. You might want to put a block of wood or a cutting board on the table to avoid damaging the surface. Say:

Elementals of the South,
Little Ones of flame and fire,
Treat this home kindly, I do ask.
Friendship is my desire.

Take the hammer and strike the air three times to the East. Say:

Begone, all those who cause fire trouble.
If human, be caught by the police.
If supernatural entity, Vulcan take them away!

Repeat this to the South, the West, and the North. Strike the table with the hammer three times. Say:

Vulcan of the flaming hammer,
Let there be peace and harmony between us.
I honor your life-giving fire,
But I do not want its destructive aspect in my home.
Honor to the god Vulcan! (Strike with the hammer three times.)

Leave the candle in a safe place to burn out completely.

Working with Nemesis

Nemesis, also called Adrasteia (the inevitable), was shown with a wreath on her head, an apple in her left hand, and a bowl in her right. She was the goddess of destiny, and divine anger against mortals who broke moral laws or taboos. Nemesis was a harsh, unremitting force representing acceptance of what must be. At times she would intercede with the Fate deity Atropos to allow a longer lifespan.

Often we have someone in our lives who consistently works at being a real trial to us. This person is sometimes called "our Nemesis," which isn't accurate. The problem, however, can fall under the power of the goddess Nemesis. She can remedy or sweep away interpersonal problems, provided we ourselves are not the cause of them. If we are contributing to the upset, she will stand back and make us work it out. So before you call upon Nemesis, be certain that you have rightfully accepted your share of the responsibility.

Use a black candle for Nemesis, anointing it from the end to the wick with patchouli or orange oil. This will help to create a balance or bring your life back into balance. Place a sliced apple in a dish next to the candle. Light the candle and sit facing it. Explain everything about the interpersonal problem to the goddess in your own words. Then say:

The hand of Nemesis balances the
scales of justice.
She untangles the threads spun by the Fates.
Lift the burden of this problem, great Nemesis.
Guide me to the solution.
If there can be no harmony, separate us one from
the other.
Untangle my life-thread, Nemesis.
This I do ask with a sincere heart.

Now sit quietly and listen with your mind. Meditation at this time can often calm you and provide possible solutions. You may even be told that you must make decisions and follow through with them. Listen, but look at everything logically. Some solutions may be too drastic and painful to implement. In this case, ask for an alternate solution to the problem.

Nemesis

Ganesha, Remover of Obstacles

One of the most popular of Hindu deities, Ganesha is looked upon with fondness and love. Known as the Lord of Obstacles, Ganesha is portrayed as a short, pot-bellied man with yellow skin, four arms, and an elephant's head with one tusk. He rides upon a rat. His titles are Elephant-Face and God of Scribes and Merchants.

Because he is thoughtful, wise, and knowledgeable of the scriptures, Ganesha is invoked before every undertaking to ensure success. He can remove the most daunting of obstacles.

During the August festival of Ganesha, called Chauti, flowers and dishes of rice are placed before his statues. It is said that if Ganesha is worshipped at this time, wishes will come true.

Ganesha rules over wisdom, good luck, literature, books, writing, worldly success, prosperity, peace, beginnings, successful enterprises, journeys, building, overcoming obstacles, and taming dangerous forces. This deity represents the combination of force and cunning.

For this ritual you will need: a yellow and a red candle; flowers (fresh or a nice artificial bouquet); an elephant statue and/or a picture or statue of Ganesha; an offering of powdered sandalwood. If you want to be really authentic, have a small amount of cooked rice as an offering to the god. Also have a piece of paper and pencil nearby.

Present the flowers and rice to Ganesha's picture or statue. Burn some of the sandalwood powder in your incense burner. Bow to the statue with your hands together, the tips touching your forehead.

> *Be joyous, for this is the time of Ganesha!*
> *The Lord of Obstacles comes riding to his festival.*
> *With his help, all success shall be mine.*
> *I greet you, Ganesha.*
> *All obstacles in my life are removed.*
> *I rejoice in your presence, Ganesha.*
> *Good luck and new beginnings flow down upon me.*
> *I praise you, Ganesha.*
> *I rejoice! For good luck and changes come!*

Light the yellow and red candles. Reach out to Ganesha with your heart and tell him what obstacles are obstructing your path to success. Listen carefully and truthfully, for Ganesha may point out a new path to take that will benefit you more than the one you have been struggling with. He may show you that you yourself are creating the obstacles for whatever reason.

Write down what you would like accomplished and put the paper under the Ganesha or elephant statue. Say:

Laughing god of creativity,
Loving, caring deity,
Of prosperity, peace, success,
I ask that you with these will bless
My life and turn life's wheel.
Positive change I would feel.

Bow to Ganesha again, with fingertips of your clasped hands touching your forehead. Extinguish the candles. Repeat the ritual for two more days; the last day let the candles burn out. Leave the statue and paper undisturbed for three days. Your requests need be written out only once.

Ilmatar, the Creatress
—Crescent Moon—

The Finnish-Ugrian goddess Ilmatar was the virgin daughter of Air. She had immense creative powers, and was known as Water Mother, Daughter of Nature, and Sky Mother. Legends say that she created the world and gave birth to the first great hero, Vainamoinen. This son was a great sorcerer and magician. He invented the zither and was such a superb musician that his playing tamed wild animals.

FOR CREATIVITY AND SPIRITUAL GROWTH: Decorate your sacred space with red eggs and flowers. Burn cinnamon incense and a pale green candle. Say:

Teacher of magick and wisdom,
Enlighten me.
Bestower of knowledge,
Open the door to ritual meaning.
Peace and contentment, I ask of you.

Sit in quiet meditation. Feel yourself riding in a boat on a gentle lake. Beside you is the goddess Ilmatar. Listen carefully to what she says. Talk with her as long as you wish. When you come back, say:

Healing, knowledge, mental powers,
All come from your creativity.
Eloquence and self-control
I ask now that you give to me.
Guidance I need and inspiration.
Teachers send with motives true.
I desire to learn, to expand my mind.
For these gifts, Ilmatar, I do thank you.

FOR CONCEPTION OF A CHILD: Again decorate your sacred space with red eggs and small flowers. Burn a pink candle and rose incense. (Pink is for birth and love, not necessarily a girl-child.) Say:

> *Mother of all mothers, hear my cry.*
> *My arms are empty, my heart full of love.*
> *Ripen my body with a little child,*
> *A soul that needs and loves me in return.*
> *Gift this child with wholeness and health.*
> *Fill my arms, Mother of all mothers.*

Sit quietly in meditation. Visualize yourself being drawn into Ilamatar's lap by her loving arms. Lay your head against her breast. Hear her loving heart beat in sympathy. Put your arms around her and tell Ilmatar of your deep desire for a child. Listen to her words of wisdom and comfort. Take as long as you need to fill up with her love and comfort. When you come back, say:

> *Ilmatar, loving and caring Mother,*
> *My heart beats in time with yours.*
> *All children come from your heart.*
> *I ask sincerely that you entrust me with a child.*
> *This child will be loved and cared for,*
> *For this is truly my desire.*

The Goddess of Opportunity
—Full Moon—

The Roman goddess Ops was a deity of crops, prosperity, and fertility. She was also honored during the Saturnalia (Cold Moon), when people exchanged gifts in her name at the festival called Opalia. Also exchanged were dolls representing the receivers as healthy and prosperous. She was invoked by sitting down and touching the Earth with one hand.

Do this spellworking on the Full Moon. Burn cinnamon or cedar incense. Either make or purchase a green cloth poppet. This is a small cloth, rough figure of a human that is stitched around the edges, with a small opening left for the stuffing. Write your name on the poppet. Stuff it with dried chamomile, vervain, and/or squill. To the herbs add several drops of mint and honeysuckle oils. Sew the opening closed.

As you hold the poppet in the incense smoke, say:

Goddess of opportunity,
Bring good things in life to me.
I'll be alert to all you send.
Goddess, be my helpful friend.

Repeat this three, five, seven, or nine times. The poppet can be left on your altar, carried with you, hung on your bedroom mirror or in your car. Each Full Moon you can renew it with this spellworking if you feel it is necessary.

Queen of the Seven Underworlds
— Dark Moon —

The goddess Ereshkigal was a deity of Mesopotamia, Babylonia, and Assyria. She was called Queen of the Underworld, and ruled over the seven hells of the Middle East underworlds. As the Crone aspect of the goddess, and sister of Ishtar (Inanna), Ereshkigal ruled over dark magick, revenge, retribution, the waning and Dark Moon, death, destruction, and regeneration.

Sometimes one is aware that negatives are coming into one's life but can't determine from where. A ritual to defeat evil is called for in these situations.

This is best performed during the Dark Moon. Have two black or very dark purple candles lit on the altar. Have ready a one-sided mirror, wand, tarot cards (or other divinatory tools), and Moon sickle (athame or sword will do) along with a small amount of blessed thistle, rosemary, and bay laurel to burn in a small metal bowl. If you use incense charcoal, these herbs can be slowly dropped on the lighted charcoal at the proper time in the ritual.

Burn a banishing incense. Cast your circle as usual. Call upon the four winds or four Elements to guard the circle. When finished, stand at your altar facing the East. Raise your arms in greeting and say:

Between the worlds I build this sacred altar.
Outside of time, this rite leads to the ancient way,
Where I may find the gods of greater powers,
And conjure magick great. Be here, I say.

Take your wand into your power hand. Hold your arms outstretched over the altar; say:

The cycle of the Moon has turned once more.
The Moon hides her light from the uninitiated.

Those who follow the Ancient Paths know that her power is not gone,
is not diminished.
The wisdom of the Dark Mother is there for all who truly seek her.

Tap the altar three times with the wand:

Hear me, O Carrier of Wisdom.
My voice flies through the night to you.
Show me new pathways I must tread
To change my life and make it new.

Crush the herbs lightly with your fingers, then hold the bowl high over the altar.

I bring an offering, fine and fair.
The scent will rise upon the air
To reach your realms. Bless me soon,
O Lady of the Darkened Moon.

Add a small amount of herbs to the burner. Continue to add small amounts of herbs throughout the rest of the ritual.

Take the Moon sickle in your power hand and the mirror in the other, the reflective side away from you. Go to the East; hold up the mirror and sickle.

I command you, all evil and unbalanced powers that come from the East,
Return to your makers!

Go to the South:

I command you, all evil and unbalanced powers that come from the South,
Return to your makers!

Go to the West:

I command you, all evil and unbalanced powers that come from the West,
Return to your makers!

Finish by going to the North:

I command you, all evil and unbalanced powers that come from the North,
Return to your makers!

Return to the altar and lay aside the mirror. Raise the Moon sickle skyward, saying:

By the symbols of the Moon goddess, I ask for protection.
I believe that by her wisdom and skills I shall be free
of all negative influences.
In the name of the Moon Lady, I ask for new ideas and beginnings
And the wisdom and guidance to act upon them.

Now is the time to silently, or aloud, ask for guidance from the Dark Moon Goddess. Explain to her what is going wrong in your life and where you would like to go. Take up the wand as you stand before the altar. Say:

Within your darkened realms
Of Earth and sky,
You change your form and face,
Reflected in the Moon on high.
Each face and form gives guidance.
I know that this is true.
Great Goddess of the Darkened Moon,
I do greet you.

Sit in meditation to receive inspiration and insight. Follow this with divination and spellworking for binding or removing of problems and influences. If you do any spellworking, before you begin, say:

Dark Lady of the waning Moon,
Mistress of the under-hells,
Grant me powers to overcome
All those who oppose my magick spells.
Give me wisdom, true insight.
I thank you, Lady of the Night.

When everything is completed, hold your wand over the altar and say:

By the spiritual fire of the gods,
By the magick of sky and Earth and sea,
All power within this circle goes
Into this spell. So mote it be.

Close the circle as usual.

Chapter 12
HARVEST MOON
September

*Also called: Wine Moon, Singing Moon, Sturgeon Moon,
Haligmonath (Holy Month), Witumanoth (Wood Month),
Moon When Deer Paw the Earth.*

The New Moon is the feast of Gauri in India.

The New Moon nearest the Autumn Equinox was the Citua, or Feast of the Moon, among the Incas.

The Full Moon was the Festival of the Pig, which honored the Greek Demeter and the Norse Freyja.

Sept. 8: In Tibet, the Water Festival, a thanksgiving feast honoring springs and water sprites.

Sept. 10: T'wan Yuan Chieh, or women's feast of reunion, a Moon festival honoring Ch'ang-O, in China.

Sept. 13-14: Ceremony of Lighting the Fire in Egypt, honoring Nephthys and the spirits of the dead.

Sept 18: The Chung-Ch'iu, or Chinese Harvest Moon festival, honoring the Moon goddess Ch'ang-O; birthday of the Moon. Usually on the Full Moon.

Sept. 19: In Alexandria, Egypt, a day-long fast to honor Thoth, as god of wisdom and magick.

Sept. 21: In Egypt, Feast of Divine Life, a celebration honoring the Triple Goddess as Maid, Mother, Crone.

Sept. 22: Autumn Equinox. Death of Tiamat in Sumeria.

Sept. 23: Festival of Nemesis, goddess of Fate, in Greece.

Sept. 23-Oct. 1: Nine-day Greek Sacred Festival of the Greater Eleusinia.

Sept. 27: Choosuk, or Moon Festival, in South Korea and Taiwan which honors the spirits of the dead. Birthday of Athene in Greece.

Sept. 30: Festival of Themis as ruler of Delphi.

Septem was the seventh month in the oldest Roman calendar. When other months were added to the seasonal calendar, the name for some reason was never changed.

The Autumn Equinox was and is celebrated still by many cultures around the world. This month is the last of the reliable harvesting months in the Northern Hemisphere. Life is beginning to wind down in preparation for the dormant months that follow. The energy flows from the Autumn Equinox through Winter Solstice to the Spring Equinox are gentler, deeper, more hidden. The Dark Moon deities, who represent the Underworld, death, reincarnation, and deep spiritual mysteries, now hold sway.

The Egyptian Ceremony of Lighting the Fire was a general festival of lights for all the gods and goddesses. Lamps of all kinds were set in front of deity statues. They were also placed before the statues of ancestors.

The Egyptian deity Thoth was the Lord of Holy Words and inventor of the Four Laws of Magick. Portrayed as ibis-headed, Thoth was a Moon god. As Supreme Magus, or the Ultimate Magician, he had control over the powers and attributes of the Moon.

In the old Incan Empire, the Citua was held on the New Moon nearest the Autumn Equinox. Everyone performed a ritual cleansing, then smeared their faces with a paste of ground maize. There followed several days of feasting and dancing. This was a Moon festival in honor of Mama Quilla, the Moon goddess.

Gauri, or the Fair One, is not a well known goddess of India. She is considered to be an aspect of the goddess Durga. Gauri is honored by eating sweets made from honey to bring sweetness to the soul.

The most famous holy celebration of this time of year was the annual Greek festival called the Greater Eleusinia. It honored Demeter, Kore-Persephone, and the holy child Iacchus. Unlike the Lesser Eleusinia held in the Spring, this celebration was open only to initiates who were under strict rule of silence about what occurred.

The Greek goddess Themis was the Titaness daughter of Uranus and Gaea. She was the mother of Atlas and Prometheus and the mother by Zeus of the Horae and the Moerae (Furies). Since she was the deity of social order and collective consciousness, the Olympians held her in high respect. Holding a pair of scales, Themis protected the innocent and punished the guilty. She ruled Delphi after her mother Gaea, but relinquished it to Phoebe who gave it to Apollo.

The annual festival of Yue-ping was held in China from the New Moon to the Full Moon. People made round cakes and painted figures of women or a hare and trees on them. These were called Yue-ping, or "Moon cakes." These cakes were presented to relatives and friends.

The Chinese said that the Moon Mother had twenty-eight "houses" (Hsiu) and rested each night in a different one. In each "house" she kept a warrior-hero consort who kept her company and did her bidding.

Correspondences

Nature Spirits: trooping faeries

Herbs: copal, fennel, rye, wheat, valerian, skullcap

Colors: brown, yellow-green, yellow

Flowers: narcissus, lily

Scents: storax, mastic, gardenia, bergamot

Stones: peridot, olivine, chrysolite, citrine

Trees: hazel, larch, bay

Animals: snake, jackal

Birds: ibis, sparrow

Deities: Demeter, Ceres, Isis, Nephthys, Freyja, Ch'ang-O, Thoth

Power Flow: rest after labor; balance of Light and Dark. Organize.
Clean and straighten up physical, mental, emotional, and spiritual clutter

Old Sayings & Lore

- A verse:

    When the Moon is at the full, mushrooms you can safely pull.
    But when the Moon is on the wane, wait ere you think to pluck again.

- Sailors believed that if the Moon, in the first or last quarter, lay in nearly a horizontal position with the horns upward, the weather would be fine. Country people say that the same type of Moon means good weather for twenty-eight days.

- Country people said that the weather was more likely to change at the four quarters of the Moon than at any other time.

- Rain is coming when the Moon has a halo around it or when an outline can be seen between the horns of a waxing or waning Moon.

- Some farmers believe that planting of plants and seeds should be done on the waxing Moon—except for runner beans and peas which grow counterclockwise, and should be planted during the waning Moon.

- One old legend says that on the Moon is everything that was wasted on Earth: misspent time, squandered wealth, broken vows, unanswered prayers, fruitless tears, unfulfilled desires and intentions, etc.

Recipes

Golden Peanutty Sauce
(Thailand)

½	cup minced onion	1	tablespoon lemon juice
1	tablespoon margarine	2	teaspoons curry powder
3	cups water	½	teaspoons dried, hot red
1	cup peanut butter		peppers, crushed

Saute onion in the margarine until tender. Add water and peanut butter, stirring until smooth. Add remaining ingredients and serve warm. Use as a dip for bite-sized pieces of cooked chicken, beef, or pork. Serve along with herb-flavored rice.

Irish Trifle

1 day-old pound cake
1 cup sherry or fruit juice
2 cups strawberries, sliced
2 cups nuts, almonds, or walnuts

1 6-ounce package strawberry gelatin
1 cup cooked custard or whipping cream, or both

Put a layer of torn cake pieces into the bottom of a 10" pan. Pour part of the sherry or juice over the cake. Add half of the strawberries and nuts. Make a second layer of these ingredients. Prepare the gelatin using only 2 cups of water; pour over the layers. After slightly set, top this with cooled custard and/or whipping cream. Refrigerate overnight.

Easy Pickled Beets

Although many people like pickled beets, the ready-made ones in the store just don't quite taste right. Here is a good recipe for busy people.

1 can small, whole beets
½ cup sugar

½ cup apple vinegar

Drain the beet juice into a saucepan. Add sugar and vinegar. Heat until the sugar dissolves. Slice the beets into a sterilized jar with a lid. Pour the hot liquid over the beets, put on the lid, and refrigerate. (If you like pickled eggs, hard-cook eggs and add to the beet juice.)

Scrumptious Baked Beans

I've given this recipe to so many people over the years that I've lost count. It takes time to prepare but is by far the most delicious baked bean recipe I've ever found.

2½ cups small navy beans
1 tablespoon salt
½ cup brown sugar
1 medium onion, chopped

½ cup chopped uncooked bacon
½ cup chili sauce or catsup
½ cup molasses

Wash and sort the beans. Soak them overnight, or boil them for 5 minutes in a generous amount of water and soak for 1 hour. Put all of the remaining ingredients into a casserole dish, and mix them together with the beans. Add enough hot water to cover the mixture. Be sure there is always enough liquid to keep the beans fully covered during cooking. Cover and bake at 275° F for at least 6 hours. Excellent served hot or cold.

Ambrosia Supreme

1 small carton sour cream
1 small can mandarin oranges, drained
1 cup small marshmallows

1 small can crushed pineapple, drained
1 cup flake coconut

Mix all ingredients together and chill. Excellent as a dessert or side-dish for a meal.

Crafts

Japanese Friendship Branch

This is a unique present for birthdays, weddings, anniversaries, or a new house. Choose a small-sized tree branch about 12-14" long with several twigs on it. Decorate it with small artificial pink blossoms to represent gaiety and joy. Other ornaments can be attached according to what you are wishing for the recipient; these can be fastened directly to the branch or enclosed in small mesh bags that are hung from the twigs. These gifts can be charms to be hung later on a bracelet, little ornaments to be set in the house, or magickal items to be used in rituals. Japanese symbols are: fish or a symbol of food for a bountiful harvest or storehouse of food; Buddha or a God/Goddess symbol to keep evil from the home; dice for good luck; money for wealth; small dolls for children. The Japanese also attach symbols that relate to the person's talent or profession.

Japanese Friendship Branch

Suede Carry-All

These are handy for almost anything, but are especially nice for transporting magickal items. Materials required:

- 2 pieces of soft, pliable, dark-colored suede, each 18" long x 16" wide; if you want a flap-top, add 5" onto the length of one piece only
- 1 piece of lighter colored suede 9" square for a contrasting motif
- 1 narrow piece of suede that can be doubled for the handle; or you can use macrame or a belt
  Strong glue suitable for use on suede
  Strong needle and button thread
  Tracing paper, pencil, and sharp scissors
- 4 Velcro self-sticking circles to use for the flap-top

With the right sides together and ¼" seams, glue the two pieces of dark suede together around three sides, leaving the top edge open. If you are making a flap on the bag, be sure that the extra piece extends above what will be the top. When the glue is completely dry, stitch around the three sides with button thread. Then stitch again within the seam allowance to reinforce the seams.

Turn 1" to the wrong side around the top edge of the bag and glue securely in place. If you are making your bag with a flap-top, skip this.

Turn the bag right side out and attach the handle. If using macrame, you will need to put metal eyelets in the top of the bag at the sides. A suede handle or belt can be attached with either thread or rivets.

Trace out your design—Moon, stars, large initials—onto the lighter suede. Carefully cut out these designs and center them onto one or both sides of the bag. Glue them in place.

To attach the closures for the flap-top, decide how far you want the edge of the top to reach down the front of the bag. Leave it loose enough at the top so you can fill the bag. Stick one of the Velcro circles at each outer edge of the flap on the underneath side.

Suede Carry-All

These circles each have a mate, so keep them matched! Space the other two along the flap. Now match these placements on the outside of the front with their mates.

Ancient India Cologne

¼	pint alcohol	1	pint distilled water
1	ounce glycerin	1	teaspoon tonka bean extract
1	ounce sandalwood powder	¼	teaspoon cinnamon
1	drop oleander oil	1	drop lemon oil

Myths

Ch'ang-O, Chinese Moon Goddess

In the beginning, Ch'ang-O (sometimes called Heng-O) was the wife of Yi, the Excellent Archer. Her husband was renowned for having shot down the ten Suns of primitive times when they decided to all rise at once and scorch the Earth. In return for this deed, the gods had rewarded Yi with a drink of immortality. Instead of drinking the potion, Yi hid the bottle and went off to spend most of his time elsewhere. Ch'ang-O grew restless being alone and under Yi's strict orders. She was powerful in her own right but never allowed to exhibit her powers. She took the bottle of immortality and drank it.

Hare in the Moon

Finally, Yi returned home from one of his long ramblings to discover the bottle empty. Immediately he guessed what had happened. Rather than have her immortal and able to use her powers, Yi decided to kill his wife. He grabbed up his sword, but Ch'ang-O fled. She made her way to the Moon where she asked protection of Hare who lived there. Yi followed her there, fully intending to do her in. Hare fought with and defeated Yi, then made him promise to give up his revenge. Ch'ang-O did not trust Yi to keep his promise if she returned to his home, so she continued to live with Hare in the Moon.

Marduk destroying Tiamat

The Death of Tiamat

In the Mesopotamian creation epic, everything began with watery chaos. Apsu, the sweet waters that produce springs and rivers, and Tiamat, the sea or salty waters, combined their forces to create the universe and the gods. Apsu did not like what his children were doing so he plotted against them. The god-children found out about the murder plot and sent the god Ea to murder their father. Tiamat had not supported Apsu's plans for destruction of her children, but at the death of her consort, she fought against them.

The goddess chose a second consort, Kingu, by whom she gave birth to thousands of monsters to help her. The god-children were afraid to go against Tiamat in war until Marduk, son of Ea, decided to take the field against her. The rest of the god-siblings promised Marduk that if he won they would make him king of the gods.

Marduk made a net and caught Kingu and all the monsters. He put them in chains and threw them into the Underworld. He then proceeded to kill his mother Tiamat. He used half of her body to make the sky, the other half to make the Earth. He created humans out of the blood of Kingu. Marduk then created a dwelling place for the gods in the sky, fixed the stars in the heavens, and regulated the length of the year.

The seas and the Moon have always been connected in one way or another. Tiamat may well have represented the triform Moon goddess whose worship was overthrown and replaced by Sun worshippers. This would account for Marduk's being credited with regulating the length of the year. The Mesopotamians originally, like most other cultures, operated on the Moon year.

Thoth, the Egyptian Moon God

The Egyptian god Thoth was called the Lord of Books and Learning, The Elder, and Lord of Holy Words, among other exalted titles. He was self-created, meaning that he came into existence without parents. The Egyptians acknowledged this deity as the inventor of hieroglyphs and numbers. He had greater powers than even Osiris or Ra, thus making him the first and greatest of magicians. He was ibis-headed and wore a lunar disk and crescent (both Moon symbols) on his head; he held the writing reed and palette of a scribe.

Thoth

His great temple and center at Hermopolis Magna in Upper Egypt was one of the greatest learning centers in the world. His priests taught that Thoth created by the sound of his voice alone. In a crypt under his main temple were kept his sacred books of magick; these were open only to his disciples. The Greeks and later races translated these into the works of Hermes Trismegistus and the Kybalion. Another of his important temples was in Lower Egypt at Hermopolis Parva. He had two wives, Seshat and Nehmauit.

Thoth helped Anubis, Isis, and Nephthys embalm the murdered Osiris after Set killed him. Later, when Isis and her son Horus were hiding in the swamps of Buto, Thoth again came to her rescue and healed Horus of terrible illnesses. During the great battle between Horus and Set, Thoth became a kind of referee, healing each of them of dreadful wounds. When the council of the gods finally declared Horus as rightful ruler of Egypt, Thoth became his grand vizier, later ruling in his place when Horus resigned earthly power.

Rituals

Feast of Divine Life

The Egyptian Feast of Divine Life was an annual celebration of the Moon and the life-giving waters they believed came from it. Egyptians believed that pigs were unclean creatures, but sacrificed a pig to the Moon at this time. Since pigs are associated with the Dark Moon Crone, one wonders if this was also part of the Egyptian belief.

Both Isis and Osiris were connected with the Moon. Isis literally means "moisture," and Osiris was said to have ascended to the Moon upon his resurrection. In another Egyptian festival, a procession marched to the seashore or riverbank. The priests carried a sacred chest which held a small gold boat. Into this boat was poured fresh water, while everyone shouted, "Osiris is found." Then spices were mixed with the water and the mixture formed into a crescent image.

However, divine life is most often connected with the Triple Goddess. This triad of goddesses was known by various names in most cultures around the world. To the Greeks, this triad was Persephone, Demeter, and Hecate; to the Romans, Proserpina, Ceres, and Hecate. To the Irish Celts, the Triple Goddess was the Morrigan (triple in herself), but also Anu or Danu, Badb, and Macha. In Wales this trio was Blodeuwedd, Arianrhod, and Cerridwen.

If you use this celebration as part of another ritual, cast your circle as usual. You will need: a green and a yellow candle and a cauldron. After you have cast the circle and called up the directional guardians, say:

> *The harvest is completed.*
> *Now all life rests before the coming of the winter season.*
> *Light and darkness stand in balance.*
> *This is a time of thanksgiving to the Triple Goddess.*

Light the yellow and green candles from the altar candles.

Carefully carry the green and yellow candles around the ritual area, beginning and ending in the East, and moving clockwise. At each Element direction, pause and say:

> *I bring the harvest of this year.*
> *Bless the harvest, Ladies of Divine Life.*

Set the candles in holders on the altar. Tap the cauldron three times with your wand and say:

> *Out of life comes death.*
> *Out of death again comes life.*
> *The universe and everything in it moves within this cycle,*
> *Ever ending, ever renewing.*
> *So it is with all humans,*
> *Both in the physical and in the mental.*
> *Remove all negative seed-thoughts that I have planted.*

Let me harvest only the seed-thoughts that will
bring me joy and abundance.
Teach me to seek better things.
For this I give all honor and praise
To the Triple Goddess of Divine Life.

Now is the time for divination for guidance and wisdom. Meditation to listen for instructions is valuable also. Close the circle.

Harvest Moon Festival
—Autumn Equinox—

The Chinese Harvest Festival was in honor of the Moon goddess Ch'ang-O. The Moon has always been associated with the psychic and divination. Chinese magicians used willow wands, wax dolls, water divining, geomancy, yarrow sticks, and magick mirrors. These mirrors were decorated around the sides with unicorns, animals representing the four sides of the universe, and other mythical beings. The I Ching (Book of Changes) is still used today.

This ritual is best done on the Full Moon. It is a consecration and blessing of divination tools. It can be included as part of a regular ritual. Burn lotus or carnation incense. Have a small amount of crushed bay laurel, pine, and mugwort in a dish, with something in which to burn them.

Put your cauldron on the pentacle in the center of your altar. Set a white or silver-gray candle on each side of the cauldron, and light them. Place the tarot cards, runes, or other tool, in or on the cauldron. Set a small magnet and a piece of silver with them.

With your wand, circle the cauldron three times while chanting:

Come, Hecate, wise and old!
Come, Ch'ang-O, bright and bold!
Come, great Pan, from the forest green!
Come, Artemis, thou woodland queen!
Bless these (name of divination article) *with future-sight.*
I ask your aid here on this night.

Remove the divination tools from the cauldron and lay them on the altar. Tap them three times with the wand. Pass them slowly through the incense smoke.

Burn tiny amounts of the crushed herbs as you read the cards, cast the I Ching, or whatever divinatory practices you use. These consecrated tools should be wrapped in their own special cloth or bag when not in use.

The Oracle Themis

Themis is a very ancient goddess of justice, known in one form to the Romans as Justicia. Oaths were taken in her name while wearing her sacred purple mantle. By taking an oath in this manner, the person was saying if they weren't telling the truth the goddess might strike them dead.

Themis was the daughter of Uranus and Gaea and the mother of Atlas and Prometheus. By Zeus she gave birth to the Horae and the Moerae. She was the advisor of Zeus and respected by all the Olympians. Carrying a pair of scales, she was another form of the Earth Mother, personifying law and order. Themis protected the innocent and punished the guilty. As the statue of justice today, she has been blindfolded, while in ancient times she saw all in the past, present, and future.

This deity was the goddess of the collective unconsciousness and social order, divine spiritual law, peace, settlement of disagreements, justice, social gatherings, oath-swearing, wisdom, prophecy, order, childbirth, courts, and judges. She was also the inventor of the arts and magick.

Themis

Do this ritual during the waxing or Full Moon. Burn jasmine or lotus incense. Lay your cards or whatever you plan to use on your altar. Fill a chalice with dark red juice or wine and set it next to your working space. Light two purple candles, one on each side of the chalice. Hold your hands over your divination tools and say:

Goddess of Moon and magick,
Goddess of Mysteries,
Show me the answer that I seek,
Reveal the destinies.

Take three sips of the juice. Shuffle your cards, and lay them out in whatever manner is usual for you. When you are finished with the divination, stand with your arms raised and say:

> *All honor to those who have helped me.*
> *My thanks I do give true and free.*
> *Your guidance I always will cherish*
> *And heed. So shall it be.*

The candles do not have to burn out, but can be used for another divinatory spell.

Anuket, Giver of Life
—Crescent Moon—

This deity's name was written as Anuket, Anqet, or Anukis. She was called the Clasper, as she was the goddess of the Nile Cataracts. Her symbol was the cowrie shell, a very ancient Great Goddess symbol. As with many other Egyptian goddesses, Anuket was considered to be self-begotten. As the second wife of the god Khnemu (a Moon deity), she had a special dwelling place on the island of Seheil. She was also worshipped at Elephantine with Khnemu.

Sometimes she was pictured as a woman wearing a tall plumed crown, sometimes as having four arms. These four arms represented the union of male and female principles.

Anuket can be called upon to greet and bless a new baby or baby animals. She was called the Giver of Life, both of humans and animals. The new sliver of the Crescent Moon is an excellent time for a family greeting and blessing of a new child or animal. Although this ritual is written for a child, you can use it in much the same manner for little animals.

Set up a miniature altar on a table. Use a white or lace cloth. Place two silver or white candles on it. In a nice bowl, pour fresh water and float a few rose petals in it; place this bowl between the candles in the center of the altar. Lay your sistrum to the right of the bowl, the ankh to the left. Burn rose incense. You can have a vase of colorful flowers to one side. Also place a chalice of milk or juice near the bowl of water. If you wish, one chalice can hold milk for the child (or animal), the other juice or wine for the other participants.

Take the child in your arms and hold her/him facing the little altar. Say:

I present this child of (parents' names) *to the Old Gods.*
Anuket, goddess of life, I ask that you bless her/him.
(Touch the child's forehead gently with the ankh)
Open her/his eyes to the Eternal Truth of Being.
Guide her/him into the spiritual path where she/he should go.

Give the child to one of the parents. Raise the bowl of water and rose petals high, then say:

These are the sacred waters of Anuket.
May Anuket always guide and protect this child.

Place the bowl back on the altar. Wet the tip of your forefinger and touch the child's forehead, mouth, and heart.

Welcome, little one. You are loved.
The Goddess loves you. We love you.
Welcome to this world.

Have one parent carry the child beside you, the other carry the ankh, as you move clockwise around the room, beginning in the East, and stopping at each direction. Take the sistrum in your power hand and shake it three times before each direction. The person holding the ankh should hold it up in presentation at each point.

Go to the East. Say:

Powers of Air, Deities of the East,
Grant this child wisdom and true knowledge.

Move to the South. Say:

Powers of Fire, Deities of the South,
Grant this child spiritual growth in the Old Ways.

Go to the West. Say:

Powers of Water, Deities of the West,
Grant this child calmness of spirit and emotions.

Finish by going to the North. Say:

Powers of Earth, Deities of the North,
Grant this child prosperity and well-being.

Go back to stand before the altar. Lay aside the sistrum and ankh. Take up the chalice of milk. Say:

> *Anuket, giver of life, nourish this child.*
> *Keep her/him under your gentle hands,*
> *Protecting and guiding her/him all the days of her/his life.*

Give the child a drink of the milk. If the child is too small to drink, wet the tip of your forefinger in the milk and put it in the child's mouth.

> *Do you,* (parents' names), *promise before Anuket,*
> *That you will love and cherish this new life*
> *She has placed in your care?*

Parents answer:

> *We do.*

Take up the chalice of juice or wine. Say:

> *Rejoice, for Anuket gives her blessings to all.*
> *Drink from this chalice, and seal your pledge to the goddess.*

First the parents, then everyone else present, takes a sip of the juice or wine.

Demeter, the Protecting Mother
— Full Moon —

The goddess Demeter was an Earth Mother, the Corn Goddess, the Sorrowing Mother. People honored her by wearing flower garlands while they marched through the streets, often barefoot. Fruits and crops of the season were made into feasts. It was believed that placing the bare feet on the Earth intensified the communication between humans and the goddess.

To the Greeks, Demeter was the creatress and measurer of time in all its forms. Her priests were called Sons of the Moon. This goddess was portrayed as a matron with beautiful hair, wearing a blue robe, and carrying a sheaf of wheat. She was crowned with ears of corn or ribbons and held a scepter. The Greeks said that Demeter gave them the first wheat seeds, taught them how to cultivate the soil, and how to make bread from the grain. She instituted the Eleusinian Mysteries.

Demeter was the protectress of women and a deity of marriage, motherhood, maternal love, and fidelity. She ruled over crops, corn, the plow, initiation, renewal, rebirth, vegetation, fruitfulness, agriculture, civilization, law, magickal philosophy, expansion, higher magicks, and the soil.

Demeter, Persephone, and a youth

The goddess Potnia of Crete was very similar to the Greek goddesses Demeter, Hera, and Rhea. Potnia was called Magna Mater, the Lady, and the Lady of the Labyrinth. She was the principal Minoan goddess. Her symbols were the labyrs (double-axe), the pillar, and the snake. It is quite likely that Potnia had a sanctuary within the Minoan labyrinth itself, as well as major temples at Kydonia, Phaistos, Mallia, and Zakro. She had a young male son/consort whose name was Velchanos, who "died" each year in the autumn and was "reborn" each spring, much the same as Persephone.

For incense in this ritual, use sandalwood, frankincense, cassia, or pine. You will need a wand decorated with colored ribbons, a wicker basket in which to place the wand, a bell, and an apple.

Cast your circle as usual, visualizing it surrounded by a circle of flame. Call upon the four winds to stand guard.

Stand at your altar facing the East and raise your arms in greeting. Say:

> *Between the worlds I build this sacred altar.*
> *Outside of time, this rite leads to the ancient way,*
> *Where I may find Demeter of high Olympus*
> *And conjure magick great. Be here, I say.*

Place the decorated wand in the wicker basket and carry it to the East. Say:

> *Persephone returns to the Underworld.*
> *Weep not, Earth Mother,*
> *For the Divine Child of love is here.*

Carry the basket to the South; say:

> *Persephone returns to the Underworld.*
> *Although the Light is fading,*
> *It shall return to the Earth.*

Take the basket to the West; say:

> *Persephone returns to the Underworld.*
> *The cold of winter comes,*
> *But only for a short time.*

Finish by carrying the basket to the North; say:

> *Persephone returns to the Underworld.*
> *The Earth shall lie in slumber*
> *Until the Light of this Divine Child*
> *Once more grows in strength and shines full upon us.*

Place the basket on the floor before the altar. Ring the bell three times. Take the ritual dagger in your power hand and the apple in the other. Say:

> *Reveal to me your hidden secrets*
> *That I may come to understand your sacred Mysteries.*

Cut the apple crosswise to reveal the pentagram in the core. Contemplate this hidden sacred symbol for several moments. Then say:

> *In life is death, in death life.*
> *All must follow the sacred dance into the cauldron,*
> *Time after time, to die and be reborn.*
> *Help me to remember that every beginning has an ending*
> *And that every ending has a new beginning.*

Take a bite of the apple. What is left put outside later to share with the birds. Say:

> *Holy Mother, Demeter,*
> *Comfort and protect me in my times of tribulation.*
> *Instruct me into the Mysteries.*
> *You, with your daughter Persephone, have the power*
> *To lead me to new understanding.*

The Great Dragon-Mother
— Dark Moon —

The goddess Tiamat of the Middle East was the goddess of the primal abyss. Her worshippers called her a She-Dragon, who was sometimes evil, sometimes good. She was portrayed as part animal, part bird, and part serpent. Marduk took her sacred Tablets of Destiny for himself. She ruled over destruction, revenge, karmic discipline, salt water, war, evil, despair, dark magick, death, regeneration, and rituals.

Knowledge of the Dark Mother is a necessity if we are to grow spiritually. We must lose the programmed fear we have been taught and realize that she is more than death of the body. The Dark Mother helps with karma, self-discipline, and despair. Tiamat helps with despair in that she can show us what caused the problems troubling us (oftentimes from past lives) and what the future may hold if we change our paths even slightly.

To contact Tiamat, the Dark Mother, burn three black candles that have been anointed from the wick to the end with wisteria oil. Set the candles in a triangular pattern, with one at the top and two at the bottom. Burn sandalwood incense. If you have a dragon statue, particularly if it is black, place that beside the candles. Dress in black or very dark robes. Hold a piece of crystal in your hands as you sit before the burning candles. Say:

> She-Dragon of the dark abyss,
> Mother of dark magick, regeneration,
> Help me to learn discipline,
> That my karmic path may be smooth.
> Lift your hand against harmful enemies.
> Lead me in the knowledge of true rituals.

Bring the crystal to your third eye in the center of your forehead. Close your eyes and watch the swift flow of pictures. You may well find yourself seeing scenes from past lives that influence your present one. Don't strain to see anything, just let it flow. When you are finished, stand before the candles and raise your arms, the crystal visible in one hand. Say:

> The Sun is black within your realms,
> Yet shine it does, a mirrored light,
> To give me insight, strengthen faith,
> To comfort me in blackest night.
> There is no end to life or growth

Unless the soul and mind be dead
To truth and knowledge, openness.
Before me gentle hands are spread
In compassion, tenderness.
O Great Dark Lady, my soul do bless.

Extinguish the candles. Sleep with the crystal under your pillow for seven nights. Pay close attention to your dreams and to what is said to you in ordinary life during this time.

Chapter 13

BLOOD MOON

October

Also called: Harvest Moon, Shedding Moon,
Winterfelleth (Winter Coming), Windermanoth (Vintage Month),
Falling Leaf Moon, Ten Colds Moon,
Moon of the Changing Season.

Full Moon: Festival of Ciuateotl, the snake woman goddess; Aztecs and
  Toltecs.

Full Moon: the Disirblot, or Disablot, of Freyja marked the beginning of the
  Winter season for the Norse.

Oct. 7: New Year in Sumeria, honoring such goddesses as Ishtar and Astarte.

Oct. 11-13: The Thesmophoria, a women only festival in Greece to honor
  Demeter and Kore.

Oct. 12: Fortuna Redux, a celebration for Happy Journeys in Rome.

Oct. 14: The Durga Puja, or Dasain, in Nepal, Bangladesh, and India,
  honoring the victory of the Great Mother Durga over evil.

Oct. 15: In Rome, purification of the city.

Oct. 16: Lakshmi Puja, or Diwalii, or Festival of Lights, in India; Lakshmi.

Oct. 18: The Great Horn Fair in Britain honoring the Horned God.

Oct. 21: Day of Orsel or Ursala, a Slavonic Moon goddess.

Oct. 22: Day of Willows, a Mesopotamian festival of Belili or Astarte.

Oct. 25: In China, the Festival of Han Lu, the Moon and Harvest goddess.

Oct. 26: The Full Moon festival of Hathor in Egypt.

Octem was the eighth month in the oldest Roman calendar. This Moon-month takes its name not from blood sacrifices, but from the old custom of killing and salting down livestock before the Winter months made it impossible to feed them. Only the choicest stock was kept through the cold season.

Today we still subconsciously begin to make preparations for the coming Winter during this time. We check the antifreeze and tires for the car, gather up garden hoses, and make plans to winterize any drafty spots around doors and windows in the house. Some of us do an ambitious fall cleaning.

The Greek festival of Thesmophoria came every year in honor of Demeter and was confined to women only. This was a three-day remembrance of Kore's return to the Underworld. At this festival the initiates shared a sacred barley drink and cakes. One feature of the Thesmophoria was a deterrent to offenders against the sacred laws and against women. Priestesses read a list of the offenders before the doors of the goddesses' temples, especially the temples of Demeter and Artemis. It was believed that anyone so cursed would die before the year ended.

The first day of the Thesmophoria was the kathodos, a ritual where purified priestesses took sacrificed piglets deep into the chasm where the sacred inner shrine of Demeter was. They left the piglets there and retrieved the remains of the ones from the previous year. The second day was the Nesteia, during which the remains of retrieved piglets were displayed on the altar. Courts were closed in honor of Demeter as lawgiver. On the third day, the retrieved piglets were sown into the plowed Earth as a symbol of Demeter's fertility aspect.

The Greeks also honored the god Hephaestus with an annual festival called Chalkeia.

In Tibet, the Buddhist Lent occurred along with the Descent from Heaven festival which celebrated the end of the rainy season.

The Durga Puja in India honors the goddess Durga for four days beginning on the New Moon. It is a time of family reunions, settling quarrels, and honoring the parents. In northern India this festival is known as Dasahara. Durga is considered a matriarchal figure and is very popular with the people. She is shown with many arms and in bright colors.

The Lakshmi Puja, or Diwalii, is a feast of lights in honor of the goddess Lakshmi. It occurs right after the Durga Puja. During this Festival of Lights, lamps are everywhere, good things to eat are produced, and Hindu wives dance for their husbands. Lakshmi, wife of Vishnu, is considered the goddess of wealth and prosperity.

In the Pacific Ocean, the ancient Hawaiians celebrated a four-month long festival called the Makahiki, beginning at the first Full Moon of this month. The god Lono had a special celebration of five days during this time, filled with games, pageantry, the hula, surfing, feasting, and tax collecting.

The Incas celebrated the Coya Raymi.

Correspondences

Nature Spirits: frost faeries, plant faeries

Herbs: pennyroyal, thyme, catnip, uva ursi, angelica, burdock

Colors: dark blue-green

Flowers: calendula, marigold, cosmos

Scents: strawberry, apple blossom, cherry

Stones: opal, tourmaline, beryl, turquoise

Trees: yew, cypress, acacia

Animals: stag, jackal, elephant, ram, scorpion

Birds: heron, crow, robin

Deities: Ishtar, Astarte, Demeter, Kore, Lakshmi, Horned God, Belili, Hathor

Power Flow: to let go; inner cleansing. Karma and reincarnation.
Justice and balance. Inner harmony.

Old Sayings & Lore

- A verse:

    O Lady Moon, your horns point toward the east:
    Shine, be increased.
    O Lady Moon, your horns point toward the west:
    Wane, be at rest.

    New Moon, true Moon, true and trusty,
    Tell me who my true love must be.

    New Moon, true Moon, true and bright,
    If I have a true love, let me dream of him/her tonight.

    New Moon, true Moon, tell unto me
    If (name), my true love, he/she will marry me.
    If he/she marry me in haste
    Let me see his/her bonnie face,
    If he/she marry me betide
    Let me see his/her bonnie side,
    If he/she will not marry me
    Turn his/her back and go away.

    The Moon and the weather may change together;
    But change of the Moon does not change the weather.
    If we had no Moon at all, and that would seem strange,
    We should still have weather that's subject to change.

- The Gaelic word for fortune comes from "that which denotes a Full Moon." The Druids believed that when the circle of the Moon was complete, good fortune was given to those who knew how to ask the gods for it.

Recipes

Herb Butter

Sometimes during the Autumn and Winter months, one needs a little something to spice up a meal. This butter, or margarine, is delicious on French bread, rolls, baked potatoes, or meat.

1 pound margarine or butter
2 tablespoons chopped fresh parsley
1 tablespoon dried basil leaves, crumbled

1 tablespoon dried tarragon leaves, crumbled
1 tablespoon chopped fresh or frozen chives

Let margarine stand in large bowl at room temperature until soft. Mix in the herbs with an electric mixer. Pack into a container with a tight cover. Refrigerate overnight to gain the flavors.

Herb Punch

This is a good non-alcoholic drink to serve at a Pagan gathering or for any get-together. Even children can enjoy it.

1 large handful lemon balm
2 large handfuls borage
1 large handful mint
1 cup pineapple or any other fruit juice

Juice of 6 lemons and 2 oranges
1 quart strong tea
Syrup made of 1 cup sugar, boiled with ½ cup water
3 quarts ginger ale

Pour 1½ quarts boiling water over the lemon balm and let steep for 20 minutes. Strain the liquid onto the borage and mint. Add the fruit juices, tea, and syrup. Refrigerate at least 8 hours. Strain into a punch bowl. Add ice, some extra mint, and ginger ale.

Brown Danish Cookies

1 cup butter
1 cup sugar
4 cups all-purpose flour
1 teaspoon baking soda
½ teaspoon ginger

1 tablespoon grated orange rind
½ cup molasses
¼ teaspoon cloves
1 teaspoon cinnamon
Blanched almonds for decoration

Cream butter and sugar. Add the rest of the ingredients. Knead together. Form into two rolls and chill. Slice cookies very thin and decorate with half an almond. Bake at 325° F for 8-10 minutes. Can be frozen to store.

Crafts

Scented Pillows

Make small draw-string bags and fill with dried lavender flowers. A citrus-smelling sachet or pillow for men's clothing drawers can be made with the following ingredients.

2 ounces dried and pounded orange and lemon peel	10 drops of lemon verbena oil
4 ounces lemon verbena	10 drops oil of bergamot

Enclose the mixture in the bags. Hang in closets to deter moths. Culpeper wrote that lavender is also good for headaches caused by a cold, cramps, or hyperventilation.

Medieval Lady Potpourri

1 pint red rose blossoms	½ pint white rose petals
3 tablespoons damiana	1 ounce dried hawthorn berries
1 ounce powdered orris root	1 tablespoon lavender flowers

Xanadu Potpourri

1 pint wisteria blossoms	4 ounces China rosebuds
1 ounce powdered myrrh gum	1 tablespoon lemon peel
1 teaspoon vanilla	

European Rose Cologne

¼ pint alcohol	1 pint distilled water
1 ounce glycerin	1 drop lemon oil or bergamot oil
2 drops rose oil	

China Forest Cologne

¼ pint alcohol	1 pint distilled water
1 ounce glycerin	1 drop pine needle oil
2 teaspoons sandalwood powder	1 drop cedar oil
1 drop rose oil	1 drop bergamot oil

Myths

Great Mother Durga

Durga, the Great Mother, was one of a triad with the goddesses Uma and Parvati. She rides on a lion and uses the gods' weapons to defend them against demons. She is the personification of the fighting spirit of a mother protecting her young. Legends portray Durga as a kind of female St. George, defending with serene dignity the gods and her children against all enemies. Serene she might be, but her calm expression can give one the feeling of menace.

Although myth says she was born out of flames from the mouths of Brahma, Vishnu, and Shiva, Indra acknowledged her as the source of his power. Her strength, ferocity, and ability became apparent when the water buffalo demon Mahisha drove the gods out of the celestial kingdom. The gods armed Durga with their own magickal weapons, one for each hand of her eight arms. The demon saw her coming and tried to capture her. Durga, however, was immune to his magick and strength. The goddess fought the demon as he changed quickly from one form to another. Finally, she killed him with a spear.

Durga-Devi's present-day role is to restore order in the world and peace in the heart during times of crises.

Lakshmi

Sri Lakshmi is portrayed seated on or holding a lotus, with a coffer and gold coins showering from her hand. She was the consort of Vishnu. Legend says this goddess was born during the churning of the milk ocean by the gods and was counted as one of the fourteen precious things brought forth by the churning. She was fully grown and beautiful as she stepped out of the ocean. All of the gods wanted her as wife, but she preferred Vishnu.

When Vishnu went through his reincarnations, Lakshmi reincarnated with him. When Vishnu became Rama, Lakshmi became Sita. When he was Krishna, she was Radha, the cow girl.

Although she is said to have four arms, she is usually shown with only two. As the goddess of fortune, Lakshmi is also described as being fickle because fortune often changes without notice.

The Great Horned God of Britain

This woodland deity has been called by a number of names and is known far beyond Britain. In Wales he was Atho, the Horned God; in Windsor Forest he was Herne the Hunter; sometimes he was also called Cernunnos. All were aspects of one deity and his powers. Whatever name and form he took, he had one common feature: antlers on his head.

Herne the Hunter is still said to haunt the woodland forests near Windsor Castle. As recently as 1964 he was said to be seen riding his fire-breathing horse through the woods.

Still today, in parts of Britain they celebrate the Great Horn Fair in the fall of the year. Men parade in the streets with antlers fastened on their heads. All this is an ancient reminder of the power of the woodland god over the fertility of the forest beasts. He is the Opener of the Gates of Life and Death, the Great Father, the Lord of all Nature. The Druids knew him as Hu Gadern, the Horned God of fertility.

Rituals

Good Journeys

Anytime you set out on a journey you need to take magickal precautions. The night before the journey, make up a little bag of dragon's blood powder, frankincense, rosemary, and vervain. A paper envelope can be used instead of a bag, if necessary. Tuck this protection talisman into your pocket or purse for carrying while on the trip. If your luggage is going separately, make small bags to put into each piece of luggage.

As soon as you get into the vehicle in which you will be traveling, close your eyes and visualize a huge gleaming sword in your hand. Mentally circle the vehicle three times clockwise with the sword. A wall of blue flame will be visible by the third pass. Then mentally stand the sword at the front of the vehicle and leave it there. This can be repeated for the return trip.

The circling ritual can be repeated at any time during the journey when you feel that extra protection is needed or the circle of flame needs to be reinforced. This technique can also be used if staying in hotel rooms.

Purification of the Home

Sometimes, no matter what we do, we get uninvited entities in our homes. Often these are difficult to get rid of. If you experience a period where you get unusually clumsy, the family is having one too many illnesses, finances and plans fall apart for no good reason, or things just feel "creepy," it is time to do a thorough spiritual house cleaning and purification.

Plan your route through the house so that you end up at an outside door. Although you can do this ritual by yourself, it is much easier if you have someone to help you. If you must perform this alone, carry everything on a tray from room to room.

Have a good banishing incense, or powdered frankincense and myrrh, in a dish with a spoon. Light the charcoal in your incense burner and sprinkle on some incense. Have a chalice of water with a little salt in it; also a bell.

Beginning at the farthest end of the house from the outside door, circle each room clockwise with the smoking incense. Be sure to get some of the smoke into all the closets. Add more incense as needed. Then make the round ringing the bell. Finally, take the chalice of water and, with your forefinger, touch each side of every window and door in the room. Do the same with all mirrors.

Move to the next room and repeat the ritual. Move through every room in the house, including the basement, ending up at the outside door. Before marking the sides of the door with water, open it and wave the smoking incense toward the door. Say with firmness:

> *Begone, you foul and disrupting entities!*
> *You are not welcome here!*

Close the door and mark the sides with the water. Lay aside your tools and raise your arms. Say:

> *Welcome to all entities of Light and helpfulness.*
> *Fill this home with your presence and blessings.*
> *Keep out all beings of Darkness,*
> *And bring my* (our) *life back into proper balance.*

When you open the door to banish the negative entities, you should feel a void around you. Then when you call upon positive entities to enter, the house should feel warm and comforting. You never want to banish entities and not call in positive ones, or they will move right back in and bring others with them. A void must always be filled.

Communication with the Horned God

The Celtic god Cernunnos was known in various forms throughout most of Europe. He was called the Horned God, God of Nature, God of the Underworld and the Astral Plane, Great Father, and the Horned One. The Druids knew him as Hu Gadern, the Horned God of fertility. He was portrayed as sitting in a semi-lotus position with horns or antlers on his head. He had long curling hair and a beard. He was naked except for a neck torque; sometimes he held a spear and shield. His symbols were the stag, ram, bull, and horned serpent. Cernunnos ruled over virility, fertility, animals, physical love, Nature, woodlands, reincarnation, crossroads, wealth, commerce, and warriors.

Everyone needs to learn how to relate to the Horned God in his powers of reincarnation, wealth, and appreciation of Nature. We already subconsciously relate to his powers of fertility and physical sex.

You will need small statues of wild animals (pictures will do), pine or fir incense, a mask (the Lone Ranger type or similar), and a drum or tambourine. Light the incense.

The Horned God

Spread a blanket on the floor and set out the statues. Lay the mask close at hand. Sit comfortably on the blanket; if you can't sit that way, use a stool or chair.

Put on the mask. Take up the drum and beat a slow, steady rhythm until you find yourself relaxing into the drum beat. Close your eyes and feel yourself sinking down into the realm of the Horned God.

Look out through the mask at the animal statues. Everything will have a slightly surrealistic quality. Pick up each statue in turn and look at it. Think about that animal, its traits and qualities. Let its image become real in your mind. Watch carefully what it does, for the animal will likely begin at some point to do things that are uncharacteristic. It may even speak to you, mind to mind.

When you have studied each animal, close your eyes again and call upon the Horned God. You will probably find yourself mentally on a forest path. Follow it until you come to a grassy clearing. There, by a huge tree, sits the Horned God, waiting for you. Sit beside him and tell him what information you need to better your life. When the Horned God is finished with what he has to say at this time, he taps your forehead, and you find yourself swiftly surfacing into this time and place.

You may well be disoriented for a few minutes, so sit quietly and let your body and mind readjust themselves. Pick up the drum and beat out a slow, steady rhythm again. Do this until you feel centered once more within your body. Thank the Horned God for his help, and remove the mask.

Job Seeking

Finding a job can be very frustrating, but there is a way to gain astral help. Of course, you first need to know what you want to do and generally where you want to be, at least in general terms. For example, if you want to get a job in another state or town, you had better have that firmly in mind when doing this spell. This ritual is best done on the night of a New Moon, but in a pinch one can perform it any time.

You will need an astral candle to represent yourself, a green candle for prosperity, a black candle to remove obstacles, and a brown candle for the job itself. Each candle needs a fireproof holder. You will also need patchouli and cinnamon oils for the candles.

Burn a good prosperity incense. Anoint the black candle from the bottom to the wick with patchouli oil; place it in a holder. Clean your hands of the patchouli oil; you don't want it on the other candles. Anoint the brown, green, and astral candles from the wick to the bottom with cinnamon (or prosperity) oil and place them in holders.

Place the black candle in the center of your work space, the brown candle to the left, and the green one on the right. Set the astral candle above the black candle. Put the candles on a safe surface since they will be left to burn out completely.

Light the astral candle and say:

I ask for change; that is my right. Open the way, clear my sight.

Light the black candle and say:

Bad luck flees. Obstacles fall. Ill-wishers vanish! Heed my call!

Light the green candle and say:

Good luck is mine and prosperity. Help me, Great Ones. Come to me.

Light the brown candle and say:

Opportunity, work, rewards I see. And as I will, so must it be.

Leave the candles to burn out completely and dispose of the wax afterward. Each night for a week, or until the candle is used up, burn a second brown candle for nine minutes while meditating and gaining balance in preparation for the good and the job to come.

During this time period, actively seek a job. Listen to all your hunches and follow up on any leads.

Festival of Lights
— Crescent Moon —

In India, the goddess Lakshmi is much loved by the people, but has no separate cult of her own. She gave Indra the drink of soma (or wise blood) from her own body so he could produce the illusion of birth-giving and become king of the devas. She was born during the churning of the milk ocean. She is a deity of happiness, good health, success, love, good fortune, beauty, prosperity, and all the wealth of the world.

Lakshmi's festival is called the Diwalii and honors this goddess as the wife of Vishnu. Hindu wives dance privately for their husbands during this festival; lamps are everywhere; good things to eat are produced. This is the Hindu New Year, a time of good luck and prosperity.

Have as many candles as possible set around the circle. Play Indian music to set the atmosphere. If you have a statue of Lakshmi, put it on your altar. Burn lotus incense.

Press your palms together in prayer and bow, touching your fingertips to your forehead. Say:

OM (long drawn-out mantra).
Eternal Goddess, Triple Mother,
Dancing God of power and might,
Bless this ritual with your presence.
Fill me with wisdom, magick, light.

Vishnu contemplating creation, with Brahma and Lakshmi

Listen for a few minutes to the music to get into its rhythm. Say:

See the dancing feet of Lakshmi as she dances for her consort.
Lakshmi, goddess of good luck, love, and prosperity,
I greet you with joy and hope.
Dance, Lakshmi, dance!
Your flashing feet bring good luck into my life.
Your dancing hands manifest prosperity for me.
Honor to the goddess! Love to the goddess!

Being careful of the lighted candles, dance about the ritual area with joy. Professional ability is not important. When the power is sufficiently raised (you can tell by the feeling in the room), go back to the altar and press your hands together. Bow and say:

With joy and hope, my heart welcomes the goddess Lakshmi.
Enter, Lakshmi, lady of good luck and prosperity.

Blow a kiss to the goddess and dance slowly around the room again, this time extinguishing each candle as you pass by.

Dancing goddess of the lights,
Good fortune shower upon your child.
Lift high the veil of depressing nights,

And bless me, dancing goddess mild.
Treasures deep within the Earth,
Precious stones and metals fine,
Wealth unending, prosperity,
Bring me these to ease the mind
And body needs. Lakshmi great,
Brighten my future. Ease my fate.

The Disirblot
— Full Moon —

The Disirblot, a Norse feast of the Disir and the goddess Freyja, was celebrated, especially in Sweden, on the Full Moon at the beginning of the Norse Winter (in mid-October). The goddess, under the name of Freyja Vanadis, was feasted with ale, pork, apples, and barley. The Norse festivals or rituals were called blots; usually, the entire community took part in these. The Disirblot was a yearly celebration of goddesses and ancestresses.

Freyja was called the Great Dis, placing her as the head of the Disir, or goddesses and female ancestors. The Disir were traditionally described as nine women dressed in

Freyja

black or white, and carrying swords. Nine is a Moon number and considered by the Norse to be one of the most sacred and mysterious of numbers. The Disir were said to bring good luck but they were also merciless in exacting justice. The Disir, called Idises in Germany, were closely associated with the Valkyries and the Norns. They were involved with divination and the dispensing of karmic justice in particular.

Some references speak of the Disir as actual humans, while other references regard them as a type of supernatural being. It is very likely that the term encompassed both goddesses and human priestesses. The Disir protected and guided the clans, dispensed fate (or wyrd), and were intermediaries between the people and the gods. They aided the volvas (priestesses) with divination and the magickal art of seidr. The Disir had the power to bind or release, using the power of the runes. The patriarchal Pagans, and then the Christians, disapproved of the Disir and their followers; both groups persecuted and killed these priestesses.

Seidr means "spell, enchantment, seething." Trances, for contacting otherworld beings and the dead, were a major part of seidr. The volva knew how to call upon the alfar, or elves, for helping or hindering. Trance was used for astral traveling to acquire information. As the volva went into trance, other priestesses sang special songs, called galdr. This was really the use of chanting and repetitious poetry that created an altering of consciousness, necessary to enter a trance.

All of the talents listed in the remaining records sound much like those used by practitioners of shamanism. Even though the patriarchal culture condemned the use of seidr, legend says that the god Odhinn practiced it after being taught by Freyja.

Calling upon Freyja and the Disir is helpful when you feel a need for more personal power. Perhaps you don't feel confident about an upcoming meeting or handling a particularly abrasive person. Maybe someone has deliberately and repeatedly torn at you and your abilities until your self-confidence is worn pretty thin. Use this ritual to re-empower yourself. It is best done on a Full Moon.

You will need a staff, a sword or dagger, a mask, and a hooded cloak. If you don't have a cloak, drape a shawl or even a towel over your head. Don't bypass this ritual because you don't have exactly everything listed. Improvise! Burn jasmine or lotus incense.

Play instrumental music that speaks to you of power. Personally, I like Wagner's "Ride of the Valkyries," as it makes me feel as if I were one with Freyja and her night-riding Disir. Choose whatever music you like.

Put on the mask and cloak with the hood pulled up. Take the staff in one hand, the sword or dagger in the other. Stand in the center of your working space and tap the staff firmly nine times on the floor. Call:

> *Freyja! Leader of the Disir!*
> *Come to my aid!*
> *My personal power is fading,*
> *And I would make it strong again!*

Raise your sword and say:

> *No one has the right to belittle me!*
> *No one has the right to take away my power!*
> *I am your daughter/son, mighty Freyja!*
> *Hear my call!*

Turn toward the East and raise your sword in warning:

Take warning, anyone in the East.
No longer will you have power over me.
My strength increases, while your control fades!

Turn toward the South and raise the sword:

Take warning, anyone in the South.
I am free of your criticism and destructive words.
My strength increases, while your control fades!

Face the West and raise the sword:

Take warning, anyone in the West.
Any harm you wish me returns to you at once.
My strength increases, while your control fades!

Finally, turn toward the North and raise the sword:

Take warning, anyone in the North.
I am shielded by Freyja and the powerful Disir.
My strength increases, while your control fades!

Tap the floor nine times with the staff. Say nine times:

Freyja protects! My enemies fail!

Stand silently while you visualize your aura becoming filled with brilliant white light. See this light expanding until it fills the room, then moves out even farther. Feel this light also entering your body and mind, making them stronger and more powerful.

If you have a special talisman or piece of jewelry that you like to wear, ask Freyja to bless it and fill it with power. Then wear it when you have to face the person who is causing you problems.

Whenever you have to meet or talk with the offending people, remind yourself that you are protected by Freyja. Project your powerful aura toward them, and watch them become confused, move away from you, or simply become more amicable.

The Awesome Mother
—Dark Moon—

The Hindu goddess Durga was often called the Inaccessible. She was one of the triad of goddesses with Uma and Parvati. In her aspect of Durga Pratyangira, she was a beautiful yellow woman with ten arms which carried a trident, sword, drum, and bowl of blood. She rode on a lion and used the gods' weapons to defend them from demons.

Her sacred festivals took place in Bengali in the Autumn. The opening phrase of the national anthem of India praises her.

Durga is the personification of the fighting spirit of a mother protecting her young. As the primary life force, this goddess is a kind of female St. George, defending the gods and her human children against all enemies with serene dignity.

Durga rules over comfort, help, power, nurturing, protection, defense, death, destruction, futility, and ruin.

Sometimes your life feels like it is stalled. You become depressed because you just can't see where you are going in terms of accomplishments. A relationship or friendship may have gone sour. Family and/or children may be driving you toward despair. Specific plans and goals may have died on the vine. Your entire life may be in the midst of upheaval. You need to take a break from the physical reality and visit with Durga the Divine Mother.

Choose a time and safe place where you are not likely to be disturbed. Burn sandalwood incense. If you have a statue of Durga, place it where you can gaze upon it. Sit in a comfortable chair and relax. Say:

> *Behold! The Divine Mother comes to protect her children.*
> *Her wrath is just and great against those who would oppress me.*
> *Trident and sword are lifted in my defense.*
> *Ruin comes to those who would persecute all people*
> *who call upon the Goddess.*

Let your entire body relax. Visualize yourself standing before a Hindu temple. There are seven steps up to the open door. Climb the steps and go inside the dim temple. Across the room from the door is a huge statue of Durga, her many arms raised around her richly-clothed body.

As you walk across the stone floor, the statue suddenly comes to life and steps down to meet you. The power emanating from Durga encircles you. The goddess dances across the floor and sweeps you into her arms. She kisses your forehead, then places you on the steps to her altar. With her trident and sword flashing in the dim light, Durga sings her magick songs of defense and protection. Her words become visible things, sailing out from the temple to right the wrongs against you. You do not see where they are going, nor can you direct them. You trust in Durga's wisdom.

The goddess dances back to you and lifts you into her lap as she sits on the altar. You feel like a small child in the arms of this great Divine Mother. Durga speaks to you about your problems, telling you what you need to do personally to correct the imbalance and confusion. If you have been at fault, Durga will not hesitate to point this out.

Then she speaks of your future, giving you insights into things to come: perhaps a new relationship, job, better goals, or new spiritual knowledge. If there are drastic changes or necessary upheavals coming, Durga will warn you and suggest ways to make the transitions easier. She will not order you to heed what she says. The responsibility of choices is up to you.

When she finishes, Durga sets you on the floor and leaps joyfully onto her altar where she dances her magick dance. You feel yourself sliding quickly away from her and re-entering your physical body. When you are once more firm in your body, chant:

> *Comfort me, Mother.*
> *Reveal to me your plan behind the cycle of my life.*
> *Lift my grief and despair.*
> *Help me to better understand your great powers.*
> *Give me faith in your goodness and greatness.*

Thank Durga for her help and wisdom. Make notes of what she told you so you can remember and be prepared when the events begin to happen.

Chapter 14
BLUE MOON
October 27 - November 1

Also called: Moon of the Dead,
Hunting Moon, Ancestor Moon,
Hunter's Moon.

Incan Festival of the Dead, the Ayamarca, this month.

Oct. 28-Nov. 2: The Isia, a six-day Egyptian festival of Isis; celebrates the search and recovery of Osiris.

Oct. 29: Iroquois Feast of the Dead, honoring the dead.

Oct. 30: In Mexico, the Angelitos, a remembering of the souls of dead children.

Oct. 31: Celtic Feast of the Dead. Feast of Sekhmet and Bast in Egypt. The Autumn festival of Dasehra in India, celebrating the battle of Rama and Kali against the demon Ravana.

Nov. 1: Reign of the Old Woman Cailleach, or Festival of the Dead,
in the Celtic countries. Day of the Banshees in Ireland. The Rite of Hel
in Scandinavian countries. Feast of the Dead in Mexico. The fifth
day of Isia, the Finding of Osiris, in Egypt.

S ince this Moon-month has not survived in the solar calendar which we now
use there is no corresponding name. All cultures which used a lunar calendar,
however, had a Blue Moon, or thirteenth month. For some, this time was considered only to be a few days long; for others, it covered an entire twenty-nine days.
Some cultures gave this month a name; others considered it a dread or especially holy
time, too sacred to name.

For convenience, I have chosen to make this Moon-month unnaturally short. Its
spiritual impact and influence on the collective unconscious of humans is, however, of
great importance. Our current observance of Halloween is really the remnant of a very
old festival of the dead. Humans around the world feel the deep subconscious need to
acknowledge death and the Underworld deities, and they accomplish this through the
use of the symbols of costume, decorations, and certain foods.

This time of year, sometimes called Between Worlds, is an opportunity for us to
face the inevitable cycle of life, both in Nature and in ourselves. It is a time for deep
reflection on where we have been and where we might be going, not necessarily from
a physical standpoint but from a spiritual one.

November 1 is a day to remember the dead in a great many countries and cultures
around the world. In Mexico, the Feast of the Dead is anything but a somber time.
Cookies and candies are made in the shapes of skeletons and skulls. People dress in
bright costumes and parade in the streets. It is a happy atmosphere, even when they
take their picnic lunches to the cemeteries.

In several Christian countries, such as England, this is called All Souls' Day. Our
trick-or-treating on Halloween came from the English custom of going from door to
door on this day begging for soul cakes, which in itself was the remnant of a much
older custom of feeding the dead.

The Scandinavian goddess Hel was known to the Germanic clans as Holde or
Bertha. She is said to ride with Odhinn on his Wild Hunt through the sky, but she is
also associated with lakes and streams. When it snowed, Germans said Holde was
turning her feather bed. She is also a maternal goddess of the hearth, spinning, and
especially the growing of flax.

The Hindus celebrated the Dasehra which commemorated the battle of Rama and Kali against the demon Ravana. At this time also they honored Samana the Leveller, or Lord of Death.

Correspondences

Nature Spirits: banshees and other beings who carry messages between worlds

Herbs: ginger, hops, wormwood, hyssop, patchouli, mugwort, nutmeg, star anise

Colors: black, white, purple

Flowers: white lily, dahlia, chrysanthemum

Scents: rosemary, dragons blood, lilac, pine, wisteria

Stones: obsidian, onyx, Apache tear

Trees: pine, cypress, yew, elder

Animals: bat, wolf, sow, dog, snake

Birds: owls, raven, falcon

Deities: Cybele, Circe, Hel, Nephthys, Cerridwen, Horned God, Caillech, Freyja, Holda

Power Flow: release, remember; communion with the dead. Prophecy. Releasing old negative memories and emotions.

Old Sayings & Lore

- A verse:

  A Saturday's change, and a Sunday's prime,
  Was never a good Moon in any man's time.

- Once in a Blue Moon doesn't mean never; it means a rare occasion. The Egyptians connected their thirteenth month with the color blue, which was a lucky color.

- It is said that cats' eyes will be open wider during a Full Moon than at any other time.

- The term "lunatic" was used as far back as Roman times to describe someone who was mentally unbalanced. Many cultures believed that sleeping out in the moonlight or where the moonlight came in through a window would cause mental illness and/or blindness.

- An old Moon belief in Tennessee says to look over your right shoulder at the Full Moon, take three steps backward and say:

  If I have a lover, let me dream of him/her tonight.
  If I am to marry far, let me hear a bird cry.
  If I am to marry near, let me hear a cow low.
  If I am to marry never, let me hear a hammer knock.

- Thessalian priestesses at one time laid curses using "Moon-dew." Even into Medieval times, people believed that such curses were incurable.

- The Gauls made ritual cakes in crescent shapes in honor of the Moon. Today in France these are called croissants, which are known as "Moon-teeth."

Recipes

Mexican Hot Chocolate

Chocolate comes from ancient Mexico where it was reserved for royalty, the wealthy, and people of high position. It was said to be a food of the gods. The name chocolate probably comes from the Indian words *xoto* (bitter) and *atl* (water). Mexican hot chocolate is dark and heavy with spices, totally unlike the weak version we usually drink.

4-6 ounces semisweet dark chocolate, broken into small pieces	1 teaspoon ground cinnamon
1 quart milk	Dash of almond extract
Dash of cloves	Sugar to taste

Gently heat the chocolate with the milk, cloves, cinnamon, almond extract, and sugar. Stir constantly until the chocolate is melted. Whip to a froth with a whisk. Serve immediately.

Cocoa powder may be substituted for the hard chocolate, and vanilla for the almond extract. Serves four.

Thyme Butter

This is good on thick slices of bread served with a soup or stew. Also good with meat and fish. Makes 1 cup.

1   cup softened margarine or butter
¼   teaspoon ground thyme

Combine and blend well. Any other of your favorite cooking herbs can be substituted for thyme.

Killarney Scones
(Ireland)

2	cups sifted all-purpose flour	½ to ⅓ cup milk
½	teaspoon salt	1 well beaten egg
1	tablespoon sugar	½ cup raisins or currants
4	teaspoons baking powder	Melted butter; sugar
4	tablespoons shortening	

Sift dry ingredients together and cut in the shortening. Add the milk to the egg and then add this to the flour mixture. Add the raisins. Knead lightly and roll the dough to ½" thickness. Cut into small wedges and place on a no-stick cookie sheet. Brush with melted butter and sprinkle with sugar. Bake at 400° F for 15 minutes. Makes 15 scones.

Pumpkin Bread
(Africa)

2	cups sugar	4 eggs
3½	cups all-purpose flour	1 cup oil
2	teaspoons baking soda	⅔ cup water
2	cups mashed pumpkin	1 cup raisins
1	teaspoon cinnamon	1 teaspoon nutmeg

Mix all the ingredients together in a large bowl. Grease 2 large or 3 small loaf pans; fill with the mixture. Bake at 350° F for 1 hour. Cool in the pans on a rack. Wrap to retain freshness; can be frozen.

Rose-Apple Conserve

2 quarts chopped tart apples (winesap, MacIntosh, etc.)	1 teaspoon cinnamon
1 pint red raspberries	2 tablespoons lemon juice
3½ cups sugar	¼ cup chopped English walnuts
1 pint powdered rose petals of a fragrant variety	1 package fruit pectin

Follow the cooking instructions for jams on the package of fruit pectin. You can substitute fresh rose petals for powdered ones. Use only flowers not treated with pesticides (not from florist). Makes about 9 cups.

Crafts

Royal Indian Love Potpourri

1 pint heliotrope blossoms	2 ounces oleander blossoms
4 ounces garden pinks	1 ounce powdered myrrh gum
4 ounces patchouli leaves	1 tonka bean

Halloween Wish Rings

Several days before Halloween, make three rings out of braided grass or straw. Hang them on the bushes outside your window and make a wish on each wreath as you hang it in place. After this, don't look at the rings again until Halloween night, or your wishes won't come true.

Halloween Wish Ring

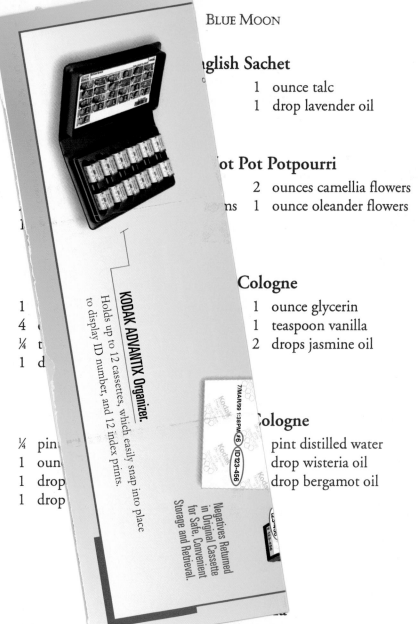

glish Sachet

1 ounce talc
1 drop lavender oil

ot Pot Potpourri

2 ounces camellia flowers
ns 1 ounce oleander flowers

Cologne

1 ounce glycerin
1 teaspoon vanilla
2 drops jasmine oil

Cologne

pint distilled water
drop wisteria oil
drop bergamot oil

One of the most d   ages of Kali Ma shows her squatting over the dead Shiva, devouring his penis with her vagina while physically eating his intestines. This image is not meant to be taken literally, or visually, on a physical level. In a spiritual sense, Kali takes the seed into her vagina to be recreated within her eternal womb. She also devours and destroys all life in order for it to be reformed.

Kali's necklace of skulls was engraved with the Sanskrit letters which were considered the magickal mantras by which she created through combining the Elements. Her worshippers were the first to use the idea of the creative Word or Logos.

Kali Ma has black skin and a hideous tusked face, smeared with blood. On her brow is a third eye. She has four arms which end in claw-like hands. Her naked body is adorned with earrings of little children, her skull necklace, a necklace of snakes,

Kali

another necklace of the heads of her sons, and a belt made out of demons' hands.

Although black is primarily the color of Kali Ma, she is also connected with the sacred gunas (threads) which are red, black, and white. She had three groups of priestesses who served her: the Yoginis or Shaktis, the Matri, and the Dakinis.

Once a demon called Raktavira was rampaging through the countryside and threatening the gods. Brahma had given the demon a boon; every drop of his blood would produce thousands more like him. Too late, the gods despaired of this power and called upon the goddess Kali to defend them. Kali engaged the demon Raktavira in single combat and pierced him with a spear. Then she lifted him high into the air and drank his blood as it poured out.

Once enraged, Kali had a blind lust for destruction and nothing could stop her. On more than one occasion her consort Shiva had to throw himself among the demons she had slaughtered and let her trample him underfoot as she did her victory dance. This was the only way to bring her to her senses and keep the world from collapsing.

The Norse Hel

In Norse-Germanic myths, Hel was queen of the dead and ruler of the Underworld realm called Niflheim. She was given her realm by Odhinn himself. Niflheim was a world of both intense ice and cold and volcanic fire.

Hel was the daughter of Loki and the Giantess Angurboda. She was terrible to look at, with one half of her body healthy, the other rotten and diseased. Although the myths said that Hel would side against the gods and humans at Ragnarok, she received all of the dead, except those who died in battle. Part of her realm was a place of rest for the good dead, even such gods as Balder, while part was a place of punishment for those who were evil.

Barbara Walker[1] writes that the expression Hella cunni (Hel's kinsmen) was later corrupted into the word "harlequin." It is recorded that during medieval times the Hellequins, or "ladies of the night," went from house to house among the commonfolk and received food and drink in exchange for good luck wishes. Whatever the Christian church thought of Hel, the commoners generally considered her more benevolent than harmful.

Another of Hel's names was Nehellania, or Nether Moon, a direct linkage with Nef-Hel, Nifl, or Niflheim, the name of her Underworld kingdom. Among the North Germanic tribes, Hel was called Holda or Bertha and was said to ride with Odhinn on the Wild Hunt. This Wild Hunt may have connections with the Valkyries led by Freyja in her dark aspect. The name of the Valkyrie Brynhild means "Burning Hel."

Skadi of the Dark North

Skadi was the goddess of the dark, cruel North with its ice and snow. Her name probably comes from the root of the Gothic skadus, which means "shadow or shade." Scandinavia was once called Scadin-auja, or the land of Skadi. The Scandinavian skalds, who were poet-shamans, said their powers and inspirations, as well as their name, came from the Dark Mother Skadi. It was believed that whatever they prophesied came true because they had a direct connection with the cauldron of all time within the realm of this goddess.

Norse myth describes Skadi as the beautiful daughter of the Giant Thjazi. After her father was killed by Thorr, Skadi came to the gates of Asgard and challenged the gods. In an attempt to dissipate her anger, Loki took a goat and went out to greet her. Since he had caused the problem in the first place, the gods considered this only proper. Loki tied one end of a rope to the goat, the other to his genitals. The goat pulled one way and Loki the other until the genitals tore free. Loki fell bleeding into Skadi's lap, bathing her with his blood. The goddess considered this payment enough for her father's death. However, Loki, by his magick, repaired the castration and went on to pursue other female deities.

The Cailleach

The Cailleach was a Crone goddess, particularly in Scotland. A derivative of her name, Caledonia, was given to that country. Her name, as well as her title as Black Mother, is too close to the name Kalika, a title of Kali, to be coincidence. Robert Graves[2] says that the Cailleach was another form of the Irish Scathach and the Norse Skadi. Medieval legend turned her into the Black Queen of a western paradise.

The Crone Goddess

Rituals

Feast of the Dead

Honoring the dead is a custom in all cultures. Many cultures celebrate their rituals for the dead at this time of year. It is an excellent time to remember your own lost ones and ancestors you never knew. If you have deceased family members or acquaintances with whom you did not get along, it is perfectly proper to ask that they NOT be allowed entrance to your house and ritual. A friend did not stipulate this; he ended up with his deceased cruel father throwing books off shelves, creating a constant turmoil, and other spooky things. It took a strong banishing ritual to get rid of the spirit. Lest anyone think it was simply the friend's imagination, the spooky acts happened in clear view of several unbelievers.

This ritual should be performed within a consecrated and cast circle for your own protection. In addition to your regular ritual tools, you will need: a cauldron, a black candle, a plate of bread and salt, and an apple. Cast your circle as usual.

With the wand in your power hand, tap the cauldron five times. Say:

> *Dark Goddess, Lord of Death, I ask your blessings.*
> *Lift the Veil for me that I may greet my ancestors,*
> *Friends and family who have gone ahead into your realms.*
> *Let only those who wish me well enter within this circle.*

Touch the plate of bread and salt with the wand. Say:

> *The feast is set. Welcome to all ancestors who wish me well.*
> *The Veil is lifted this night that all may once more rejoice*
> *together in fellowship.*
> *The bread of life, the salt of the Earth, are prepared as a banquet.*
> *As we eat, may we remember the eternal presence of the Gods,*
> *And may we also remember that what we call death is but*
> *a fleeting existence*
> *In the cycle of birth and rebirth.*

Take a piece of the bread, dip it into the salt, and eat. Anything left after the ritual must be placed outside or buried.

Light the black candle in the cauldron.

This is a time of remembrance of all those gone into
the realm of the Dark Mother.

Silently think of family, friends, and pets who have departed this Earth. Then say:

The Thin Veil has been lifted.
My ancestors have come to the Feast of the Dead.
I thank them for their presences and words of comfort.

Take up the apple. Say:

Beautiful Maiden, you are the dispenser of the seed of life,
Life that awaits, hidden in the sacred cauldron.
Fruitful Mother, your ripeness of power nurtures the seed
Bringing it into existence and helping it to grow.
Dark Mother, your magick cauldron is the well of death and rebirth,
An experience each of us undergoes again and again.
Let there be no fear in me, for I know your gentleness.
Here is the secret symbol of life in death and death in life,
The hidden, mystical symbol of the Triple Goddess.

Cut the apple crosswise to reveal the hidden pentagram in the core. Incline your head toward the altar and say:

My deepest thanks to the Triple Ladies.
May I always walk in peace beside you.

Eat part of the apple. Put the remainder outside as an offering to the birds and animals. Break the circle. Say:

This rite is ended, the circle cut.
The power goes out to manifest.
Yet though its light is gone to sight,
By lingering power I am blessed.

Remembering Lost Children

Every year there are a great number of children who die, who are kidnapped, or who are runaways. Others are lost in crime, drugs, prostitution, or horrible family environments. We should remember all of them, whether or not we know them personally.

For children who have died, light a white candle in remembrance. Ask the Gods to comfort the family members left behind, and guide and comfort the souls of the deceased. Let all of the candles burn out.

For children who are kidnapped, burn a red candle. Ask that they be given strength and wisdom to endure and escape. Ask the Gods to lead the authorities to them.

Light a blue candle for those children who are runaways or caught in terrible circumstances. Request for them the wisdom to get help and the courage to break free of whatever binds their minds and bodies.

Although these seem like very simple rituals, their power to change circumstances is great.

Thoth, Moon God of Wisdom

The Egyptian god Thoth was also known as Tehuti, Thout, Djehuti, and Zehuti. He was the Lord of Books and Learning, Judge of the Gods, director of the planets and seasons, and scribe of the gods. The Greeks identified him with Hermes. He was considered to be self-begotten and self-produced.

Thoth

Thoth was called "Lord of Holy Words" for inventing hieroglyphs and numbers. As The Elder, he was the first and greatest of magicians, the Supreme Magus. He had greater powers than either Osiris or Ra. He was the patron of priests and god of all magick. Thoth was the inventor of the Four Laws of Magick.

This deity was ibis-headed and wore a lunar disk and crescent on his head; he held the writing reed and palette of a scribe. He had two wives, Seshat and Nehmauit. The ibis was sacred to this god and associated with the Moon.

At his sacred center at Hermopolis Magna in Upper Egypt, his priests taught that Thoth created by the sound of his voice alone. In a crypt under his main temple were kept his books of magick which were open only to his initiated disciples, and which the Greeks and later people translated into the works of Hermes Trismegistus and the Kybalion. In Lower Egypt his center was at Hermopolis Parva.

Thoth ruled over writing, inventions, the arts, divination, commerce, healing, initiation, music, success, wisdom, medicine, astronomy, geometry, surveying, drawing, sciences, measurement of time, all calculations and inventories, archives, judgment, rituals, the law, astrology, alphabet, speech, grammar, arbitration, balance, mental powers, the Moon, botany, theology, hymns and prayers, reading, peace, learning, books, truth, the Akashic records, fate.

For this ritual, you will need your usual ritual tools, plus a sistrum or rattle, a caduceus (or wand entwined with two pieces of blue cording), and a piece of candy. Sweets were part of Thoth's ancient rituals.

Take the caduceus in your power hand and beginning in the East, draw a protective boundary around the ritual area. Move clockwise and end in the East. Stand before the altar facing East, caduceus still in hand, and say:

> *In Thoth is a balance of all powers and wisdoms.*
> *I encircle myself with balance.*
> *Within this circle of balance*
> *May Thoth and all the Gods help me to draw*
> *Upon infinite wisdom and power.*

Shake the sistrum three times. Say:

> *Hail to thee, Thoth,*
> *You who are self-begotten,*
> *The oldest of the Gods, the wisest.*
> *Supreme Magus, you who gave the Four Laws of Magick,*
> *Harken to my call. Instruct me in all things.*
> *Hail to thee, Thoth!*

Touch the caduceus to the center of your forehead. Say:

> *The silvery Moon sends forth mystic energies.*
> *Its luminous rays bless the healing herbs.*
> *Dreams float on its shimmering light.*
> *Visions and intuition ride its magickal beams.*
> *Bless me, O Thoth of the Moon.*

Point the caduceus at the East. Shake the sistrum three times; say:

> *I call upon Thoth and all the Gods of Air*
> *To send eloquence and new ideas.*

Point the caduceus at the South. Shake the sistrum three times; say:

> *I call upon Thoth and all the Gods of Fire*
> *To send will power, determination, and fresh goals.*

Point the caduceus at the West. Shake the sistrum three times; say:

> *I call upon Thoth and all the Gods of Water*
> *To send psychic knowledge and greater skill in magick.*

Point the caduceus at the North. Shake the sistrum three times; say:

> *I call upon Thoth and all the Gods of Earth*
> *To send practical skills.*

Hold up the caduceus in salute over the altar. Shake the sistrum seven times. Say:

> *The sacred fire is laid.*
> *The fire shines.*
> *The incense is laid upon the fire.*
> *The incense shines.*
> *The fragrance rises to the Gods.*
> *Thy awakening is in peace, O Thoth.*
> *Turn back the followers of evil.*
> *Sweet is the truth you bring, thou Judge of the Gods.*
> *Sweet is the truth that I seek through you.*

Take a piece of candy and eat it. Think upon the goals that you seek, the skills that you need and desire.

> *Lord of Holy Books, Healing, and Learning,*
> *Your aid is greatly needed by this child.*
> *I seek knowledge and success.*
> *I seek healing and psychic powers.*
> *Teach to me the ancient knowledges.*
> *Open to me the record of my past lives in your Holy Books,*
> *the Akashic Records.*
> *Grant me power and the wisdom to use it wisely.*

Now is the time for meditation and spellworking. When you are finished, ground the power by placing your hands flat on the floor. Close the circle as usual.

> *Truth is revealed; magick expands.*
> *Good fortune and health flow from your hands.*
> *Riches and honor, these are my right.*
> *Pour out your blessings. Shower me with light.*

Dark Faeries

There are a number of Little Ones who can be considered Dark Faeries. These are the entities who are primarily connected with the Earth. Sometimes they are called Dark simply because they like to live in dark places such as under stairs and in basements, not because they are evil.

The Coblynau of Wales are mine spirits who knock where rich ores can be found. The Knockers from Cornwall (also called Buccas) are like the Coblynau of Wales. The Gnomes are Earth Elementals, who live underground and guard the treasures of the Earth; they are also wonderful metal workers, especially of swords.

Goblins or Hobgoblins originally were not the nasty, evil creatures portrayed today; they were a small, grotesque but friendly type of brownie. The Bwca or Bwbachod of Wales is also a type of brownie. The Brownie himself (called Bodach in Scotland, Fenodoree in Manx, and Pixies or Pisgies in West England) dresses in brown clothing and makes himself responsible for the house where he lives; unless offended, he is an amiable little creature.

Dark Elves and Faeries of the Unseelie Court can be unfavorable to humans. They have had good reason not to trust us. They often shelter in dark areas, under stairs, or in the attic or basement. Ordinarily, the most they do to humans is make them feel very uncomfortable in their inhabited areas. Sometimes they were called the Sluagh or Host.

Dwarves are probably the best known of the Dark entities. They are not the stupid, silly creatures portrayed by Disney, but keepers of the Earth, its minerals, and gems. They are marvelous workers in metal: swords, magickal items, jewelry, etc. One should not take things from their kingdom without asking their permission.

Rather than being frightened of these entities, you would be wise to cultivate their friendship. Those dwelling within your house will protect and bless it if you are their friend. Those who dwell outside or in the ground (and they are everywhere!) will bless your property, making the plants and trees grow better and once in a while allowing you to turn up some stone or other treasure that will help you in your magickal work.

Gnomes and dwarves like a clear dark green color or a rich brown. You can entice them to your altar with candles of these colors. Also use pyrite (fool's gold) and steel or iron. Spicy scents, such as ginger and cinnamon, draw their attention.

Elves like the colors of silver, light green, or light blue. They are fond of ginger, lily of the valley, fir, and floral scents. You can attract them by laying out silver, quartz, rock crystal, and moonstone.

All of these Dark Faeries or beings are attracted to ginger, honey, and milk, as well as by rock crystal. If you call them to participate in a ritual, keep it light and full of fun. They like happy music and dancing.

To commune with these Dark Faeries and creatures, set out a little ginger beside some crystals. Light Earth-colored or the appropriate candles. Have cookies and juice for a party. Chant:

> *Little Ones, from dark places shady,*
> *Come to me, both Lord and Lady.*
> *Dressed in magick clothes and flowers,*
> *Teach me in the twilight hours.*
> *As the clouds flow past the Moon,*
> *Sing to me an eldritch tune.*
> *Whisper magick of the land,*
> *Mushroom ring and wooded strand.*
> *Keep this home a happy place,*
> *Of merry heart and smiling face.*
> *Welcome here, you are to me.*
> *Let us be friends happily.*

Now is the time to sing and dance and be merry. Share the cookies and juice with them. Leave the ginger and crystals on the altar overnight.

Keeper of the Golden Apples
— Crescent Moon —

Idunn, or Idunna, was the Aesir goddess of immortality. She was the wife of Bragi and keeper of the golden apples for the Norse gods. When Loki arranged to have Idunn and her apples stolen by the giants, the gods immediately began to age. This goddess rules over youth, responsibility, beauty, and long life.

This ritual is for renewing your life forces and energies after a mental, emotional, or physical crisis. When such a crisis occurs, you need to cleanse, protect, and renew both yourself and your home. If the crisis is caused by another person within the home, this ritual may well cause them to either move out or be forced to face what they are doing. Performing this ritual doesn't, however, absolve you of the responsibility of doing whatever is necessary to remedy the situation.

You will need a white and a black candle; apple blossom or lotus incense; a single-sided mirror; frankincense and myrrh incense.

Set up your altar with a lighted white candle on the right, a black candle on the left. Burn apple blossom incense if you can find it; otherwise, use lotus. Stand before the altar and chant:

Most lovely Idunn of the Crescent Moon,
Guide me in the choices right
For my life each Moon-filled night.
O, Distant One, give me a boon.
Sweet Idunn, give victory.
Apple-Keeper, prosperity.

Spend as much time as needed to talk with Idunn about the crisis you have experienced, or are experiencing. If you have had any responsibility in the problem, be sure to state this. The goddess does not help whiners who are always shifting responsibility for their actions. Then chant:

Comfort me. Guide me, great Lady of power.
Come to me in this silent hour.
Strengthen my faith. Balance my life.
Free me of sorrow, confusion, and strife.

Take the mirror in your power hand and pass it slowly through the incense smoke. Stand with the mirror heart-high, reflecting surface away from you. Say:

No other being, physical or spiritual, has a right to interfere in my life!
I am worthy of the Goddess's love and gifts.
Under her hands I stand, protected from all evil and jealousy.

Take the mirror counterclockwise around each room in your home with the reflecting side away from you. At each door and window, stop and say:

No evil in thought, word, or being may enter this place,
I am a favored child under the protection of the goddess Idunn.
And she is a revengeful protector of her children.
Beware, all those who wish me ill!
Enter here, and you create your own destruction!

Return the mirror to the altar. Carry a good protection incense, or frankincense and myrrh, through every room in the house to purify and bless.

The Moon Goddess Selene
— Full Moon —

Selene, sometimes known as Mene, was the second aspect of the Moon to the Greeks. She was the daughter of Hyperion and Theia, a Titaness, and the sister of Helios and Eos. Selene personified the Moon as bride and lover. She was pictured as a beautiful woman with a golden crown. This deity had great importance in magick, spells, and enchantments.

Often we find ourselves out of synch with the rhythm of the Moon and her powers. Usually this happens when we have been too involved in material, physical matters and have not given enough time to spiritual development. This meditation is good for correcting that condition. It is also useful when we need to renew our spiritual initiation and communication with the Moon Goddess.

Set up an altar with a silver or white cloth. Light a white candle and set it in the center. If you wish, have a vase of white flowers on the altar. Before the candle, place a chalice of water or white juice or wine. Burn a little powdered gum mastic and mugwort. Dress in white or silver.

Put a comfortable chair near the altar and sit there. If you like, play soft, dreamy instrumental music. Say:

> *Silently, she rides the night,*
> *The Silver Mother, crystal clear.*
> *Her gifts are subtle, changing my path,*
> *Yet lovingly erasing fear.*
> *Mother of the magick Moon,*
> *I chant your sacred name divine,*
> *And follow to true destinies*
> *That lead to higher realms than mine.*

Close your eyes and relax your body. Before you is a silver path that leads from the Earth up to the Moon. You find yourself swiftly ascending that path. The spiritual Moon is not at all like the physical Moon. The Moon garden of Selene is full of pale flowers and green trees. In the center of this garden, before a shallow pool filled with water lilies, stands a small round temple with open sides. Its columns are covered with flowering vines. Inside sits the goddess Selene, waiting for you.

You sit beside Selene and gaze into her deep eyes. Her long silver-blonde hair falls to her hips. Her white dress is held at the waist by a silver belt. She smiles and gathers you into her arms in an embrace.

"Sister (Brother)," she says in her soft voice, "I am glad you came."

Selene speaks to you about your spiritual goals and what you have accomplished in that area so far. She may make suggestions as to what would help you. You can tell her about your problems if they touch upon the spiritual, especially if you are being persecuted or ridiculed for your beliefs.

When your conversation is over, Selene takes your hand and leads you out to stand beside the lily pond. A group of men and women come to stand with you. They are all dressed in white. One of them hands the goddess a silver chalice. She lifts it to your lips and you drink.

Then she stoops and picks a water lily. With great solemnness, Selene places the flower on the top of your head. You feel it sink down into your body. She tells you that this flower will help to balance and realign your sacred centers in the astral body. You feel the flower begin to work its spiritual magick. You become aware of a subtle heart beat rhythm all around you. Selene says that this is the rhythm of the Moon, an influence all humans could hear and feel if they would listen.

Another of the Moon attendants holds out a bright silver disk on a chain. The goddess slips this over your head. Selene whispers that this emblem is a sign of your Moon initiation, that it is a key to her realm whenever you want to return.

The attendant who brought the pendant comes forward and takes your hand. This person is to be one of your spiritual teachers and guardians. Selene kisses you once more and goes back to her temple. The new teacher goes with you back down the path of moonlight to the Earth. Beautiful music is heard all around you. You slide back into your physical body and open your eyes.

Gaze again at the candle. Say:

> *Moon magick, visions, dreamy inspiration.*
> *The Moon is darkened in the sky.*
> *Astral travel, healing, intuition.*
> *The Moon is a silver sliver in the sky.*
> *Prophetic dreams, luck, divination.*
> *The Moon is a crystal ball in the sky.*
> *Three phases of the Moon, three phases of my life,*
> *Youth, maturity, great wisdom.*
> *Let me be guided by your deep symbolism.*

Sprinkle water from the chalice around your working space and onto yourself. Call upon your new teacher whenever you need help in ritual, magick, and spiritual insight.

The Courts of Hel
—Dark Moon—

Hel, or Hella, was Queen of the Dead and Ruler of Niflheim. Her home was called Sleet-Den or Sleetcold. She ruled over dark magick and revenge.

Another name for the goddess Hel was Nehellania, or Nether Moon, a direct linkage with Nef-Hel, Nifl, or Niflheim, the name of Hel's underworld kingdom. Among the North Germanic tribes, she was called Holde, Holda, or Bertha and rode with Odhinn in the Wild Hunt. Holly was sacred to her, and the Germanic followers of this goddess often made magick wands from its wood. Even in the tenth century, witchcraft tracts said that Pagan women rode under her leadership in wild night rides.

The Dark Mother Hel is a powerful deity. Often she works with her special animals, the wolves. If you feel that you have been under psychic attack, bombarded by negative thoughts, or in physical danger, call upon the goddess Hel and her wolves.

Perform this ritual during the Dark Moon. Cast your circle as usual, but moving counterclockwise, from the East. When you are finished, stand before the altar with your arms raised and say:

> *Dark Mother, let your power flow through the body of your daughter/son*
> *and out again to repel and destroy all negative thoughts and deeds that are*
> *directed against me.*

Stand in silence as you draw down the power. Then go to the East, raise your sword (dagger) in greeting and say:

> *Hail, Dawn-Treader, great wolf of the East,*
> *Whose yellow eyes see all in the Element of Air!*
> *I do summon you here to protect and defend me.*

Move to the North; say:

> *Hail, Ice-Leaper, great wolf of the North,*
> *Whose green eyes see all in the Element of Earth!*
> *I do summon you here to protect and defend me.*

Go to the West. Say:

> *Hail, Night-Stalker, great wolf of the West,*
> *Whose blue eyes see all in the Element of Water!*
> *I do summon you here to protect and defend me.*

Finish by going to the South. Say:

> *Hail, Sun-Chaser, great wolf of the South,*
> *Whose red eyes see all in the Element of Fire!*
> *I do summon you here to protect and defend me.*

Move counterclockwise back around until you once again stand before the altar. Say:

Great Dark Mother, I call upon you to build up this protection,
To send back all the evil that has been sent against me.

Raise your sword high.

Dark Mother, Queen of the Night, there are those who stand against me.
Let their efforts fail. Let them go down into darkness.
Let them stand in the courts of Hel.
May their efforts always be lost in the darkness with no light to guide them.
I am your child! Protect me, Dark Mother!

Rest the sword point down at your feet. Say:

Dark Mother, help me reach my goals, live my life to the fullest,
walk a path of Light and balance.
Sweep away all barriers built by those who want me to fail.
Crush the evil sent against me!
Sweep its evil remains back into the bodies and brains of those who sent it!
The evil is dead! The attackers taste their just rewards!
Their mouths are full of ashes, their thoughts of nightmares,
their lives of unfulfillment!
I stand under the sword and hand of the Goddess!
So mote it be!

As you draw a pentagram on the floor between your feet with the sword, say:

It is done!

Lay aside the sword. Say:

Your hands protect me, from Dark Moon to Dark Moon.
Your sword covers me, from Dark Moon to Dark Moon.
The wolves guard me, from Dark Moon to Dark Moon.
All love and honor to the Dark Mother!

This is the time for any spellworking and to finish any other ritual matters.
Then take the sword and go to the East. Raise it in greeting, and say:

Farewell, Dawn-Treader!
My thanks for your protection and defense.
Depart in peace. Blessed be.

Move to the North; say:

Farewell, Ice-Leaper!
My thanks for your protection and defense.
Depart in peace. Blessed be.

Go to the West; say:

Farewell, Night-Stalker!
My thanks for your protection and defense.
Depart in peace. Blessed be.

Finish by going to the South. Say:

Farewell, Sun-Chaser!
My thanks for your protection and defense.
Depart in peace. Blessed be.

Stand before the altar again, with arms raised.

My thanks to the Goddess and to all who have helped here this night.
Depart in peace. Blessed be.

Cut the circle.

Endnotes

1. *The Woman's Encyclopedia of Myths & Secrets.*
2. *The White Goddess.*

Chapter 15
SNOW MOON
November

Also called: Dark Moon, Fog Moon, Beaver Moon, Mourning Moon,
Blotmonath (Sacrifice Month), Herbistmanoth (Harvest Month),
Mad Moon, Moon of Storms, Moon When Deer Shed Antlers.

Nov. 3: The last day of Isia in Egypt; the rebirth of Osiris.

Nov. 6: The birthday of Tiamat in Babylon.

Nov. 8: The Fuigo Matsuri, a Shinto festival honoring Inari or Hettsui No
Kami, goddess of the Kitchen Range, in Japan.

Nov. 10: Kali Puja in India, for Kali, the destroyer of evil.

Nov. 9-10: Night of Nicnevin in Scotland.

Nov. 11: Feast of the Einheriar (Fallen Warriors), Norse.

Nov. 15: The Shichigosan (Seven-Five-Three Day) for safety of children of
these ages in Japan. In India, Children's Day. In Rome, the Feronia
for the goddess of forests and fertility.

Nov. 16: Night of Hecate in Greece; begins at sunset. Festival of Bast
in Egypt.

Nov. 24: Feast of Burning Lamps in Egypt for Isis and Osiris.

Nov. 27: Day of Parvati-Devi, the Triple Goddess who divided herself into Sarasvati, Lakshmi, and Kali, or the Three Mothers.

Nov. 30: Day of Hecate of the Crossroads in Greece, the Dark Moon. Skadi among the Norse. Day of Mawu, African creatress of the universe from chaos.

Novem was the ninth month in the oldest Roman calendar. In the Celtic tradition this was the beginning of a new year. The Celtic year ended on the eve before Samhain and began again on the day after. They considered it a Moon-month of beginnings and endings.

The Isia, or rebirth of Osiris, in Egypt was time of the receding waters of the Nile floods. This rebirth does not mean reincarnation, but a rising from the dead. After an enactment of the story of Osiris' death at the hands of his brother Set, the people followed the mourning Isis to her temple. There the drama continued with the combat between Horus and Set. Images of Osiris were made of paste and grain; they were watered until the barley sprouted and then floated down the Nile with candles as part of the planting ceremonies. James Frazer, in *The Golden Bough,* translates a "Lamentation of Isis" which has the goddess say that she is Osiris's sister, child of the same mother, and that the god shall never be far from her.

The Japanese festival honoring the goddess of the kitchen range honored the women who prepared the daily meals in a back-handed way. Commonly called Kami (deity), this goddess was important because, through use of the harvested food, she protected and provided for the family.

The goddess Hecate had many celebrations throughout the year. November 16 was known as the Night of Hecate, the Three-formed. Hecate is part of the most ancient form of the triple Moon goddess as Crone or Dark Moon; Artemis was the Crescent Moon and Selene the Full Moon. Most of Hecate's worship, and especially on this night, was performed at a three-way crossroad at night. Food was left there as an offering to her. She was known to rule the passages of life and transformation, birth and death. Her animals were the toad, the owl, the dog, and the bat.

Nicneven was a Scottish goddess, whose name means "Divine" or "Brilliant," a form of Diana the Huntress. In Scotland she was said to ride through the night with her followers at Halloween (the Celtic Samhain). During the Middle Ages she was called Dame Habonde, Abundia, Satia, Bensozie, Zobiana, and Herodiana.

In Tibet, they celebrated the Feast of Lanterns, a Winter festival of the shortest days of the Sun. Among the Incas it was a time of the Ayamarca, or Festival of the Dead.

Correspondences

Nature Spirits: subterranean faeries

Herbs: grains of paradise, verbena, betony, borage, cinquefoil, blessed thistle

Colors: gray, sea-green

Flowers: blooming cacti, chrysanthemum

Scents: cedar, cherry blossoms, hyacinth, narcissus, peppermint, lemon

Stones: topaz, hyacinth, lapis lazuli

Trees: alder, cypress

Animals: unicorn, scorpion, crocodile, jackal

Birds: owl, goose, sparrow

Deities: Kali, Black Isis, Nicnevin, Hecate, Bast, Osiris, Sarasvati, Lakshmi, Skadi, Mawu

Power Flow: take root, prepare. Transformation. Strengthen communication with the god or goddess who seems closest to you

Old Sayings & Lore

• To cry for the Moon is an old saying that means you are craving or demanding something that you can't have.

• The word moonshine has two meanings. In the U.S., it means "illegally distilled liquor," also known as "white lightning." An older meaning was "total nonsense."

• A waning Moon was considered an unlucky time for a marriage or birth.

• In English, French, Italian, Latin, and Greek, the Moon is feminine; but in all the Teutonic languages the Moon is masculine. In Sanskrit, the word for the Moon is *mas,* which is masculine.

• To the Chinese, the Old Man in the Moon was Yue-lao. It was his duty to predestine the marriages of mortals. They said he tied the future husband and wife together with an invisible silk cord that never parted as long as they lived.

• Although the Koran expressly forbids worshipping the Sun or Moon, many Moslems still clasp their hands at the sight of a New Moon and offer a prayer.

Recipes

Mandelformer
(Swedish Tarts)

This delicious, delicate finger-dessert is only one of many such treats served on holidays. Fluted tartlet pans are needed to make them authentic; these are generally available in boxed sets in any shop that sells kitchen supplies. If unable to find these pans, tiny muffin tins can be used.

1	cup sweet butter or margarine	1	cup ground, sweet roasted
⅗	cup white sugar		almonds
1	whole egg		A few sliced almonds
2⅓	cups white enriched flour		

Mix together the butter, sugar, egg, and flour; blend in the ground almonds. Carefully coat the insides of the tartlet pans with butter. Press the dough into the buttered tins until evenly and thinly coated. Bake at 350° F until lightly brown.

Since the pans are quite small, you may find it necessary to arrange them on a cookie sheet for baking. When the tarts are done, remove the pans to a wire rack to cool. When cool, carefully remove from the pans. This confection is so delicate that any rough treatment will cause them to crumble. Fill with pudding, jam or jelly, cooked mincemeat, fresh sliced strawberries or other fruits, or pie fillings. They may be garnished with whipped cream and sliced almonds.

Mead

I am including this recipe for its interest more than for its practical use. It is from an old 1842 hand-written recipe book that I discovered; unfortunately, the book was lost during a move, except for my copy of this recipe. I never could figure out a convenient modern translation for its use.

32	pounds new honey	2-3	handfuls ground malt
13	gallons water	1	round of toast
1	handful each of rosemary,		Yeast
	thyme, bay leaves, and	1½	ounces each of cloves, mace,
	sweet briar		and nutmeg

Boil the new honey in the water; skim it well. Add the handfuls each of rosemary, thyme, bay leaves, and sweet briar. Boil the mixture for one hour, then put it into a tub with the ground malt. Stir until lukewarm, and strain through a cloth into another tub. Spread a round of toast with yeast and put it in the liquid. When the mead is covered with yeast, pour it into a cask. Tie the cloves, mace, and nutmeg in a bag and hang it in the cask. Close the cask for six months, then bottle. Make sure all containers are sterilized before use.

Crafts

Pomander Balls

Start with an orange, lime, or lemon that is firm and free from blemishes. Warm the fruit to room temperature before beginning. Using a darning needle to pierce the skin of the fruit, insert whole cloves in rows that touch each other. When completely covered, put the fruit in a dry place for at least a month to dry out.

Blend together equal amounts of orris root powder, cloves, nutmeg, cinnamon, allspice, and rosemary. Roll the fruit in this mixture until coated; then leave it in the powder for another two weeks.

Enclose the clove-decorated fruit in a square of netting and tie at the top with a ribbon loop for hanging.

Forest Potpourri

2 ounces geranium leaves (pine-scented)	1 teaspoon vanilla
	2 ounces German rue
1 ounce balsam fir needles	2 tablespoons pine needles
4 ounces sweet woodruff	1 ounce powdered orris root
3 tablespoons cedar chips	1 drop bergamot oil
1 tablespoon violets	

Road to Mandalay Potpourri

4 ounces orange blossoms	2 ounces heliotrope blossoms
2 ounces ylang ylang blossoms	1 ounce frankincense
1 teaspoon nutmeg	1 teaspoon orange peel
½ teaspoon cinnamon	1 teaspoon vanilla

Meadow Flower Sachet

2 ounces cornstarch	1 ounce talc
½ ounce powdered benzoin gum	¼ ounce sweet woodruff
¼ ounce heather	1 teaspoon vanilla
1 drop violet oil	

Magick Hands Poster

This is a project that is easy for a child or an inexperienced adult to make for themselves or to give as a gift. Healers and magicians can use it as a focal point at the beginning of meditation.

Trace onto paper the outline of both your hands with the fingers outspread. Transfer these outlines to white felt and carefully cut them out. Cut out a 3" diameter circle from the white felt also. Using a golden color felt, cut out the two wings, one for each side of the globe. Arrange these pieces onto a square of blue felt and glue into place.

If you are handy with needle and thread, the same design can be cut from cloth instead of felt, with the pieces appliqued in place. This can then be used as either a wall hanging or a banner.

Myths

Sarasvati

The *Vedas* list Sarasvati originally as a water deity, the goddess of a river which flowed west from the Himalayas. Later her powers increased. She became known as the goddess of hymns and speech, the inventor of Sanskrit, and the discoverer of the sacred drink soma. She became the power behind all phenomena.

Brahma and Sarasvati

Still today Sarasvati is called the consort of Brahma and mother of the Vedas which sprang from his heads. She is portrayed as a graceful woman with white skin, wearing a Crescent Moon on her forehead; she rides on a peacock or swan, or is seated on a lotus blossom. She is goddess of all the creative arts, particularly poetry and music, learning, and science.

One myth says that originally Sarasvati was one of three wives of Vishnu, along with Lakshmi and Ganga. These goddesses quarreled so much that Vishnu finally gave Ganga to Shiva and Sarasvati to Brahma. Another myth says she took so long at her toilet, keeping Brahma waiting to start the sacrifices, that he married Gayatri, the daughter of a sage. When Sarasvati arrived, she cursed Brahma to be worshipped only once a year. Things quieted between the goddess and Gayatri when the girl promised to always remain the second and lower wife.

Mawu from Africa

The African goddess Mawu was originally called Mawu-Lisa and was sometimes seen as female-male twins, sometimes as an androgynous being. She was associated with the night, the Moon, fertility, gentleness, and motherhood. She gave birth to all the other deities. One of her first children stayed in the sky and founded the Thunderer pantheon, or Sogbo. One of the others, Sagbata, was sent to Earth to reproduce. When it came time to choose which child went to Earth, Mawu chose Sagbata because he was the eldest. Sogbo was jealous and made the rains stop so that the people on Earth had no water or crops. When the people started complaining, Mawu sent Legba to find out what was going on. Legba had put Sogbo up to stopping the rains in the first place, but Mawu was unaware of this. The trickster Legba sent a bird to start a huge fire on Earth. When the smoke cloud rose, Legba told Mawu that the absence of rain was burning up the Earth. Mawu then ordered Sogbo to release the rain.

Mawu

Parvati

Parvati was the daughter of Himavan (god of the Himalayas) and sister of Ganga, goddess of the Ganges River. She was an incarnation of Sati, one of Shiva's wives. She waited patiently for Shiva to recognize her in her new form but the god embarked on a career of asceticism and showed no interest. Parvati took up practicing austerities, changing her natural black skin to a golden color. Still Shiva was unmoved. So Kama, the god of love, shot a fiery arrow into Shiva's heart, but Shiva controlled the passion and emotions.

As a last resort, Parvati took her practices to the extreme. She ate nothing, lay in icy water, tortured her body. One day a Brahman priest came to her and ask why she was doing this. Parvati told him she wanted to marry Shiva. The Brahman called the god a dirty old man who haunted cemeteries. Parvati agreed but said she still loved him. When the priest called Shiva much worse things, Parvati covered her ears and shouted at him to go away. Then the priest revealed that he was really the god Shiva. He told Parvati to stop her austerities and he would marry her. Although this was basically a happy union, Shiva and Parvati had frequent quarrels. These usually occurred because Shiva wanted to curse someone who Parvati wanted to bless.

Rituals

Festival of the Kitchen

Everyone who works in a kitchen, especially those at home, need to be appreciated and honored for their work, done day in and day out, usually without thanks. Honor your household cook by taking him/her out to dinner or preparing a nice meal yourself. Be sure that you do all the cleaning up afterwards!

The Chinese kept plaques in the kitchen that honored the kitchen god or goddess. Each year a new plaque was put up and the old one taken down. Today it is not unusual in Pagan households to find a little kitchen witch on her broom hung up in the kitchen to bless it.

Honor your kitchen and all the unseen supernatural helpers who live there by giving the room and the appliances a good cleaning. Perhaps the room could use a new coat of paint, or something as simple as new curtains or cupboard handles to brighten things up. The kitchen is an important part of your family existence. Keep its supernatural beings, and your physical ones, happy with their residence.

Personal Peace & Happiness

It can be a simple task to make a demon trap for your home. This device will trap incoming negative entities before they can disrupt the harmony of your residence.

Take a white piece of paper. When you wrote the following words on it, write them in a spiral, leading from the outer edge to the center of the paper.

Write: "All you spirits of disruption and disharmony, into this trap are you drawn. From the center you can only return to your original domain."

Place this flat under the rug by the front door. If anyone enters with such creatures in their wake, the "demons" will be trapped at the door. This was a very ancient device used by the people of Mesopotamia.

Kali, Keeper of the Books of Reincarnation

Kali Ma is a Hindu goddess with a dual personality, exhibiting traits of both gentleness and love, revenge and terrible death. She was known as the Black Mother, the Terrible, Goddess of Death, and Mother of Karma. As the Kalika, or Crone, she governs every form of death but also rules every form of life. She represents the three divisions of the Hindu year, three phases of the Moon, three sections of the cosmos, three stages of life, three types of priestesses at her shrines. The Hindus revered the trefoil as an emblem of Kali's three-fold divinity. The Hindus say that if one cannot love Kali's dark face, then one cannot hope to become enlightened.

Kali commands the gunas, or threads of Creation, Preservation, and Destruction, and embodies the past, present, and future. These gunas are symbolized by threads of white, red, and black. She is said to control the weather by braiding or releasing her hair. Her karmic wheel devours time itself.

Kali is pictured with black skin and a hideous face smeared with blood, four arms, and bare breasts. She wears a necklace of skulls and is draped with snakes. Her brow has a third eye. Her four hands hold weapons and heads. Violence against any woman is forbidden by her. This goddess rules over sexual activities, dark magick, fear, revenge, regeneration, and reincarnation.

Cast your circle as usual if this is to be part of a regular ritual. A cast circle isn't necessary, though. This ritual is asking to be shown what past lives influence the present one. You are also contemplating physical death, which you have experienced many times, so that you can understand that physical death is not an absolute end.

You will need a cauldron, a black cloth, a black or indigo candle.

Set the cauldron in the center of your altar. Cover the cauldron with a black cloth. Have a black or indigo candle near the cauldron. Stand in silence, looking at the covered cauldron. See it as a symbol of the end of a physical life, but also the container of a sacred Mystery—the beginning of another life.

Slowly remove the cloth from the cauldron and say:

> *Kali Ma is the dancer of death.*
> *Her belly is the cauldron of rebirth.*
> *Beneath her stamping, dancing feet all humans die.*
> *She presses out the life-blood like wine.*
> *No human may escape her Dance of Death in Life.*

Set the black or indigo candle inside the cauldron and light it.

> *Yet Kali Ma is also the Great Mother.*
> *Out of her cauldron comes new life on the wheel of karma.*
> *Her Dance of Death in Life returns us to her warm, dark embrace*
> *That we may rest, may set new goals for another life.*
> *When our rest is done, Kali dances her Dance of Life in Death*
> *And we are once more reborn.*
> *To truly love the Goddess, we must love her Dark aspect*
> *as well as the Light.*
> *To gain complete spiritual understanding, we must honor all her faces.*

Contemplate the beauty and mysteries of the Dark Goddess, the necessity of her existence for your spiritual growth. Then press your hands together and bow toward the cauldron.

Great Kali Ma, show me my past lives
That I may learn from them.
I seek your help and guidance that I may not repeat
Old patterns and past mistakes.
Show me what is needful, Great Kali Ma.

Now is the time for meditation on past lives. Don't try to direct where you go or what you see. Let it flow.

When you are finished with the meditation, say:

Your cauldron of rebirth boils with your power.
Your dance of death is a dance of regeneration.
Black Mother, I honor you in all your aspects.
Through you comes rebirth of the mind, of the heart, as well as of the body.

Feast of the Einheriar

This is a Feast of Fallen Warriors. The Einheriar were the fallen warriors who went to Valhalla, the Norse heaven for brave warriors whether men or women. This roughly corresponds to our Veterans' Day. This remembrance, however, is in honor of all heroes, not just those who fell in battle.

You will need your regular ritual tools for circle casting. Other items needed are cookies in animal and human shapes as a symbolic sacrifice, a plate of bread and salt, an apple, a cauldron, and three candles (black, red, white). Set the cauldron in the center of your altar with the white candle inside it. Place the black candle to the right of the cauldron and the red candle on the left.

Cast your circle as usual. After calling upon the guardians of the quarters, stand before the altar.

Light the black candle. Salute the altar with your sword or athame. Say:

This is the time to honor all fallen warriors. Great Odhinn, Allfather, you
who have gathered to you all brave warriors who die in battle, I salute you.

Light the red candle to the left of the cauldron. Salute the altar with your sword. Say:

Freyja, Queen of the Valkyries, you who have gathered your share of the
fallen heroes, I salute you.

Light the white candle. Salute the altar again with your sword. Say:

> *Hail to the fallen warriors who now dwell in Valhalla. I honor your
> courage, your willingness to die in defense of your family, your property,
> your community, your country. Well do I know that brave warriors do not
> all fall in wars. Well do I understand that not all heroes are men. Heroes
> sacrifice themselves as policemen on the streets. They greet the Valkyries
> when rescuing others in peril. They meet the Allfather as firemen on duty.
> They answer Freyja's call as parents defending their children. The fallen
> warriors of Valhalla have walked all paths of life, yet because of their deeds
> were found worthy by the Valkyries, those warrior-women who see the
> truth in the heart of each person.*

Lay the sword before the altar. Take up the dagger and apple:

> *As there is death in life, so must there be life in death. The symbol of the
> Lady and life eternal is hidden inside the sacred fruit of Idunn, the
> Maiden. Only those who seek and know may find it.*

Cut the apple crosswise to reveal the pentagram made by the core and seeds:

> *Behold! The star of Life! Symbol of the Triple Goddess who, with the
> Allfather, brings forth new beginnings out of the cauldron of
> death and rebirth.*

Eat part of the apple, saving the rest to be placed outside for the birds and animals:

> *The secret of this sacred fruit is forbidden only to those who walk in
> darkness. Those who turn away from the great knowledge that life
> never ends shall not understand the Mystery. Like a dried Autumn
> seed, each passing soul falls into the sacred cauldron, to rest, then
> to be reborn in another time and place.*

Lift high the plate of bread and salt. Say:

> *Behold, the staples of life! The seed of grain which must die in the soil
> to produce new grain. The grain which is ground and baked into bread
> to sustain the body. Salt which is mined from the Earth, which is tasted
> in tears and blood. Salt which preserves food and enriches life. Each
> time I taste salt and bread may I remember that all life turns in
> cycles of life and death.*

Dip a piece of bread into the salt and eat it. Raise the plate of cookies high, then set it on the altar. Go to the East. Salute by holding up your hand, say:

> *Rulers of Air, give your blessings to the fallen warriors. Grant them rest in Spring fields caressed by gentle breezes.*

Go to the South. Salute with your hand and say:

> *Rulers of Fire, give your blessings to the fallen warriors. Grant them sunny days and warm nights of feasting.*

Move to the West and salute that direction. Say:

> *Rulers of Water, give your blessings to the fallen warriors. Grant them warm pools of refreshing water where they may dream of rebirth.*

Finally, go to the North. Salute and say:

> *Rulers of Earth, give your blessings to the fallen warriors. Grant them changing seasons, green forests, and sweet meadow flowers to soothe their minds and spirits.*

Return to stand before the altar. Hold up your hand once more and say:

> *Great Odhinn, you who see beyond all actions to the truth, carry my greetings and blessings to the heroes of Valhalla. Although we may grieve their loss among us, yet do we rejoice that they rest with you. Let them know they are not forgotten.*

Now raise both arms and say:

> *Great Freyja, Queen of the Valkyries, you who know the secrets of life and death and rebirth, carry my words to the heroes of Valhalla. Teach them what they must know in preparation for their return in another form to this world. Let them know they are not forgotten.*

Close the circle as usual. Put out your offering of leftover bread for the Nature spirits. Tie the cookies and pieces of the apple to tree limbs for the birds and animals. If it is appropriate and acceptable to your thinking, visit the graves of these loved ones.

Forest Goddess

The Forest Goddess is an aspect of many goddesses. She is the spirit that protects and nourishes all woodlands and their creatures. She is often seen in the company of the Horned God, Pan, Faunus, Puck, and Cernunnos. By honoring her, you show your respect and appreciation for her work.

The most obvious way of honoring the Forest Goddess is to treat her realms with respect. Don't litter. Be careful with fire. Don't wantonly harm her creatures or the woodlands. If you must cut plants or trees, leave a gift of milk and honey, and ask first! I don't approve of hunting animals, unless it is necessary. If you do hunt, be sure to thank the goddess and the spirit of the killed animal. Native Americans have the right idea about this. And if you hunt, don't waste what you have taken.

If you want to wander the woodlands and feel welcomed by the Forest Goddess, take a little bag of fertilizer with you. When you find a spot that appeals to you for contemplation, sit down with your back to a tree. Listen carefully to the sounds of Nature. Feel the strength of the tree as it lets part of its energy slide into you. Feel the power of the Earth seeping up through your body. Send your love out to all the woodlands. I don't recommend meditating outdoors unless you can be sure of no danger.

When you rise to leave, sprinkle the fertilizer around the tree where you sat. This offering will be well received. You may even be given the unexpected gift of a leaf or nut falling at your feet. Thank the tree and the Forest Goddess for letting you renew yourself in the woodlands.

Night of Hecate

The goddess Hecate was a deity of the night, crossroads, life and death. She was called Most Lovely One, the Distant One, Queen of the World of Spirits, goddess of witchcraft. To the Thracians especially, Hecate was goddess of the Moon, the dark hours, and the Underworld. Midwives were connected with her.

Some myths say Hecate was the daughter of the Titans Tartaros and Night; other versions say of Perseus and Asteria (Starry-Night), or of Zeus and Hera. We do know her worship did not originate in Greece.

One of her sacred animals was the toad, a symbol of conception. She was called the goddess of transformations as she ruled over the various passages of life, and could change forms or ages. Hecate was considered to be the third aspect of the Moon, the Hag or Crone (Carrier of Wisdom). The Greeks called Hecate the Hag of the Dead.[1] An ally of Zeus, she was accompanied by a pack of hounds.

As an aspect of the Amazon goddess, Hecate's chariot was pulled by dragons. Her symbols were the key and the cauldron. The women who worshipped her often stained their palms and soles with henna. Her festivals were held at night by torchlight. Every year on the island of Aegina in the Saronic Gulf, a mysterious festival was held in her honor.

This was a huntress goddess who knew her way in the realms of spirits; all secret powers of Nature were at her command. The Greeks and Thracians said she had control over birth, life, and death. Hecate was called the patroness of priestesses, goddess of witches. She was associated with healing, prophecies, visions, magick, the Dark Moon, dark magick, charms and spells, vengeance, averting evil, riches, victory, wisdom, transformation, purification, choices, renewal and regeneration.

You will need a ritual dagger, a small cauldron, an apple, a piece of black cloth, and a small amount of salt, in addition to your regular ritual items. Put the apple in the cauldron and cover the cauldron with the black cloth. Cast your circle as usual.

With the wand in your power hand, tap the cauldron five times. Say:

> *Hecate, Wise One, I ask your blessings.*
> *Lift the Veil for me that I may greet my spirit helpers,*
> *Long-ago friends from other lives, and those who are new.*
> *Let only those who wish me well enter within this sacred place.*

Uncover the cauldron. Take out the apple, raise it in offering, and lay it on the altar.

> *Hecate, your magick cauldron is the well of death and rebirth,*
> *An experience each of us undergoes again and again.*
> *Let there be no fear in me, for I know your gentleness.*
> *Here is your secret symbol of life in death.*

Cut the apple crosswise with the dagger. Contemplate the revealed pentagram in the core. Put the two halves of the apple back into the cauldron and cover them again with the black cloth.

> *Only the initiated may know your hidden Mysteries.*
> *Only the true seekers may find the spiral way.*
> *Only those who know your many secret faces*
> *May find the Light that leads to the Inner Way.*

Put a pinch of salt on your tongue:

> *I am mortal, yet immortal.*
> *There is no end to life, only new beginnings.*
> *I walk beside the Goddess in her many forms.*
> *Therefore, I have nothing to fear.*

Open my mind and heart and soul
To the Deep Mysteries of the Cauldron, O Hecate.

Do a meditation on seeking the Dark Moon goddess. Listen to her messages. Be aware of any new guides and teachers who may come through to help you.

Goddess of Skills
— Crescent Moon —

The Celtic goddess Brigit was sometimes called a Triple Goddess. In Britain she became known as the Three Mothers or the Three Blessed Ladies. Her sacred shrines, such as the one at Kildare, were served by female virgins, much like the Vesta Virgins of Rome. One of the tasks of these priestesses was to keep burning an eternal flame. Brigit was the patroness of the Bards, the goddess of poetry, the arts, crafts, smithcraft, agriculture, childbirth, agriculture, inventions, and healing. Certain wells and springs became sacred to Brigit as healing waters. Many of these wells and springs can still be seen today in Ireland and Britain.

The Icelandic rune the wishing well is a charm that has a lunar origin; the four "dippers" at the edge of the well are Crescent Moons. Making a wish at a sacred well, followed by an offering, was a form of prayer to the resident Water-deity, usually a goddess.

Icelandic Wishing Well Rune

Carefully draw out the Icelandic rune of the wishing well on a small piece of paper while thinking of a specific wish you would like fulfilled. Fold the paper around a silver coin, with the coin in the center of the wishing well. Say:

Crafts and skills, make me endowed
Of knowledge old that makes me proud
To use my hands. O, Brigit, great,
Put your skills within my fate.

Tap the paper and coin with your wand. Say:

I call upon the goddess of Bards,
Great one of skill and creativity.
Give me to drink from your sacred well
That my arts may grow and flourish.
With wand I invoke you.
With chant I bless you.
Come, Brigit of gifts great and wondrous.

Place the folded paper and coin in a bag or envelope and carry with you until the wish is granted. When it has been fulfilled, remove the coin and burn the paper.

African Great Mother
—Full Moon—

Mawu of Africa was the Supreme Goddess, the creatress of all things. The god Lisa is often spoken of as her son. It is said that she sent him to Earth to teach humankind useful arts and to watch that they observed her rules. But Mawu is considered a gentle goddess, as seen in the proverb, "Lisa punishes, Mawu forgives." The Fon of Benin in West Africa worship Mawu as Moon goddess.

Place a one-sided mirror face up on the altar between two lighted blue candles. On the mirror set a picture of the person or animal to be healed. If you don't have a picture, at least have a piece of paper with the person's name on it. Lay a crystal on the picture or paper.

With the wand in your power hand, hold it over the mirror, crystal, and picture. Say:

You are cleansed. You are purified.
You are healed. You are whole.
By the powers of the Ancient Healers,
By the great powers of Mawu,
All wrong is made right.

Lay aside the wand. Take up the mirror and picture. Hold the picture so that it faces the reflecting side of the mirror. Say:

*The Great Mother Mawu and all the Great Healers see your image as
whole and complete again.
Look into the mirror of Mawu, (person's name).
See yourself as you are seen by the Gentle Mother.*

Lay the mirror on the altar with the picture face down upon it. Leave them there overnight. In the morning, bury or burn the picture and cast the ashes to the winds.

The Lioness
—Dark Moon—

Sekhmet of Egypt was known as the Terrible One, the Powerful, the Beloved of Ptah. As a lioness-headed goddess, she was the dark sister of Bast, representing the destroy-

ing power of the Sun. She was crowned with a disk and a coiled cobra. Sekhmet ruled over war and battle, and physicians and bone-setters.

The lion was sacred to Sekhmet. The Egyptians listed other lion deity names as Aker, Ari-Hes-Nefer, Urt-Hekau, Hebi, and Ma-Hes. These may be aspects of the goddess Sekhmet.

Sometimes you need a quick protection and don't have the time or opportunity to do a complete banishing and protection ritual. If you do these chants with enough conviction and emotion, you should immediately attract the attention of the goddess Sekhmet and gain her aid.

*Ramses II offers flowers to
the goddess Sekhmet*

Grasp whatever talisman you are wearing and chant softly:

*Lady of the lion, of battle and the sword,
Sekhmet, goddess terrible, set 'round protective ward.
Break all the walls enclosing me. Help to set me free
Of enemies and obstacles. Great Lady, do help me.*

Picture Sekhmet with her lioness's head, her sharp teeth showing. Feel her standing right behind you, her arms stretched over you in protection, her claw-like nails ready to tear your enemies.

Lioness of destruction and revenge,
My enemies crowd about me, seeking my downfall.
Release me from their powers. Grant me freedom.
O Powerful and Terrible One, beloved of Ptah,
Hear my plea for protection.

Endnotes

1. The word "hag" may have come from the Egyptian word *heq*, meaning a matriarchal ruler who knew magickal words of power.

Chapter 16

Chapter 16
COLD MOON
December

Also called: Oak Moon, Wolf Moon, Moon of Long Nights,
Long Night's Moon, Aerra Geola (Month Before Yule),
Wintermonat (Winter Month), Heilagmanoth (Holy Month),
Big Winter Moon, Moon of Popping Trees.

Dec. 1: Day of Pallas Athene/Minerva in Greece and Rome.

Dec. 3: The Roman Feast of Bona Dea (the Good Goddess), deity of justice.

Dec. 8: Festival of Ixchel among the Maya. Festival of Neith in Egypt. The Astraea in Greece, for the goddess Astraea, deity of justice.

Dec. 10: Festival of Lux Mundi (Light of the World), honoring the Roman goddess Liberty.

Dec. 13: St. Lucia or Lucy's Day in Sweden.

Dec. 17-23: The Saturnalia in Rome.

Dec. 19: The Opalia, for Ops, in Rome; success and fertility. The Pongol in India; the Hindu Solstice festival to Sarasvati.

Dec. 21: Winter Solstice. Celtic Festival of the Stars. Osiris' return to Isis in Egypt.

Dec. 23: Day of Hathor in Egypt. The Night of Lamps, or final entombment of Osiris, in Egypt.

Dec. 24: Modresnach or Mother Night among the Anglo-Saxons. Night of the Mothers in Germany.

Dec. 25: End of Saturnalia in Rome. Day of the Geniae in Greece; Athene also honored. Celebration of Astarte in the Semitic countries.

Dec. 26: Birthday of Horus in Egypt.

Dec. 27: Birth of the Norse Freyja.

Dec. 31: Hecate's Day in Rome. Lucky Day of Sekhmet in Egypt. The Norns in Scandinavia. Faery of the Van in Wales. Hogmanay in Scotland; ward off evil spirits by wearing costumes, such as hides and horns. In Sicily for Strenia, goddess of gifts. In France for Dame Abonde for presents. In Mexico called Wishing Night.

*D*ecem was the tenth month on the old Roman calendar, the month containing the care-free Saturnalia. The Franks called it Heilagmanoth, or Holy Month, because of its large number of sacred festivals. On the old Tibetan calendar December 1 was the beginning of a new year.

The ancient Mayan goddess Ixchel is still honored in southern Mexico with processions and rituals that bless boats and fields. She was also known as Lady Unique Circular Darkness, Lady Splotch of Blood, Lady of the Night, and Lady All Embracer. Her worship at one time extended through southern Mexico, the Yucatan Peninsula, and as far as El Salvador.

In Sweden, the Sun goddess Lucina is still honored on St. Lucy's Day. At daybreak a daughter of the house wears a candle crown and serves the family with cakes. There are processions and treats. Young girls often wear white dresses, and many of the men dress as elves, who are known as Lucy's helpers.

The very ancient god Saturn was honored at the Roman Saturnalia, a seven day celebration. He was pictured with a half-bare chest and a sickle or ears of corn in his hand. His consort was the goddess Ops, deity of fertility. Gifts were exchanged, and there was much wine and singing. It was a time of temporary freedom for slaves, when they could supposedly say what they wished to their owners. This festival is the origin of all carnivals and revels that we still observe today.

The Winter Solstice, a time when the Sun turns from its fall into darkness back into gaining light, was and is celebrated around the world. Around the world it is the time when Virgin mothers give birth to sacred sons: Rhiannon to Pryderi; Isis to Horus; Demeter to Persephone. In Japan it was the time when the hiding Sun goddess Amaterasu came out of her cave. The birth of Horus was celebrated about December 23, shortly after Winter Solstice, the time of Osiris's final entombment. At this time of the year, Isis and Nephthys were said to have circled the shrine of Osiris seven times, symbolizing their mourning and search for his scattered body parts. Set was driven away by the shaking of Isis's sistrum.

In the ancient Middle East countries, celebration of the Great Goddess Astarte goes back to Neolithic times. This goddess was called Athtar by the Arabs, Attar-Samayin in Aramaic, Ashtoreth by the Canaanites. She was known as the morning star, the celestial ruler, mother of all the gods.

Mother Night, or Modresnach (Anglo-Saxon), was a Germanic-Scandinavian festival. Many of its traditions still live on in our present Christmas celebrations. The decorated evergreen tree was a symbol of the Tree of Life, or World Tree. The crackling Yule log was lit in honor of the returning Sun. The star atop the tree represented the pole star of the Star Goddess. The dinners and gifts were in honor of the food and prosperity given by the Mother Goddesses to their human children. The elves connected with our current Santa Claus are remnants of the supernatural Nature folk of the Old Religion. The reindeer are symbols of old shamanic abilities used by the people. The mistletoe is said to have first been picked and used to collect kisses by the goddess Frigg, before it became a weapon to kill her son.

In the Slavonic cultures, the festival of Koleda began at Winter Solstice and lasted for ten days. In Russia, this festival was called Kutuja, which was later applied to Christmas Eve. Although the Slavonic name comes from the god Kolyada, it was in honor of the goddess Lada, the goddess of love, Spring, youth, and fertility. She was said to be reborn each year at this time. Each family burned a Yule log and invited their personal household gods to join in the festivities. Groups of children went from house to house singing; as a reward, they were given little gifts. One of the big events was the use of prophecy for the coming year.

In Scotland, December 31 is still called Hogmanay; it is the Scottish New Year. Traditional foods served at this time are: bannocks, oarsmen, shortbread, black buns, and ankersocks (a type of gingerbread). A long time ago it was customary for the men to dress in animal skins, often wearing horns or antlers. At midnight people opened all the doors and windows in their homes to let out the old and let in the new.

In Wales, some people still believe that the Cwn Annwn, or the Underworld hounds, run through the air at midnight New Year's Eve, looking for victims to carry back to their master. Pots and pans are banged to drive these supernatural animals away.

In the Incan civilization, the great feast of Capac Raymi, or Magnificent Festival, was held at the Solstice. This month was also a time for the Huarachico, or puberty ceremony for young boys.

In the Southern Hemisphere, this Solstice was equal to the Summer Solstice in the North. In Tahiti, they celebrated the parara'a matahiti, or first-fruit festival, honoring the god of Paradise, Roma-tane. In Tonga, there was a similar festival where the men indulged in wrestling, club-fighting, and boxing. In Fiji, they said that at this time of year the Lord from the Underworld came to push the yam shoots through the soil.

This is a month for contemplating the coming new year and what one plans to do with it. Ideas are formed and allowed to germinate until the new year has started, but one must begin thinking about it.

Correspondences

Nature Spirits: snow faeries, storm faeries, winter tree faeries

Herbs: holly, English ivy, fir, mistletoe

Colors: blood red, white and black

Flowers: holly, poinsettia, Christmas cactus

Scents: violet, patchouli, rose geranium, frankincense, myrrh, lilac

Stones: serpentine, jacinth, peridot

Trees: pine, fir, holly

Animals: mouse, deer, horse, bear

Birds: rook, robin, snowy owl

Deities: Hathor, Hecate, Neith, Athene, Minerva, Ixchel, Osiris, Norns, Fates

Power Flow: to endure, die, be reborn; Earth tides turning. Darkness. Personal alchemy. Spiritual paths. Reach out to friends and family, the lonely and needy

Old Sayings & Lore

- The Irish say never cut your hair, begin a journey, move into a new house, start a business, or cut out a dress on a Friday in particular, and especially if a New or Full Moon falls on a Friday.
- In Ireland it is said that if you walk nine times around a faery rath or hill at the Full Moon, you will be able to find the entrance.
- The name Mount St. Helens means "Moon Mountain."
- The word "create" comes from the same word-root as the word "crescent."

- In some legends, the Egyptians said that the Dark Moon and the Full Moon were the two eyes of Horus.

- The horseshoe is a symbol of the lunar crescent. Certain ancient British coins had the horse and the crescent on them. For the horseshoe, and the Crescent Moon, to be lucky and hold the luck, the horns must be turned upward.

- The natives of Madagascar call their isle the Island of the Moon.

- To aim at the Moon means to be very ambitious, to set your sights extremely high.

- The feldspar gem known as moonstone is said to become brighter and clearer when the Moon is full.

- The eastern branches of the Eskimo clans say that their people came from the Moon to Earth.

Recipes

Bourbon Balls

This recipe makes about thirty one-inch candies, but be warned that they won't last long.

1	6-ounce package semisweet chocolate pieces	½ cup sugar
3	tablespoons light corn syrup	1¼ cups crushed vanilla wafer cookies (about 36)
¼	cup bourbon	1 cup finely chopped pecans

In a double boiler, melt the chocolate pieces, stirring constantly. Remove pan from the heat. Blend in the corn syrup and bourbon; stir in the sugar, vanilla wafers, and pecans until well blended. Allow to cool slightly. Pat about 1 teaspoon of the mixture into a ball with your hands. Roll each ball in the remaining sugar and place on a cookie sheet. Cover and chill several hours. To store, put in a wide-mouthed jar with a tight-fitting lid.

Cheese Logs

2	3-ounce packages cream cheese	½ teaspoon grated or dried onion
1	5-ounce jar smoky cheese spread	½ teaspoon Worcestershire sauce
1	5-ounce jar sharp Cheddar spread	¼ cup undiluted evaporated milk
1	5-ounce jar Roquefort cheese spread	½ cup finely chopped pecans or walnuts

Let the four cheeses stand at room temperature for an hour or so. Put them in a bowl with the onion and Worcestershire sauce. Mix with a fork until smooth and well-blended (I usually use my hands). Stir in milk, a little at a time, until blended in thoroughly. Cover and chill until firm—overnight or about 4 hours. Shape into long rolls about 2" thick. Roll each cheese-roll in the chopped nuts. Wrap in waxed paper or saran wrap and chill until ready to serve with crackers.

Scottish Shortbread

1½	cups sifted all-purpose flour	1	cup (2 sticks) butter
1½	cups sifted powdered sugar		

Sift the flour and powdered sugar into a medium size bowl; cut in the butter until the mixture is crumbly. Work the dough into a ball with your hands and knead about 10 minutes. Pat the dough into a ¼" thick rectangle, 14"x12", on a large ungreased cookie sheet. Cut into 2" squares or diamonds with a sharp knife. Decorate with colored candies, if desired. Bake at 300° F for 45 minutes or until firm and lightly golden.

Recut the shortbread at the marks and separate very carefully. Handle with extreme care! Remove from the pan to a wire rack. Store with waxed paper between the layers in a container with a tight-fitting lid. If stored for a few weeks, this shortbread mellows to a delicate delicious taste.

Crafts

Frosted Holly Leaves

In the 1800s this craft provided decoration when fresh flowers were not available. Tucked in among mistletoe and fir boughs, frosted holly leaves are quite pretty.

Choose the nice stems and leaves of the holly, and wipe them with a clean dry cloth. Dry them thoroughly but do not allow to shrivel. Dip the edges of each leaf in thin clear glue, then sprinkle with coarse sugar. Leave to dry in a warm place.

Rose Sachet

2	ounces cornstarch	1	ounce talc
½	ounce powdered orris root	2	drops rose oil
¼	teaspoon cinnamon		

Cornucopia

Cornucopias and Cornets

The cornucopia is also called the horn of plenty, originally used by the Greeks as a decoration. A large one can be made by rolling a sheet of fairly stiff paper into a cone shape and taping the edges. Then lay it on its side and fill it to overflowing with candies, fruits, and small decorations. If you embellish it with lace, trim, ribbon, and/or gold foil, it makes a beautiful centerpiece.

Small cornets, or cones, can be made in the same way and used as tree decorations. Attach a strip of ribbon to the open top on opposite sides for hanging. These can hold small gifts, candy, etc.

Christmas Tree Sachet

5 ounces cornstarch
1 ounce powdered benzoin gum
1 drop bergamot oil
½ teaspoon cinnamon

3 ounces talc
1 drop pine oil
¼ teaspoon nutmeg

Yule Potpourri

4 ounces peppermint leaves
1 ounce powdered benzoin gum
½ teaspoon cinnamon

2 ounces rose petals
1 teaspoon vanilla

French Hot Pot Potpourri

4 ounces jasmine flowers	2 ounces violets
1 ounce rue	1 ounce cut orris root
1 vanilla bean	

India Cologne

1 pint distilled water	4 ounces alcohol
1 ounce sandalwood powder	1 ounce glycerin
1 tablespoon powdered myrrh gum	1 tablespoon powdered frankincense gum
1 drop patchouli oil	1 drop tonka bean extract
¼ teaspoon nutmeg	½ teaspoon cinnamon

Royal Japanese Cologne

1 pint distilled water	¼ pint alcohol
1 ounce glycerin	1 drop cherry oil
1 drop carnation oil	1 drop oleander oil
1 drop rose oil	1 teaspoon vanilla
1 drop synthetic musk oil	

Myths

The Birth of Horus

After the goddess Isis recovered the body of her husband/brother, she took it to the swamps of Buto in the Nile Delta. There she hid it from the vengeful Set. Isis had learned strong magick from the greatest magician, Thoth. She called upon that magick to make light with her hair and stirred the air over Osiris with her winged arms. This magick reanimated the body long enough for her to conceive a child. Now, more than ever, Isis needed to remain hidden from Set, for the evil god would surely destroy the rightful heir to Egypt's throne.

When it came time for the child Horus to be born, Isis was attended only by the cobra goddess Buto. Buto helped Isis to hide the child from Set and to raise him in the swamps. As a child, Horus was exposed to many dangers. He was attacked and bitten by wild beasts, stung by scorpions, burned, and suffered with intense intestinal pains. Thoth drove out the scorpion's poison; his mother's great powers saved him at other times.

One day while Isis was away from the body of Osiris, Set found it while hunting in the swamps. He cut the body into fourteen pieces and scattered them throughout Egypt. Isis was heartbroken. She searched until she found all the pieces except his phallus, which had been eaten by a Nile crab. She and her sister Nephthys joined the pieces together and, with the help of her nephew Anubis, the grand vizier Thoth, and her young son Horus, performed the first embalming. Osiris then ascended to the immortal world and became king of the dead and the Moon.

Saturn

Saturn is a very ancient Roman god, also known as Father Time, Father of the Gods, the Great Lesson-Giver, and Ruler of the Golden Age. Today, his name is mostly familiar through astrology; people dread being told that Saturn is forcing them to learn lessons and balance karma.

Saturn was a working god and an agricultural deity, besides his other duties. He is often shown with either a sickle or ears of corn in his hands. His consort was the fertility goddess Ops. His annual festival of the Saturnalia saw a general suspension of public activity. No law courts or schools were open; commercial and military operations were suspended.

His temple in Rome was near the Capitol; the State treasury was kept there, as well as the standards of the legions not on campaign. Except for during the Saturnalia, the god's statue was bound tight with woolen bands to prevent him leaving Roman territory.

The image of this god has survived into modern times as the hooded and bearded figure of Father Time at New Year's Eve. The sickle has become the scythe, and the hourglass symbolizes his control over time itself. Rather than look upon Saturn as a figure of dread, we should consider him as the greatest teacher we can have. Time gone by cannot be reclaimed. Use it wisely.

Saturn

Sekhmet, the Lion-Headed

This Egyptian goddess was called "the terrible one," the Powerful, the Beloved of Ptah. She represented the destroying power of the Sun and was crowned with a disk and coiled cobra. Although she was the goddess of war and battles, she was also patroness of physicians and bone-setters. As an aspect of Hathor, she once nearly annihilated humans for disrespect to Ra.

At this time of year, when the Sun's rays are weakest, Sekhmet presents a more gentle side. Like many Sun gods, her life and powers seem to ebb and flow with the yearly cycles of the Sun. However, Sekhmet is never to be treated lightly. Her power always deserves the utmost respect and consideration before calling upon her aid. In Egyptian legend it is said she torments the evil and law-breakers in the Underworld. Today, she can be called upon to right wrongs, not by our narrow standards, but by her more expansive ones. She is a protector of the under-dog and the helpless. Social status means nothing to her when she sets out to balance the scales of justice.

The Norns

The Scandinavian Norns are similar in many ways to the Greek Fates. This trio of goddesses guard the Well of Urd which lies under a root of the World Tree Yggdrasil in Asgard. The Norn Urd (Fate) was defined as "that which is becoming"; Verthandi (Necessity) as "that which is becoming"; Skuld (Being) as "that which should become." Predestination and predetermination were unknown to the Norse. They believed that what each person did influenced her/his future.

The Norns were almost as important as the Aesir themselves. In fact, these goddesses were said to weave the destinies of men, gods, giants, dwarfs, and every other living being. Each day the Norse gods held their council at this Well in the presence of the Norns.

It is rare for a person to know exactly where their future is going, including all the sidetracks that we invariably go on. It is difficult to even get a clear glimpse of the broader picture. Learning to work with the Norns and listen to their advice is important to avoid major pitfalls. If they point out coming problems, and we manage to change our life direction to avoid them, then we have taken responsibility in the molding of our future. If the problems revealed by the Norns seem to stay in our path regardless of our efforts, then we must work through them, learning the necessary lessons.

Rituals

Rebirth of the Lost Lord
—Winter Solstice—

Many cultures celebrated the rebirth of a god at the Winter Solstice. In fact, most of the Christian story was lifted almost word for word from an ancient Hindu myth. Some of it was also taken from the celebration of Mithras, the Sun god, who was worshipped by the Roman armies as far away as Britain. Mithras' birthday was celebrated on December 25.

The Winter Solstice is a turning point of the Earth tides. The Sun is at its lowest point. If you wish, you can use a nativity set to represent the Great Mother, her consort, and the newborn Sun Child. After all, this idea has been around much longer than Christianity.

If you have others celebrating with you, give them the parts to answer for the Mother and the Elemental Powers.

Use as many candles as possible around your ritual area. Cast your circle as usual. Have an extra white candle on the altar.

Light the white candle and carry it to the East, say:

> *O Powers of Air, I seek the newborn Child.*
> *Is he within your realm?*
> *The Powers of Air answer:*
> *Follow the star to the hidden cave.*

Go to the South, say:

> *O Powers of Fire, I seek the newborn Child.*
> *Is he within your realm?*
> *The Powers of Fire answer:*
> *Follow the star to the hidden cave.*

Go to the West, say:

> *O Powers of Water, I seek the newborn Child.*
> *Is he within your realm?*
> *The Powers of Water answer:*
> *Follow the star to the hidden cave.*

Finish by going to the North, say:

> *O Powers of Earth, I seek the newborn Child.*
> *Is he within your realm?*
> *The Powers of Earth answer:*
> *Follow the star to the hidden cave.*

Return to the altar and set the white candle inside the cauldron.

> *I have searched everywhere for the newborn Child,*
> *Yet I have not found him.*
> *Behold, the Great Mother speaks words of wisdom:*
> *Seek the Holy Child of Light within the hidden cave of your heart,*
> *For ever is he there, and not without.*

Raise your arms in praise and say:

> *I have found the Child!*
> *He is always with me, wherever I may be.*
> *All praise and honor to the Lord of Light!*
> *All praise and honor to the Lady and her consort!*

Close the circle.

Success & Prosperity

This spellworking is best done during the waxing Moon or on the Full Moon. The first Full Moon after the Winter Solstice is considered to be the most powerful one of the whole year. Have ready a small green or brown talisman bag and three silver coins. Set the cauldron on the pentacle. Place a small dish inside the cauldron with a small amount of cinnamon and cedar chips on it. Beside the cauldron, lay your wand.

Tap each coin with the wand as you chant:

> *Glistening silver, coin of the Moon,*
> *Shiny and round, bring me a boon.*
> *Draw to my hands many more of your kind.*
> *Multiply, grow, like the image in my mind.*

Place the coins in the cauldron with the herbs. Stir the air clockwise seven times over the cauldron. Chant:

> *Earth elementals, cunning and bright,*
> *With me share your treasures here on this night.*
> *Share with me riches of silver and gold,*
> *Successes, prosperity, all I can hold.*

Put the coins and the herbs in the talisman bag.

Birth of Freyja

The Norse Vana-Goddess Freyja was very important to the welfare and existence of the Gods. This went far beyond her aspect as a fertility goddess, for there was a long series of battles between the Gods and the Giants over Freyja. Freyja had many names: Syr, Lady, Great Goddess, Mardoll (She who shines over the sea). She was the sister of Freyr and the daughter of the sea god Njord.

Myths hint at her marriage to a mysterious god named Od who disappeared. Although Freyja is linked closely with the powerful Odhinn, she is not his wife, nor the wife of any god. When she weeps, her tears fall as drops of gold; when the tears fall into the sea, they become amber. Her magickal cats, Bygul (Bee-gold, honey) and Trjegul (Tree-gold, amber), pull her chariot, but she also has a battle-boar (Hildisvini) which she rode. She owns the necklace Brisingamen and keeps half of the slain warriors in her hall.

Freyja is the mistress of cats, leader of the Valkyries, a shape-shifter, and the Sage or "sayer" who inspires all sacred poetry. Thirteen is her number and Friday her day. Her special magick seidr was primarily women's magick, a type of shamanism and prophecy. Some myths hint that the runes were hers long before Odhinn gained them.

Freyja has power over love, beauty, animals, sex, cats, childbirth, fire, horses, enchantments, witchcraft, gold, wealth, trance, jewelry, wisdom, foresight, magick, luck, long life, fertility, the Moon, the sea, death, music, poetry, and protection.

To petition Freyja for aid in developing psychic talents and performing magick, anoint a green candle with juniper or pine oil, working from the wick to the bottom. Wear a necklace or pendant of amber in honor of Brisingamen; or at least hold a piece of amber in your hand. Wear a green robe or one with green in it. Sit in a comfortable chair where you will not be disturbed. Chant:

She-Falcon! The Moon sails through the trees.
Freyja! I call the weeper of gold!
Lady of Sorcery! I stand before you unafraid.
Keeper of Brisingamen! Reveal to me secrets of knot and braid.
Freyja! Moon Goddess! Queen of the Valkyries!
Give me the key to deep magicks.

Close your eyes and breathe deeply. Feel your body relax. Before you will be a brilliant door of light. Visualize yourself walking through it. You are in Freyja's hall in Asgard. The goddess is sitting on her throne. There is a stool at her feet. She beckons to you, and you walk down the hall to sit on the stool. Spend as much time as Freyja allows talking with her and listening to her wisdom.

When you are dismissed, return through the door of light to your physical body. Breathe deeply again. Then repeat the chant and thank Freyja for her help.

Winter Faeries

During the Winter months, the Nature spirits usually sleep while their plants and trees sleep. However, if you make those of your area welcome within your home, they will spend the cold months inside with you, checking on their charges when needed. It may take some patience and coaxing, especially if previous dwellers were unsympathetic to their existence and unkind to their plants and trees. They are wonderful friends to both humans and animals. They are especially fond of small children.

The Little Ones are a good barometer to the state of vibrations in the house, also. If negatives get dragged or sent in, they become very quiet and withdrawn. They bring it to my attention if I don't notice right away.

This celebration for the Little Ones does not need a cast circle. You will need powdered ginger and a small spoon. Set out candles at the compass directions: yellow in the East; red in the South; blue in the West; green in the North. Place a crystal or other stone beside each candle. Stand in the center of the room and send out thoughts of welcome to the Little Ones. Chant:

O spirits of plants and Earth and trees,
O Little Ones of every form,
Show yourselves to me, I ask.
From me shall come no harm.
Join me in friendship and in love.

Rejoice with me in magick old,
For together with the Ancient Gods
We can re-create all things in gold.
Guardian spirits, watchers fair,
Our lives are joined. All things we share.

Go to the East. Sprinkle a little ginger by the candle, and say:

All you Nature spirits and faeries,
Hear my call.
Enter this magick circle.
Welcome, all.

Go to the South, sprinkle ginger, and say:

All you little ones of the sunbeams,
Hear my call.
Enter this magick circle.
Welcome, all.

Go to the West, sprinkle the ginger, and say:

All you nymphs and water sprites,
Hear my call.
Enter this magick circle.
Welcome, all.

Finish by going to the North. Sprinkle ginger and say:

All you little ones of the moonbeams,
Hear my call.
Enter this magick circle.
Welcome, all.

Sit quietly for a time, thinking about the Little Ones. Be aware of their feather-light touches on your body. Listen for their musical voices in your mind. Talk to them if you wish. When your communication is finished, stand in the center of the room. Raise your arms high, saying:

All thanks and blessings be,
To those of air, Earth, sky, and sea.

Wishing Night

The end of December was the celebration of Wishing Night in Mexico, when wishes were said to be granted to those who deserved them, rather like gifts from Santa Claus.

A Mayan god seated upon symbols for the moon

Since this falls on what we call New Year's Eve, it becomes a kind of combination gifts and resolutions time.

If it is safe for you to do so, go outside when it is completely dark. If it isn't safe or possible, at least stand near a window in a totally darkened room. Look up at the sky. Listen to the night sounds. Try to hear the music of the stars and the Moon. Think about the night as if you were in an isolated country with the dark woodlands nearby, the owls ghosting silently across the snow-covered hills. Let your primal being thrill to the call of wolves in the distance.

Have in mind what is important to you in the way of desires for the coming year and what things you would like to delete from your life. Don't be shy; this can include troublesome people. Just be prepared to accept what will come when your desires are answered.

Breathe each thing you want gone, one at a time, into the palm of your hand. Then blow them away into the darkened sky on the winter winds. Do the same with each desire you wish to enter your life. Take your time.

When you are finished, go inside and light a red candle. Place it in a safe place to burn out completely. This candle is a symbolic guiding spot to draw the desires to you.

Goddess of the New Dawn
— Crescent Moon —

Hebe was the youngest daughter of Zeus and Hera. Among the Romans she was called Juventas. She was the goddess of the dawn, the East, and youth. Hebe was cup-bearer to her father before Zeus brought the youth Ganymede to Olympus. Hebe was also a personal servant to her mother Hera, helping to yoke the goddess's chariot.

Before the goddess Hebe was replaced by the boy Ganymede, she served the Olympian Greek gods their nectar. The very lives of the deities depended upon their receiving this nectar. The Greeks called it the supernatural red wine of Hera, or the menstrual blood of the Great Mother. Many cultures around the world have tales of this "wine." In India it was called *soma;* in Britain, red claret of the Faery Queen; in ancient Egypt, it was *sa.* This drink spiritually represented the fact that everything, including the gods, came from the womb of the Great Mother.

Traditionally, claret was the drink of kings, a remnant of their being appointed by a priestess of the Great Mother. An old saying goes: "The man in the Moon drinks claret." The word claret means "enlightenment."

A self-initiation ritual is a very spiritual act. It can be repeated privately, whenever the individual feels that she/he has undergone so many personal changes that they are more or less beginning a new life. It is best done on or near a Full Moon.

Prepare yourself with meditation and silence for at least one hour before entering your ritual area. Wear a magickal robe or go nude. If possible, have your magickal name chosen and your magickal tools consecrated. If you have outgrown your original magickal name and wish to choose another, now is a time to present yourself under that name to the gods.

You will need the regular ritual tools, plus a bell or rattle, some frankincense oil and a piece of special jewelry. If you already have a consecrated talisman, you can recharge it at this time.

Cast your circle as usual and set up the directional guardians. When finished, face the East and raise your arms in greeting:

> *Behold, I stand beyond the Veil of Mysteries*
> *Where magick dwells and the Gods are near.*
> *The infinite circle of power and protection*
> *Is all around me.*

Stand with your feet together and arms outstretched. Say:

> *I call upon the Ancient Gods! I now stand before the temple Veil of Mysteries, awaiting the call to enter and be initiated. Hear my call, O Great Ones! True initiation comes from the Great Goddess and her consort. It is my desire to walk the secret paths of old, to stand within the pillared temples and receive instruction.*

Put a pinch of salt on your tongue. Say:

> *Although I am mortal, I know that I am loved and cared for by the Goddess and her consort. Through the Goddess, all women/men are born into*

*this world. In time all women/men must return to stand in the Hall of
Judgment before the Lords of Karma.*

Set the frankincense oil on the pentacle. Kneel before the altar and say:

> I, (magickal name), *come into this sacred temple of pillars for instruction.
> I dedicate my life to the Old Gods, whose powers are still strong. May the
> Lord and Lady witness my words!*

Rise, take the bell, and go to the East. Ring the bell three times, say:

> *Behold, O Guardian of the East.*
> I, (magickal name), *am a daughter/son of the Lord and Lady.*

Go to the South, ring the bell three times, say:

> *Behold, O Guardian of the South.*
> I, (magickal name), *am a daughter/son of the Lord and Lady.*

Move to the West, ring the bell three times and say:

> *Behold, O Guardian of the West.*
> I, (magickal name), *am a daughter/son of the Lord and Lady.*

Finally, go to the North, ring the bell three times and say:

> *Behold, O Guardian of the North.*
> I, (magickal name), *am a daughter/son of the Lord and Lady.*

Return to the altar. Take the oil and, with a drop on the forefinger of your power
hand, lightly anoint your forehead. Say:

> *May the goddess Athene expand my mind
> to encompass greater knowledge and magick.*

Anoint your upper lip. Say:

> *May the goddess Hera keep me silent among unbelievers.*

Anoint your heart, say:

> *May the god Apollo teach me truth in all things.*

Anoint the palms of your hands. Say:

*May the goddess Artemis guide
my hands to greater skills.*

Anoint the tops of your feet. Say:

*May the goddess Hecate place
my feet on magickal journeys.
Bless me, all you Ancient Ones!*

Stand in silence to receive the blessing. Lay your piece of jewelry on the pentacle, saying:

*Through the power of the God
and Goddess this (name of
jewelry) is blessed. Through it
shall come magickal power
from ancient temples and past
lives.*

Hebe

When this is finished, hold the wand over the jewelry and say:

*By the powers of the Goddess and her consort,
I bind all power within this circle
Into this (name jewelry). Be done!*

Close the circle as usual.

The Great Earth Mother
—Full Moon—

Gaea, sometimes spelled Gaia, was the Great Mother, the "Broad-bosomed Earth," the Primeval Prophetess, Mother Earth herself. The great center at Delphi was hers before Apollo took it over. Sacred oaths were often made in her name. She had sanctuaries at Dodona, Tegea, Sparta, and Athens. Her priestesses were the sacred Sibyls, wise Pythias, and devout Mellisae. Into her sacred cauldron at Delphi, the priestesses threw barley and laurel. She was the goddess of motherhood, marriage, agricultural fertility, dreams, trance, divination, oracles, and healing.

This is a good time of year to call upon Gaea to heal the Earth and its creatures. This can be part of a regular ritual or can be performed by itself. Place some barley and bay laurel leaves in a cauldron on your altar. Set a lighted brown candle behind the cauldron. Place stones and crystals all around the cauldron and candle. Burn earthly-type incense, such as vervain, bayberry, powdered orris root, or even patchouli. If you want, put a picture of the Earth nearby. Have another brown candle ready in a holder.

Place both of your hands, palms down, on the altar. Chant:

> *Mother Gaea, Goddess of the Earth,*
> *I give you honor,*
> *For without your care and being*
> *I would have no home.*
> *Earth Mother, hear my words.*
> *I have need of your divine presence.*

Light the extra brown candle and carry it to the East.

> *Awake, Earth Mother!*
> *Your winds are heavy and foul.*
> *Sweep them clean again!*

Carry the candle to the South.

> *Awake, Earth Mother!*
> *Your children need your cleansing rays of light.*
> *Our atmosphere is in trouble!*

Go to the West.

> *Awake, Earth Mother!*
> *The plants and animals and humans are in danger.*
> *Protect your children!*

Finally, move to the North.

> *Awake, Earth Mother!*
> *The planet itself is sick.*
> *Do not destroy us in order to restore balance.*
> *Rather inspire us all to work together as healers of our world.*
> *Come again to your children, Gaea!*

Place the candle on the altar. Stand with upraised arms.

Awaken our minds and souls, Gaea!
Teach all humans to respect their home.
Teach us all responsibility,
Whether it be of chemicals or population.
Awaken us all to the needs of our Earth!

Thank Gaea for her presence and extinguish the candles. Put the barley and laurel outside as an offering to the Earth. And do your part in healing the Earth!

Talking with the Fates
—Dark Moon—

The Greek Fates and the Nordic Norns are very similar. It may be that these goddesses all came from pre-Aryan cultures in the Far East, before these cultural groups migrated to their respective areas to settle.

The Greek Fates ("portions, shares") were also called the Moerae or Moirai (Part), and became known as the Parcae during the Middle Ages. These three serious daughters of Nyx (Night) were Clotho, Lachesis, and Atropos. Clotho spun the life thread; Lachesis measured it, assigned the destiny, and added a portion of luck; brooding Atropos with her shears cut that thread at any time without warning. Not even Zeus could go against a decree by the Fates. The goddess Nemesis was the only one who could influence Atropos to let the thread spin into a longer length.

They were often accompanied by the Keres (Dogs of Hades), who were three beings with sharp teeth and robed in red. Although this trio was feared, the beings were also invoked at weddings for a happy union.

In many aspects, the Nordic Norns were quite similar. This trio of Fate goddesses lived at the Well of Urd near one of the roots of the World Tree Yggdrasil. They were Urd (the Past), Verthandi or Verdandi (the Present), and Skuld (the Future). The fact that the water from the Well of Urd turned everything white may tie these deities to the three phases of the Moon.

Certain records also speak of the helpers of the Norns, who were the Disir; in some writings these were called elves. The Hamingjes were like guardian angels to humans. There were elf-maids who cared for unborn babies. The decrees of Urd were carried out by the Giptes. Other Disir oversaw certain families or clans. There were even supernatural women, not Valkyries, who brought the souls of the dead to Hel's realm.

The English knew of the Norns by the name of the Weird Sisters. The Anglo-Saxons called them Wyrd; in Old High German Wurd. These Weird Sisters are quite likely direct descendants of the Greek Moerae or Fates.

Although there is no record of sacrifices to the Norns, the Nordic clans held them in awe and high regard. In Greece and Rome, the Fates were taken very seriously. They were given sacrifices of honey and flowers. Well into Medieval times three rings were used in special rituals to invoke the Fates. The three gunas, or colored threads (white, red, black), of India were said to run through every life as ordained by the Fates. Ovid, Theocritus, and others wrote of the same colored life-threads in Greek literature.

Take three cords, one each of white, red, and black, and braid them together. Knot both ends separately. If you wish, you can make this long enough to tie around your waist and use the braided cord as part of your ritual garments. While braiding, chant:

> *Over, under, threads of fate.*
> *As in my life, so in all things.*
> *Weaving the pattern, soon or late,*
> *I see the result that action brings.*

Kiss the finished braid and tie it around your waist, or drape it over your shoulders. Visualize the Greek Fates or the Nordic Norns before you. Lift your hands to them. Chant:

> *A new year dawns. The threads weave on,*
> *To ultimately reveal my destiny.*
> *O Fates of Life, I ask your aid*
> *To clear my path and set me free.*
> *Let old things die and blow away.*
> *Let new come in to prosper me.*
> *O Fates of Life, I ask your aid*
> *To clear my path and set me free.*

Sleep with the braided cords under your pillow and pay attention to your dreams. And be prepared to do whatever is necessary and proper to straighten out your life and make your path smoother.

APPENDICES

Moon Deities

and

Symbols

MOON DEITIES

*D*eities from around the world have long been associated with the Moon. The majority of these archetypal powers have been goddesses. Although their names change from culture to culture, many of them are similar in nature and powers. The following list of deities is given as an aid for anyone who wishes to add a specific name to her/his rituals, spellworkings, or just plain talks with the Moon. Included in the list are such creatures as angels and archangels, who were also connected with the Moon. This list is not meant to be complete.

Aine of Knockaine (Ireland): Moon Goddess; patroness of crops and cattle. Connected with the Summer Solstice.

Akua'ba (Ashanti of Africa): A lunar fertility deity.

Al-lat (Arabia): Full Moon goddess. Once the ruling goddess over shrines that are now forbidden to women. In ancient times represented by a huge uncut block of white granite in the village of At Ta'if near Mecca.

Al-Uzza (Arabia): The Mighty; Crescent Moon goddess. Virgin warrioress of the morning star. In very ancient times, she was considered enshrined in the black stone of Mecca, the Ka'aba, where she was served by priestesses. Today the stone is served by men who are called Beni Shaybah (the Sons of the Old Woman). Her sacred grove of acacia tress once stood just south of Mecca.

Anahita/Anat/Qadesh/Anait/Anatu (Phoenicia, Canaan, Ur, Persia): The High, Powerful, Immaculate. This goddess carried an ankh and wore horns and a Moon disk. Her sanctuary at Erex in Akilisene contained her golden statue.

271

Andraste (British Celts): A Moon goddess worshipped by Queen Boadicea. Connected with the hare and divination.

Anna Perenna (Rome): Two-headed goddess of time, with one head (Prosrsa) looking forward, and the other head (Postverta) looking backward; much like the god Janus. According to Ovid, a Moon goddess. Beginnings, endings, alphabet.

Aphrodite (Greece): "Foam-born"; Moon Goddess; "She Who Binds Hearts Together"; "She who came from the sea"; Goddess of the Western Corner. She was pictured as beautiful, voluptuous, with blue eyes and fair hair. At one time her name was Marianna or "La Mer," meaning "the Ocean." She was called virginal, meaning that she remained independent. Her priestesses were not physical virgins, but celebrated sexual rites; men were excluded from many of her rituals. Frankincense and myrrh were burned in her temples.

    The love of women, in whatever form, was sacred to her. Her birds were the heron, lovebird, swan, and dove (yonic symbol). Patroness of prostitutes. Goddess of love, beauty, the joy of physical love, sensuality, passion, generosity, all forms of partnerships and relationships, affection, fertility, continued creation, renewal.

Aponibolinayen (Philippines): Sky woman who supported the heavens by a vine wrapped around her waist. Probably a Moon goddess as she bore children to the Sun.

Ariadne (Crete): Her name means "High Fruitful Mother"; another form of the Cretan Moon goddess Britomartis. Robert Graves wrote that she was the consort of Dionysus. Images of her with snakes in her hands represent her oracle priestesses.

Arianrhod (Wales): "Silver Wheel"; "High fruitful mother"; virgin; goddess of reincarnation; Full Moon goddess. Her palace was called Caer Arianrhod (Aurora Borealis). Keeper of the circling Silver Wheel of Stars, a symbol of time or karma. This wheel was also known as the Oar Wheel, a ship which carried dead warriors to the Moon-land (Emania). Honored at the Full Moon. Beauty, fertility, reincarnation.

Artemis (Greece): Virgin Huntress; goddess of wild places and wild things; the Huntress; Maiden; Bear Goddess; Moon Goddess; Hunter of Souls; shapeshifter. In Ephesus she was called Dea Anna, "many-breasted", and was the patroness of nurturing, fertility, and birth. In Greece she was sculpted as tall, slim, lovely, and dressed in a short tunic. Her chariot was pulled by silver stags. She roamed the forests, mountains, and glades with her band of nymphs and hunting dogs. She acted swiftly and decisively to protect and rescue those who appealed to her for help and was quick to punish offenders, although violence itself was abhorrent to her. She knew the deep secret places in Nature where one could rest and regain strength.

    The Amazons (Moon-women), who were loyal to her, worshipped one aspect of Artemis (the New Moon phase). As Goddess of the Hunt, she carried a silver bow and was accompanied by a stag and her pack of hounds, the Alani. She could bring destruction but was usually benign. The sixth day of the New Moon was hers. Defender of women who were harassed or threatened by men. Acorns and wormwood were sacred to her.

Patroness of singers; protectress of young girls; mistress of magick, sorcery, enchantment, psychic power, women's fertility, purification, sports, good weather for travellers, woodlands, the hunt, mental healing, wild animals, mountains, woodland medicines, healing.

Astarte (Babylonia, Assyria, Phoenicia): Lady of the Mountain; Queen of Heaven; Lady of Byblos; Mistress of horses and chariots; Maiden; Virgin; Mother Goddess. Her temples had sacred prostitutes; sacred marriages were made by her priestesses with the kings. In her war aspect, she wore the horns of a bull. Her priestesses were famous astrologers. Revenge, victory, war, crescent Moon, astrology, sexual activities.

Ataensic (Native American, Huron): Moon god; the Huron word for water comes from this name.

Athene/Athena (Greece): Bright-Eyed; Holy Virgin; Maiden Goddess; Mother Goddess of Athens. Sometimes called Pallas Athene in memory of her close friend. Sacred to her were the owl, olive, oak, intertwined snakes. She wore a helmet and breastplate and carried a shield and spear. Goddess of freedom and women's rights; patroness of craftsmen, especially smiths, goldsmiths, potters, dressmakers, shipbuilders, weavers and spinners. Protection, writing, music, the sciences, wisdom, crafts and arts, renewal, true justice, prudence, wise counsel, peace, strategy.

Atius Tirawa (Pawnee, Native American): Creator god; god of the Sun, Moon, and stars.

Auchimalgen (Chile): Moon goddess of the Araucanian Indians. Protection against disasters and evil spirits, primarily through the fear she can create. They considered a red Moon to be the sign of the death of an important person.

Ba'alat (Phoenicia): Lady of Byblos; she wore either a cobra headdress or a disk between two horns. Similar to the Egyptian Hathor. Also known as Belit, Belit-ili, Beltis.

Ba'alith (Canaan): Great Goddess. Love, the Moon, the Underworld, trees, springs, wells.

Bast/Bastet/Pasht (in her dark aspect) (Egypt): Cat-headed goddess; mother of all cats. She was identified with Artemis or Diana, who was also called the mother of cats. The cat was Egypt's most sacred animal but the black cat was especially sacred to Bast; Egyptian physicians used the black cat symbol in healing. Cats were kept in her temple and embalmed when they died. Bast carried a sistrum in her right hand and a basket in her left. She was usually draped in green.

Goddess of fire, the Moon, childbirth, fertility, pleasure, benevolence, joy, sexual rites, music, dance, protection against disease and evil spirits, warmth, all animals but especially cats, intuition, healing.

Bendis (Greece, Thrace): Goddess of the Moon and fertility. Her rites included orgies.

Blodeuwedd (Wales): The Ninefold Goddess of the Western Isles of Paradise, she was connected with death and reincarnation. Like Athene, owls were sacred to her. Robert Graves writes that Blodeuwedd had nine powers, a blending and multiplication of the Triple Goddess. She dealt with lunar mysteries and initiations.

Bomu Rambi (West Africa, Zimbabwe): A Moon goddess associated with wisdom, comfort, and the calming of emotional stress. Her followers wear necklaces with a Crescent Moon.

Brigit/Brid/Brig/Brigid/Brighid (Ireland, Wales, Spain, France): "Power"; "Renown"; "Fiery Arrow or Power" (Breo-saighead). Called the poetess. Often called the Triple Brigits, Three Blessed Ladies of Britain, the Three Mothers; associated with Imbolc. Her exclusive female priesthood at Kildare numbered nineteen, the number of the Celtic "Great Year", and the number of the Moon's cycle. Goddess of the hearth, all feminine arts and crafts, fertility, martial arts. Healing, physicians, agriculture, inspiration, learning, poetry, divination, prophecy, smithcraft, animal husbandry, love, witchcraft, occult knowledge.

Britomartis (Crete): Virgin forest Moon goddess; sometimes called Dictynna. Similar to Artemis and Diana.

Caillech Beine Bric/Calleach (Celts, Scotland): Great Goddess in her destroyer aspect; called the "Veiled One." Another name was Scota, from which Scotland comes. Originally Scotland was called Caledonia, or land given by Caillech.

Centzon Totochtin (Aztec): "Four hundred rabbits." Gods connected with the Moon. Depicted with black and white faces, crescent-shaped nose ornaments. Associated with pulque beer.

Ceres (Rome): Moon and Grain goddess; identified with the Greek Demeter. Her daughter was Proserpina.

Cernunnos/Cernowain/Cerneus/Herne the Hunter (All Celtic cultures in one form or another): The Horned God; God of Nature; god of the Underworld and the Astral Plane; Great Father; "the Horned One." From very ancient times a companion of the Moon goddess. Horns in whatever form always connected a deity with the Moon. The Druids knew him as Hu Gadern, the Horned God of fertility. He was portrayed sitting in a lotus position with horns or antlers on his head, long curling hair, a beard, naked except for a neck torque, and sometimes holding a spear and shield. His symbols were the stag, ram, bull, and horned serpent, all Moon creatures. Virility, fertility, animals, physical love, Nature, woodlands, reincarnation, crossroads, wealth, commerce, warriors.

Cerridwen/Caridwen/Ceridwen (Wales): Dark Moon goddess; Great Mother; goddess of Nature; grain goddess. Her cauldron and the white corpse-eating sow represented the Moon. Welsh Bards called themselves Cerddorion (sons of Cerridwen). Death, fertility, regeneration, inspiration, magick, enchantment, divination, astrology, herbs, science, poetry, spells, knowledge.

Chandra/Soma (India): Moon god whose name came from the intoxicating, hallucinogenic drink made for the gods. God of pleasant forgetfulness. The Moon is called Sasin or Sasanka (hare mark or spot) because Chandra carries a hare. One folktale says that the Moon is a crystal ball filled with silver water. Chandra rides in a chariot pulled by antelope and protects the world from ignorance and chaos. Psychic visions and dreams, rising on the inner planes.

Ch'ang-O/Heng-O (China): Goddess of the Moon. Her palace there is called the Great Cold on the Moon. At the Full Moon of the Autumn Equinox there was a female-only celebration where women offered the goddess crescent Moon cakes (called "Yue-ping") and statues of little hares.

Changing Woman (Native American, Apache): Moon goddess. Mother of All. Dream work, shape-shifting, insight, wisdom, birth, joy. Associated with flowers and rainbows. See Estsanatlehi.

Charities/Graces (Greece): Triad of Moon goddesses who were Aphrodite's companions. Usually portrayed nude and dancing. They were Aglaia (the shining one, glorious), Thalia (the flowering one, abundance), and Euphrosyne (the one who makes glad, joy).

Circe (Greece): "She-Falcon"; Dark Moon Goddess; Fate-Spinner. Called the death-bird (kirkos or falcon). As the circle, or cirque, she was the fate-spinner, weaver of destinies. Ancient Greek writers spoke of her as Circe of the Braided Tresses because she could manipulate the forces of creation and destruction by knots and braids in her hair. The isle of Aeaea was a funerary shrine to her; its name is said to come from the grief wail. She was the goddess of physical love, sorcery, enchantments, precognitive dreams, evil spells, vengeance, dark magick, witchcraft, cauldrons.

Coyolxauhqui (Aztec): "Golden Bells"; Moon goddess. Shown with golden bells on her cheeks. The actual physical Moon was called Mextli. In Teotihuacan, north of the present Mexico City, is an ancient Aztec city with a Pyramid of the Moon. The beneficent giver of harvests and children, but also goddess of the night, dampness, cold, and illness.

Cybele/Kybele (Greece, Phrygia): A goddess of the Earth and caverns; Great Mother. One of her symbols was the crescent Moon. She was the goddess of the natural world and its formation; wild beasts, especially lions; dominion over wild animals; dark magick, revenge.

Danu/Danann/Dana (Ireland): Probably the same as Anu. Ancestress of the Tuatha De Danann; Mother of the gods; Great Mother; Moon goddess. Patroness of wizards; rivers, water, wells, prosperity and plenty, magick, wisdom.

Demeter (Greece): Moon and Grain goddess; identified with the Roman Ceres. Mother of the Kore, who became Persephone after her return from the Underworld. The Eleusinian Mysteries centered around her spiritual teachings.

Diana (Rome): Goddess of the wildwood, lady of beasts; Moon goddess; sometimes called Many-Breasted. Goddess of mountains, woods, women, childbirth. Her title "Queen of Heaven" was the Roman name for the Triple Goddess; her aspects were the Lunar Virgin, Mother of Creatures, and the Huntress or Destroyer. Her animals were the dog and the stag. Patroness of outlaws and thieves. Often associated with the forest god Sylvanus or Pan. In ancient Italy, her oldest and most famous place of worship was at a volcanic lake, known as the Mirror of Diana. In a grove (Nemus) on the only accessible shore of the lake was her sanctuary. This goddess was known for her liking for exclusively female society. There are records from the tenth century referring to women who attended night meetings with the Pagan goddess Diana.

Dictynna (Crete): A virgin forest and Moon goddess; sometimes called Britomartis.

Diiwica (Slavic-Russian): Goddess of the Hunt who ruled over forests, horses, wild animals, and victory. Possibly identified with the Roman Diana.

Dione/Nemorensis/Nemetona (Goddess of the Moon-grove) (Greece, Rome): Dione was originally the oracle goddess of Dodona before the shrine was taken over by Zeus. In Italy, the woodland lake of Nemi, which lies in a volcanic crater in the Alban Hills, had a woodland sanctuary dedicated to Diana or Dione. The reigning priest was called the King of the Wood and held his post by right of combat. Any man, free or slave, could challenge him.

Ereshkigal (Mesopotamia, Babylonia, Assyria): Queen of the Underworld; the Crone aspect of the Goddess. Dark magick, revenge, retribution, the waning Moon, death, destruction, regeneration.

Estsanatlehi (Navaho, Native American): "The woman who changes"; Changing Woman; a shape-shifter. The Moon, transformation, immortality.

Eurynome (Greece): Sometimes known as Aphrodite Eurynome; a Moon goddess. Her statue was a mermaid carved in wood in her temple in Phigalia in Arcadia.

Fates/The Moerae (Greece): Their name means "portions, shares." During the Middle Ages these goddesses were known as the Parcae. They were the daughters of Nyx, or Night. Clotho spun the life thread; Lachesis measured it, assigned the destiny, and added a portion of luck; Atropos cut the thread with her shears at any time without warning.

Fleachta of Meath (Ireland): Moon queen of Ireland.

Freyja/Freya (Norse): Syr (seer); "Lady"; Great Goddess; Mardoll ("She who shines over the sea"); Vanir goddess. Mistress of cats, leader of the Valkyries, a shape-shifter, the Sage or "sayer" who inspires all sacred poetry. Thirteen is her number and Friday her day. Love, beauty, animals, sexual activity, childbirth, horses, enchantments, witchcraft, wealth, gold, trance, wisdom, foresight, magick, luck, long life, fertility, the Moon, the sea, death, music, poetry, writing, protection.

Frigg/Frigga/Frija (Norse): "Well-Beloved Spouse or Lady"; Aesir Mother Goddess; queen of the goddesses; a shape-shifter; knower of all things. Daughter of Nott (Night). Independence, childbirth, cunning, cleverness, physical love, wisdom, fate, foresight, marriage, children, fertility, destiny, the Moon, magick, enchantments.

Furies/Erinyes (the Angry Ones)/Eumenides (the Kindly Ones) (Greece): The daughters of Nyx; Children of Eternal Night. Particularly associated with Demeter in her chthonic aspect. They were Alecto (Neverending, the Unnameable), Tisiphone (Retaliation-Destruction), and Megaera (Envious Anger, Grudge).

Gabriel (Archangel): Prince of Change and Alteration; Archangel of the Annunciation. One of the two highest ranking angels. Ruling prince of Paradise and sits on the left hand of God. The angel of resurrection, mercy, vengeance, death, revelation, truth, hope. His planet is the Moon, his color blue. He rules the Element of Water and the West. Angel of visions, magick, clairvoyance, scrying, astral travel, herbal medicine. His Arabic name is Jibril or Jabrail.

Ganesha/Ganesa/Ganapati/Gajani (India): "Elephant-face"; Lord of obstacles; elephant-headed god of scribes and merchants. Pictured as a short, pot-bellied man with yellow skin, four arms, and an elephant's head with one tusk. Rides on a rat. Removes obstacles from life. Thoughtful and wise, he is invoked before every undertaking to insure success. It is said that if Ganesha is worshipped at the August Hindu festival, wishes will come true. However, it is unlucky to see the Moon during this festival.

Wisdom, good luck, literature, books, writing, worldly success, prosperity, peace, beginnings, journeys, overcoming obstacles, taming dangerous forces, combination of force and cunning.

Ge (Dahomey in Africa): Moon god; son of Mawu.

Gidja (Australia): Moon god and totemic ancestor of the Dreamtime. God of dreams and sex.

Green Man (Ireland, Britain, Wales): In Old Welsh his name was Arddu (The Dark One), Atho, or the Horned God. Identified with Cernunnos. A horned deity of trees and green growing things of Earth; god of the woodlands. Connected with several Moon goddesses. The very first deities were the White Goddess (Moon goddess) and the Horned God.

Han Lu (China): A Moon and Harvest goddess.

Hathor/Athyr/Het-Hert (House or Womb Above)/Hat-Hor (House or Womb of Horus) (Egypt): "The golden"; "Queen of the West" (or the Dead); "the Lady of the Sycamore"; "House of the Face"; Mother Goddess; mother of all gods and goddesses; Queen of Heaven; Moon goddess; similar to Aphrodite. Considered self-produced. She carried the Sacred Eye of Ra. The mirror and sistrum were sacred to her.

Hathor's appearance could be as a cow-headed goddess or a human-headed woman with horns, cow's ears, and heavy tresses. She liked to embody herself in the sistrum to drive away evil spirits; another of her instruments was the tambourine. She cared for the dead, carrying them to the afterworld.

Protectress of women; goddess of joy, love, pleasure, flowers, the Moon, tombs, motherhood, beauty, marriage, singers and dancers, artists, vine and wine, happiness, protection, astrology, prosperity, strength, good times in general.

Hecate (Greece, Thrace, Rome): "Most lovely one"; "the Distant One"; Silver-Footed Queen of the Night; goddess of the Moon, the dark hours, and the Underworld; the Crone; Queen of the world of spirits; goddess of witchcraft; snake goddess; Great Mother; Great Goddess of Nature; Lady of the Wild Hunt. Another goddess of the Amazons, her chariot was pulled by dragons. It was said she wore a shimmering headdress and was second to none in powers of sorcery. A very old statue, from the eighth century BCE, shows Hecate with wings and holding a snake.

She could change ages or forms and rejuvenate or kill. She was the third Moon aspect as the Hag (Dark Moon) or the Crone (revered as the Carrier of Wisdom). One of her symbols was the cauldron. A three-faced image represented her triple aspects; she was then called Triformis. As Hecate Trevia, Hecate of the Three Ways, her images stood at three-way crossroads where offerings of dogs, honey, and black ewe lambs were left on Full Moon nights. Divination and communications with the dead were performed in these places.

The oldest Greek form of the Triple Goddess, her festivals were held at night by torchlight. A huntress goddess who knew her way in the realm of spirits; all secret powers of Nature at her command; control over birth, life, and death. Patroness of priestesses; goddess of witches. The waning Moon, dark magick, prophecy, charms and spells, vengeance, averting evil, revealing karmic events, enchantments, incantations, riches, victory, wisdom, transformation, reincarnation, dogs, purification, endings, choices, crossroads, curses, hauntings, renewal and regeneration.

Heimdall (Norse): Vanir god of Light and the rainbow; "The White God." He is called "the Son of the Wave" because he was born from nine waves by Odhinn's enchantment; nine is a magick Moon number. Guardian, beginnings and endings, morning light, seriousness, defense against evil.

Hel (Norse): Ruler of Niflheim; Nether, or Dark, Moon. Goddess who ruled over the land of the dead; her realm was not necessarily a place of punishment as there were separate areas for the good who died peacefully and those who were evil.

Hera (Greece): The Greek equivalent of the Roman goddess Juno.

Hina (Hawaii): Moon goddess with the dual aspects of life-giver and life-destroyer.

Holda/Holde/Holle/Hulda (Benign)/Bertha/Berchta (White Lady) (Germany, Norse): North Germanic name for Hel. "White Lady"; "Black Earth Mother"; goddess of winter and witchcraft; the Crone aspect of the Moon. Among the North Germanic tribes, it was said she rode with Odhinn on the Wild Hunt. Even as late as the tenth century, tracts said that Pagan women rode under her leadership in wild night rides. Holly was sacred to her. Fate, karma, the arts, dark magick, revenge.

Horned God (Many cultures): Also called Cernunnos, the Green Man, Herne the Hunter, Lord of the Wild Hunt. Connected with the Moon goddess from very early times. Very similar to the Greek Pan and the Roman Sylvanus. The masculine, active side of Nature. Growing things, the forest, Nature, wild animals, alertness, annihilation, fertility, panic, desire, terror, flocks, agriculture, beer and ale.

Horus (Egypt): Although this god was basically a falcon-headed Sun and sky god and identified with Apollo, his two eyes were said to be the Sun and the Moon. He was also associated with cats. The Moon boat, called Yaahu Auhu, was sometimes called the Left Eye of Horus. Egyptians said that this Moon boat carried the souls of the dead over a vast sea to the Sun.

Huitaca (Columbia, South America): A Moon goddess who weaves dreams, especially instructive ones.

Hur (Chaldea): Moon god, whose capital city Ur was named after him.

Idunn/Iduna(Norse): Goddess of eternal youth who kept the golden apples (sometimes a symbol of the Moon). Childbirth, Spring; clear vision and enlightenment, especially for newborns.

Igaluk (Eskimo, Native American): Moon god; Supreme God. Natural phenomena, animals, sea animals.

Inanna (Many cultures in the ancient Middle East): Identified with Ishtar.

Ishtar/Inanna/Ashtart/Ashtaroth/Ashtoreth/Astarte/Anaitis/Anat/Atar/Athtar/ Mylitta/Esther (Mesopotamia, Babylonia, Assyria, Sumeria, Arabia, Phoenicia, Canaan): Lady of sorrows and battles; Queen or Lady of Heaven; Goddess of the Moon and evening; Great Mother; Shining One; Mother of Deities; Producer of Life; Creator of People; Guardian of Law and Order; Ruler of the Heavens; Source of the Oracles of Prophecy; Lady of Battles and Victory; Lady of Vision; Possessor of the Tablets of Life's Records. As Sharrat Shame (Queen of Heaven), this goddess was offered kamanu, sacrificial cakes. She was the sister of Ereshkigal.

As a warrior goddess, she carried a bow and rode in a chariot drawn by seven lions. Other images show her seated on her lion throne with horns, bow and arrows, a tiara crown, a double serpent scepter, holding a sword, or with dragons by her sides. She wore a rainbow necklace much like that of the Norse Freyja.

During the night of the Full Moon (known as Shapatu), joyous celebrations were held in her many temples. At these rites, which were called the sacred Qadishtu, women who lived as priestesses in her shrines, took lovers to express the sacredness of sexuality as a gift from Ishtar. These sexual rites enabled the men to commune with the goddess.

Goddess of the positive and negative sides of all she ruled; patroness of priestesses; guardian of the law; teacher. Love, fertility, revenge, war, resurrection, marriage, lions, double-serpent scepter, lapis lazuli, amorous desire, the dying and begetting power of the world, purification, initiation, overcoming obstacles.

Isis/As/Ast/Aset/Eset/Tait (Egypt): Supreme Egyptian goddess; Moon goddess; Great Mother and Goddess; Giver of Life. Isis literally translates as "moisture." As Tait, Isis was the weaver and knotter of the threads of life. She was identified with Demeter, Hera, and Selene. With Osiris, Isis (the mother) and Horus (the divine child) made up a Holy Trinity. The cow was sacred to her, as were the magick Buckle of Isis and the sistrum. Her sistrum was carved with a cat image that represented the Moon. Sometimes she was portrayed with protecting winged arms.

As High Priestess, she was a powerful magician. Goddess of marriage and domestic life, the Moon, motherhood, fertility, childbirth, magick, purification, initiation, reincarnation, success, womanhood, healing, domestic crafts, advice, divination, agriculture, the arts, protection. The patroness of priestesses.

Ixchel (Maya): "The Rainbow." The Mayan Moon was represented by a U-shaped (uterine) symbol. Goddess of childbirth, fertility, lunar cycles, weaving of the fabric of life, healing, medicine, the Moon, pregnancy, floods, weaving, domestic arts. Identical to Spider Woman. During the rite of passage, young Mayan women traveled to her temple on the sacred Isle of Women.

Ixchup (Maya): "Young Moon Goddess."

Jahi the Whore (Persia): Great Mother who, as Lilith, mated with the serpent Ahriman. The Moon, women, menstruation, sex.

Jezanna (West Africa, Zimbabwe): Full Moon goddess. Wisdom, understanding, comfort, enlightenment.

Juno (Rome): Moon goddess; Queen of Heaven; "Lady"; Earth goddess; "She who warns"; Great Mother; protectress of women in general. As Juno Lucetia and Juno Lucina, she was the celestial light. Sometimes she held a scepter, thunderbolt, veil, or spear and shield. Protectress of marriage, the home, and childbirth. Light, women's fertility, the Moon, renewal, purification, death, pain, punishment.

Kali/Kali Ma (India): "The black mother"; Dark Goddess; the Terrible; goddess of death; Great Goddess; the Crone; Mother of Karma. Patroness of witches. Dual personality exhibiting traits of both gentleness and love, revenge and terrible death. Governs every form of death but also rules every form of life. She is always a trinity manifested in three forms: three divisions of the year, three phases of the Moon, three sections of the cosmos, three stages of life, three types of priestesses at her shrines. Said to command the weather by braiding or releasing her hair. Her karmic wheel devours time itself.

She is pictured with black skin and a hideous face smeared with blood, four arms, and bare breasts. She wears a necklace of skulls and is draped with snakes.

Her brow has a third eye; her four hands hold weapons and heads. Violence against any woman is forbidden by her. Regeneration, revenge, fear, dark magick, sexual activities, time, reincarnation, intuition, dreams, defender of the helpless such as women and children.

Khensu/Khons/Khonsu (Egypt): "Traveller"; "The Navigator"; "He who crosses the sky in a boat"; God of the New Moon. He wore a skullcap topped by a disk in a crescent Moon. His head was shaved except for a scalp-lock tress. His human body was swathed tightly, and he held a crook and flail. Under the New Kingdom Khensu gained popularity as an exorcist and healer.

Khepera/Khepra/Khepri (Egypt): "He who becomes"; god of transformation; the scarab beetle, symbol of creative energy and eternal life; a Creator God. Although Khepera was known as God of the Rising Sun, he was also known as God of the Moon. Exorcism, healing, new beginnings, gentleness, literary abilities, miracles, compassion.

Kore (Greece, Rome): Persephone before she descended into the Underworld; daughter of Demeter. A crescent New Moon goddess.

Kuan Yin (China): Goddess of fertility, compassion, children, childbirth.

Kuu/Kun (Finnish-Ugrian): Moon deity, sometimes seen as male, sometimes as female.

Lakshmi (India): Goddess of love and beauty; legend says she gave Indra the drink of soma (or wise blood) from her own body. She was born from the churning of the milk ocean. Good fortune, prosperity, success, love, feminine beauty.

Leucippe (Greece): The night mare. White horses were sacred to her.

Lilith/Lilithu (Hebrew, Babylonia, Sumeria): Moon Goddess; patroness of witches; female principle of the universe; demon goddess to the Jews and Christians. Her sacred bird was the owl. Her name may have come from the Sumerio-Babylonian goddess Belit-ili or Belili. A tablet from Ur, about 2,000 BCE, mentions the name Lillake. Protectress of all pregnant women, mothers, and children. Wisdom, regeneration, enticing sorcery, feminine allure, erotic dreams, forbidden delights, the dangerous seductive qualities of the Moon.

Luna (Rome): The second aspect of the Moon; the Full Moon as lover and bride; giver of visions. Daughter of Hyperion and sister of the Sun. Enchantments, love spells.

Mah (Persia): Moon god.

Maia (Greece): Full Moon goddess connected with May, the Hare Moon.

Mama Quilla (Inca): "Mother Moon"; Moon goddess; Mother of the Incas; her image was a silver disk with a human face. Adjoining the Temple of the Sun in Cuzco, Peru, was a small chapel of the Moon. Although she had no widespread worship, this deity was connected with the calendar and festivals. Protectress of married women, the calendar, religious festivals.

Manat (Arabia): "Time"; "Fate"; Karma. The Arabic word "mana" which comes from this name is used in the sense of luck. Dark Moon goddess. On the road between Mecca and Medina was a large uncut black stone which was worshipped as her image.

Mani (Norse): Moon god who kidnapped the boy Hjuki and the girl Bil, whom he placed on the Moon. Mani directs the course of the Moon and regulates Nyi (the New Moon) and Nithi (the waning Moon).

Mari/Mariham/Meri/Marratu (Syria, Chaldea, Persia): Basic name of the Great Goddess; she wore a blue robe and a pearl necklace, both symbols of the sea. Fertility, childbirth, the Moon, the sea.

Mawu/Mawa (Dahomey in West Africa): Supreme Goddess; creatress of all things; Great Goddess. The Fon of Benin in West Africa worship Mawu as a Moon goddess and creatress. She was known as a gentle and forgiving goddess. Remembering dreams, seeing divine influence in our lives, revelation of Mysteries.

Men/Mene (Phrygia): Moon god. Not to be confused with the goddess Selene.

Meztli/Teccezeiecatl (Aztec): The material Moon at its height; "He from the sea snail." Represented as an old man with a white shell on his back and sometimes with butterfly wings. Was replaced by the goddess Coyolxauhqui.

Minerva (Rome): Virgin; Maiden Goddess; goddess of women's rights and freedom. She wore a breastplate and helmet and carried a spear. Her sacred bird was the owl. Patroness of craftsmen. Protection, writing, music, the sciences, arts and crafts, renewal, prudence, wise counsel, peace, medicine.

Morrigan, The/The Morrigu/Morrighan/Morgan (Ireland, Wales, Britain): "Great Queen"; "Supreme War Goddess": "Queen of Phantoms or Demons"; "Specter Queen"; shape-shifter. Great Mother; Moon goddess; Great White Goddess; Queen of the Faeries. Reigned over the battlefield, helping with her magick, but did not join in battles. Associated with ravens and crows. Patroness of priestesses and witches. Rivers, lakes, fresh water, revenge, night, magick, prophecy.

Muses, The (Greece): Nine Moon goddesses; three (the number of the Triple Goddess) times three makes the Moon number nine. Each goddess presides over a specific area of inspiration and art: history, music, comedy, tragedy, poetry, art, astronomy and astrology, eloquence of speech.

Myesyats (Slavic): Moon god; sometimes male, sometimes female. In Serbia, this god was called Bald Uncle. Spring, healing.

Nanna/Nana/Anna/Inanna (Norse): Aesir goddess; "The Moon"; Great Mother; Earth goddess. Love, gentleness.

Nanna/Nana/Nina (Sumeria, Assyria): Lady; Ancient Mother; Holy One of Many Names; Great Mother; the tripartite Moon. The Judge of humankind on the last day of every year. An image of a winged lioness guarded her temple. A very ancient name, this goddess was represented with a fish-tail or serpent-tail. Herbs, the Moon, healing, magick, intercession, interpretation of dreams, crops, civilization.

Nehellania (Norse): Nether, or Dark, Moon. Sometimes connected with Hel.

Neith/Neit/Net/Nit (Egypt): "The Huntress"; "Opener of the Ways"; Great Goddess; Mother of the gods; goddess of the lower heavens; warrior-goddess and protectress; Lady of the West. Universal mother; the Spirit behind the Veil of Mysteries; Primal Abyss. Her name means "I have come from myself," or self-begotten. The Greeks identified her with Pallas Athene, who also had a dual role of warrior and woman skilled in domestic arts. She wore the red crown of Lower Egypt and held a bow and two arrows. Part of her sanctuary at Sais was a school of medicine, the House of Life. Her ceremonies were of a mystic nature.

Herbs, magick, healing, mystical knowledge, rituals, meditation. Patroness of domestic arts, weaving, hunting, medicine, war, weapons. Protectress of women and marriage.

Nemesis (Greece): Dark Moon goddess of karmic retribution.

Nephthys (Egypt): Dark Moon goddess; sister of Isis and mother of Anubis by her brother Osiris. Her symbols were the cup and the lotus. Rebirth, reincarnation, building good upon the ashes of hopelessness. The great revealer and giver of dreams; understanding the Mysteries.

Ngami (Africa): Moon Goddess.

Nkosuano (Ghana): The Moon-egg.

Norns/Weird Sisters/Wyrd/Wurd (Norse, Germanic, Anglo-Saxon): Very similar to the Greek Fates. They tended the Well of Urd near one of the roots of the World Tree Yggdrasil. They were named Urd (the Past), Verthandi or Verdandi (the Present), and Skuld (the Future). The water from their well turned everything white, thus connecting them with the three phases of the Moon.

Eostre/Ostara/Eostra/Ostarra (Germany, North European): A Moon goddess whose name survives in the word Easter. As a fertility goddess of the Spring Equinox, she was associated with hares, rabbits, and eggs.

Osiris (Egypt): Lord of life after death; Universal Lord; Lord of Lords; God of Gods. Although he was sometimes called a Sun deity, he also was connected with the Moon. A great number of inscriptions call Osiris Lord of the Moon, sometimes the Great Hare. He was sometimes shown standing, sometimes seated on his throne, tightly wrapped in mummy cloth, his freed hands on his breast holding the crook and flail. Sometimes his face was green; on his head he wore a high white miter flanked by two ostrich feathers. Texts written in the main hall of the Temple of Hathor at Dendera call Osiris the Moon.

Patron of priests; god of fertility, harvests, commerce, success, initiation, death and reincarnation, water, judgment, justice, agriculture, crafts, vegetation, grains, religion, architecture, codes of law, power, order, discipline, growth, stability.

Pan (Greece): Much the same as the Celtic Horned God. "Little God"; Horned God; goat-foot god; very ancient. A woodland deity often associated with Moon goddesses. Positive Life Force of the world. Creative powers, Moon influences, fertility in all its forms, music, Nature spirits, wild animals, dance, medicine, soothsaying.

Pandia (Greece): One of a female trinity of Moon goddesses representing the phases of the Moon. The others were Erse and Nemea.

Pasht (Egypt): The destroying aspect, or Dark Moon, of Bast. Known as the Tearer or devouring Sphinx. Associated with cats, particularly the black cat. Healer-destroyer of diseases; remover of obstacles and barriers, particularly if these are people.

Pe (Pygmies of Africa): Moon goddess. A special New Moon feast for her occurs just before the rainy season begins.

Persephone/Proserpina (Greece, Rome): Daughter of Demeter (Ceres) who was first called the Kore. She took the name Persephone after she descended to the Underworld.

Samhain/Samen (Ireland, Celts): Although the name of the festival we now celebrate as Halloween, also at one time a Moon goddess. An old Irish saying to wish a friend happiness was: "The blessings of Samen (Moon) and Bel (Sun) be with you."

Sarasvati (India): "Stimulator"; inventor of Sanskrit and discoverer of soma in the Himalayas. Represented as a graceful woman with white skin, wearing a crescent Moon on her brow, and seated on a lotus flower. The highest spiritual body center is the thousand petalled lotus called the place of the hidden Moon. The creative arts, science, music, poetry, learning, teaching.

Scathach/Scota/Scatha/Scath (Ireland, Scotland): "Shadow, shade"; "The Shadowy One"; "She Who Strikes Fear." Dark Moon goddess. Patroness of blacksmiths, healing, magick, prophecy, martial arts.

Selene/Mene (Greece): The second aspect of the Moon; the Full Moon as lover and bride. She was pictured as a beautiful woman with a gold crown. The woodland god Pan fell in love with her. Great importance in magick, spells, enchantments.

Seshat/Sesheta (Egypt): "Mistress of the house of books"; "the secretary"; "mistress of the house of architects." The female equivalent and wife of Thoth, this goddess was in fact older than Thoth. Very early Seshat was pictured as a woman wearing on her head a star, a reversed crescent, and two long straight plumes; sometimes this image was only a star on top of a pole surmounted by a downturned crescent. Later the crescent was replaced with two long down-turned horns. She was the record-keeper of the gods. Goddess of writing, letters, archives, measurement, calculation, record-keeping, hieroglyphics, time, stars, history, books, learning, inventions.

Shing-Moo (China): Our Lady Moon.

Shiva/Siva/Mahakala (India): Lord of the Cosmic Dance; Lord of the World; Lord of Stillness and of Motion; Lord of Yoga; Great Lord; Beneficent One; He who gives and takes away; demon-slayer. His power depends upon his union with Kali, without whom he cannot act. He wears his hair in an ascetic's knot, adorned with a crescent Moon and trident. He is pictured as a fair man with a blue throat, five faces, four arms, and three eyes. Three serpents coil around him, darting out at enemies. He is the god of all humans who have no place in society. His dance movements symbolize the eternal life-death rhythm of the universe.

Cattle, mountains, medicine, fertility, physical love, destruction, lightning, storms, long life, healing, strength, magick, weapons, rivers, death, dance, meditation, righteousness, judgment.

Sinn/Sin (Mesopotamia, Ur, Assyria, Babylonia, Sumeria): Moon God; "the Illuminator"; Lord of the calendar; Lord of the diadem. He was shown as an old man with a long beard the color of lapis and wearing a turban. He rode in a boat (a brilliant crescent Moon) across the skies, with the Full Moon as his diadem. Mt. Sinai (Mountain of the Moon) was sacred to him. The Babylonians believed that this god revealed the evil traps laid for men by evil spirits. Enemy of all evil-doers; god of measurement of time. Destiny, predictions, air, wisdom, secrets, destruction of all evil, decisions.

Skadi (Norse): "Harm"; daughter of the Giant Thjasi and wife of Njord. Rightful retribution, mountains, Winter, revenge, dark magick.

Soma (India): Also called Chandra. He symbolized the Moon and immortality. Soma was also the name for a sacred plant that made a religious-ecstasy drink. Soma, both god and plant, was created from the churning of the primordial sea by the gods. His wives, the daughters of Daksha, are considered to be the twenty-seven lunar stations.

Spider Woman (Native American, Southwestern): Sometimes called Spider Grandmother. Connected with the Moon.

Sylvanus (Rome): The Roman equivalent of the god Pan.

Tanit/Tanith (Phoenicia, Carthage): Moon Goddess; Great Goddess; similar to Ishtar.

Thoth/Tehuti/Thout/Djehuti/Zehuti (Egypt): "Lord of Books and Learning"; Judge of the gods; director of the planets and seasons; scribe of the gods; identified with the Greek Hermes. Considered self-begotten. Thoth was called "Lord of Holy Words" for inventing hieroglyphs and numbers; "The Elder" as the first and greatest of magicians. He had greater powers than Osiris or Ra. He was ibis-headed and the inventor of the Four Laws of Magick. He wore a lunar disk and crescent on his head and held the writing reed and palette of a scribe.

Patron of priests; Supreme Magus; god of all magick, writing, inventions, the arts, divination, commerce, healing, initiation, music, prophecy, tarot, success, wisdom, medicine, astronomy, geometry, surveying, drawing, sciences, measurement of time, archives, judgment, oracles, rituals, astrology, alphabets, mathematics, speech, arbitration, balance, mental powers, the Moon, botany, theology, hymns and prayers, peace, advice, learning, truth, Akashic records, fate.

Tlazolteotl (Aztec): "Goddess of filth"; "Dirt Goddess"; Earth goddess; Lady of Witches. Goddess of the crescent Moon. Associated with the snake and bat, her worship was performed at crossroads, much like the Greek Hecate. She rode naked on a broom through the night skies, wearing a peaked hat and holding a red snake and a blood-stained rope. Four aspects of herself were recognized as separate goddesses: Tiacapan, Teicu, Tlaco, and Xocutxin. Physical love, fertility, death, witchcraft, sexuality, gambling, temptation, and black magick.

Triple Goddess: A trinity of goddesses, or a goddess having three aspects. Known around the world in various forms. Almost always connected with the three phases of the Moon.

Tsuki-Yomi (Japan): Some references call this deity a god, others a goddess. Anne Rush writes that until very recently this deity was female. Deity of the Moon and sibling of the Sun goddess Amaterasu. Moon meditations were a frequent practice in Japanese culture and were said to clear the mind and calm the soul.

Tzaphiel/Tsaphiel (Angel): Angel of the Moon.

Ursala/Orsel (Slavic-Russian): Moon goddess. Also connected with bears.

Venus (Rome): Moon goddess; patroness of vegetation and flowers. She was strong, proud, and loving. She was called virginal, meaning that she remained independent; her priestesses were not physical virgins. Goddess of love, beauty, the joy of physical love, fertility, continued creation, renewal, herbal magick.

Wahini-Hai (Polynesia): Creatress of the world and Mother goddess; also called the Moon and the first woman. Joseph Campbell says that her name was used in the word *wahine,* meaning "woman."

White Shell Woman (Native American, Navajo): Moon goddess.

Xiuhtecuhtli (Aztec): God of the calendar and spiritual fire.

Xochiquetzal (Aztec): Goddess of all women; a Mexican type of Aphrodite. She was also a Moon virgin, the complete Triple Goddess, and had a son/lover much like Adonis. She presided over love, marriage, sacred harlots, music, spinning and weaving, magick, art, and changes.

Yue-Lao (China): Old Man in the Moon. It is said he holds in his hands the power of predestining the marriage of mortals; he ties together the future husband and wife with invisible silk cords which never separate.

MOON SYMBOLS

Certain symbols have been associated with the Moon and Moon deities for thousands of years. Many such symbols recur in diverse cultures who had no contact with each other. Ancient spiritual leaders knew how to communicate with the collective unconscious, which is the storehouse of all knowledge, and hear the deities' voices which speak there. Using these symbols today in meditation, ritual, or spell-working will intensify your connections with the archetypal powers of the Moon.

Ambrosia: The feminine mysteries of the menstrual cycle; the re-creative power of menstrual blood. Called soma among the Hindus, red claret of the faeries, wise blood.

Bat: A creature often associated with the Moon and darkness. In China, good fortune and happiness; in Europe, a companion creature of the goddess Hel. The Christians made the bat evil and demonic in an attempt to dissociate the people from the Goddess.

Blood: The words "blessing" and "blood" are related. Red was always considered the color of life; it is also the color of the Mother aspect of the Triple Goddess, a sign of Her fruitfulness through menstruation and birth. Staining of the hands and feet with henna was practiced by followers of Hecate, Anath, and many Hindu goddesses. Originally, altars and people were consecrated by sprinkling with blood; now objects and people are sprinkled with salted water.

Boat: The Babylonians called the Moon the Boat of Light. The Egyptians portrayed the crescent Moon with the horns turned upward either as part of headdresses of their lunar deities or carved sky-boats, such as the ones pictured in the temples of Isis.

Bull: At first this was a lunar symbol of the Great Mother, the horns representing the crescent Moon. Later, when it came to represent Sun gods, it often was still connected with a Moon goddess such as Cybele and Attis.

Cat: The Egyptian word for cat was Mau. To the Egyptians especially, this was a Moon creature. Cats were sacred to such goddesses as Isis, Bast, Artemis, Diana, and Freyja. When Diana became known as Queen of the Witches during the Middle Ages, the cat was associated with witchcraft, or Goddess worship.

Circle: Long before this symbol was taken over by the Sun gods, the circle was a symbol of the Moon. The stone circles in the Orkney Islands of Scotland are still called Temples of the Moon. The ancient Greek divinatory tool known as Hecate's Circle was a gold sphere with a sapphire in its center; it was hung on a thong of oxhide.

Color: The primary colors connected with deities of the Moon were white, red, or black, depending upon the Moon phase. The Hindu goddess Kali and many European triple goddesses specifically used these three colors to designate their various aspects: white, Maiden; red, Mother; black, Crone.

Cow: A feminine symbol of both the Earth and the Moon. The Egyptian goddesses connected with both the Moon and the cow were Isis, Hathor, and Neith, among others.

Crescent: The New Moon; the very first sliver of Moon that marks its change from the Dark Moon. In Old European designs, the lunar cycle is represented by a right crescent, a circle, and a left crescent. Sometimes the circle was replaced by a large snake coil. Semicircles also symbolized the crescent, as did bull horns. U-shaped marks not only represented crescents, but also were combined with dots to symbolize owls—Moon birds. The croissant, or any crescent-shaped cake, was sacred to the Moon deities.

Crow: Because of its black color, this bird was sometimes associated with the Dark Moon goddesses, such as the Morrigu. It represented the necessity of destruction before new life could begin.

Crystal: This stone most often represented the Full Moon and its divinatory powers.

Dew, Rain: These forms of condensation are associated with the Moon in many cultures. The early dew after a Full Moon was said to heal and improve beauty if rubbed onto the skin. Certain phases and signs of the Moon are said to be conducive to rain.

Dog: Dogs have long been associated with Moon deities, especially goddesses of the crescent New Moon. Among the Norse was the story of Managarmr (Moondog), the mightiest of all dog-wolf supernatural beings.

Dragon: Although primarily connected with solar and lunar eclipses, dragons are associated with the Moon. This idea of dragons and eclipses was held in China, Northern Asia, Finland, Lithuania, North Africa, Persia. Legends say that dragons often flew about in the moonlight.

Eye: Often associated with the Moon, especially in ancient Egypt. Many little Eye Goddesses have been found in Mediterranean and European sites.

Fan: Among the ancient Asiatic and Oriental cultures, the fan represented the phases of the Moon.

Fish: In some cultures, the Moon was symbolized by a fish instead of a snake. Some Moon goddesses were shown as having fish-tails, rather like mermaids.

Frog: Many times a lunar symbol; sometimes called a toad. In Egypt, Hekat the frog goddess was connected with birth.

Grotto, Garden: The Moon goddess or god was often worshipped in a grotto or garden; this sacred space usually contained either a Moon tree (such as an olive), a sacred stone, or a spring, or all of these.

Groves: Groves of trees were often sacred to the Moon Mother, especially if they held springs, pools, or lakes. Ceremonies of drawing water and pouring it were part of her rituals. If a grove contained a grotto where water came directly out of a rock, it was especially sacred.

Hare or Rabbit: Many cultures around the world, including Tibet, China, Africa, Ceylon, and some Native Americans, said that a hare lived on the Moon along with the ruling Moon deity. Especially associated with lunar goddesses.

Horns: Bull or cow horns very early were connected with the Moon and Moon deities. Cattle and bison horns have been found that have thirteen notches carved into them; the Great Goddess of Laussel is such an example. These notches represent the thirteen Moon months of a seasonal year. The Greek Hera was also called Keroessa ("Horned One") in her aspect of Io, the Moon-cow.

Horseshoe: A crescent Moon symbol and also a yonic emblem.

Hounds, Dogs: Packs of hounds, such as the Alani of Diana, represent the dangerous energies of the Moon.

Labyrs, Double Axe: A Goddess and Moon symbol; said to have been one of the weapons preferred by the Amazons. A thunderbolt said to have been given in this shape to the Amazons by Hera. In Crete and at Delphi, both originally Goddess centers, the labyrs was a ceremonial scepter.

Lamp: The Moon is often called the lamp of the night. Additional titles to goddess names show their close connection with the Moon's light and its powers: Juno Lucina, Diana Lucifera.

Mirror, round: In Central Asia, and many other parts of the world, the Moon is called the heavenly mirror. A Goddess symbol sometimes called a soul-carrier or soul-catcher. Some cultures believed that the souls of the dead went to the Moon to await reincarnation.

Moonstone: A whitish, cloudy form of feldspar gemstone; said to contain an image of the Moon. The Hindus said that it was formed from congealing of the Moon's rays. Pope Leo X (1475-1521) was said to own a moonstone that waxed and waned in brilliance with the Moon. This stone is said to cure nervousness and bring luck to the owner.

Old Man, Old Woman: The markings on the surface of the Moon were often called the Old Man or Old Woman in the Moon. Some cultures, such as the Asians, the Mayans, and the Aztecs, called these markings the hare, frog, or toad.

Owl: The night-hunting owl with its large eyes has long been associated with the Moon. To the Egyptians, the owl was a symbol of death, night, and cold. However, to the Greeks, it was an emblem of wisdom and the goddess Athene. Its staring eyes connected it with the Eye Goddesses, Lilith, Minerva, Blodeuwedd, Anath, and Mari, among others. The owl has long been associated with the Moon, wisdom, sacred lunar mysteries, and initiations.

Ox: In Greece and Rome, this animal was seen as a lunar animal.

Pomegranate: Because of its blood-red juice, its many chambers and seeds, the pomegranate is symbolic of blood, the Dark Moon deities, and the land of the dead.

Pillar, Cone: The earliest representation of the Moon; sometimes this stone was a meteorite. Often this was grouped with a circular stone which represented the Full Moon. Some pyramids fall into this category.

Raven: A black bird associated with the Dark Moon goddesses, such as the Morrigu and Rhiannon.

Scythe, Sickle: A symbol of the crescent Moon. Used by the Amazons and women who worshipped Moon goddesses, particularly Crone deities. Even the Druids used a Moon-shaped sickle for their sacred ceremonies.

Semicircle: The semicircle represents the crescent Moon in symbology.

Shell: A symbol of the Great Mother and related to the Moon.

Silver: This metal has long been regarded as the Moon's metal. Silver was used for divinatory cups.

Snake: The snake, a Goddess symbol, is the same as the spiral when it is coiled. Sometimes each turn of the coil marks a day in the lunar calendar. Zigzag lines represent snakes. Serpents were associated with the Dark Moon because they were considered related to the Underworld. Some Dark Moon goddesses were depicted with snakes as hair. There are pictures showing Cybele offering a cup to a snake. In the mythology of Mexico are tales of the woman serpent (Moon) who is devoured by the Sun, a description of an eclipse or the phases of the Moon.

Soma: A sacred liquid connected with the Moon. In India it was called soma; the Persians knew it as haoma, and the Celts as red claret. See **Blood.** The Chinese goddess Ch'ang-O drank this sacred liquid, then fled to live on the Moon.

Sow: The white sow has been associated with Moon deities from the Celtic lands to the Mediterranean. It was connected with Astarte, Cerridwen, Demeter, Freyja, the Buddhist Marici.

Spiral: The spiral, whichever way it turned, represented an aspect of the Great Goddess, and also the Moon. The upward and downward spiraling, or in and out, can be compared to the waxing and waning of the Moon. The Greek Crane Dance, probably performed originally in Crete by the bull-dancers, was danced around a horned altar which was part of the labyrinth. Spirals appear on some ancient Goddess statues, primarily replacing what would be eyes.

Toad: Some cultures saw a toad, instead of a hare, in the Moon. In some parts of Asia, Africa, and North America, the toad is a symbol of the Moon and fertility.

Tree: Frequently a tree, called a Moon tree, was an emblem of the Moon. This is seen in many Assyrian pictures. Sometimes rather than an actual depiction of a tree, it is more like a maypole with ribbons hanging on it. Often the Moon tree was guarded by animals.

Triple Symbols: Many groups of triple symbols represent the three phases of the Moon. Hecate Triformis is an example of the Triple Moon Goddess, as is the Celtic Morrigu. The tripod, triangle, and trident are all connected directly with the three phases of the Moon goddesses, or with gods who are consorts of these goddesses.

Wishing Well: There is an Icelandic charm of this name which has four crescent Moons as dippers about its edge. The Moon has long been associated with water and the granting of wishes or prayers. Several goddesses, such as the Greek Demeter and the Celtic Brigit, had sacred Moon wells where rituals, large and small, were held for the granting of desires.

Wheel: Although the wheel was most often a Sun symbol, there were occasions when it represented the Moon. Arianrhod's Silver Wheel or Oar Wheel is really the Moon.

Willow: A Moon tree sacred to such Dark Moon deities as Hecate, Circe, and Persephone. The willow (helice) gave its name to the Helicon, abode of the nine muses, the orgiastic priestesses of the Moon goddess.

Wings: Long before the Persians adopted the winged disk as a symbol of their Sun god, the Moon goddess was shown with wings. Sometimes the Moon itself, whether crescent or Full, was pictured with wings. Certain birds, such as doves and pigeons, were associated with the Moon.

Wolf: Many gods and goddesses, who had connections with the Moon, also had the wolf as their symbol. The wolf howls at the Moon, as do dogs; they hunt and frolic by moonlight. The Moon priestesses of many cultures were adept at astral traveling and shape-shifting, both talents usually practiced at night. They also practiced rituals, dancing and singing, outdoors under the Moon. A Roman festival, the Lupercalia, was in honor of the wolf-goddess Lupa or Feronia. The Norse believed that the giant wolf Hati dogs the courses of the Moon, and in the final days will eat this celestial body.

Yin and Yang: This Chinese symbol represents the joined powers of male and female, positive and negative; in other words, a cyclical alternation of duality. At one point in ancient Chinese history, this design symbolized the phases of the Moon, the light and dark cycles. Much of the ancient world spoke of the Two Ladies or Two Mistresses of the Moon.

Appendix 3

THE CHARGE OF
THE GODDESS

*I*n 1899 Charles Godfrey Leland first published *Aradia: Gospel of the Witches,* a small book on surviving Italian witchcraft. In it he gives the Charge of the Goddess which has become a standard part of Wiccan ritual today. This Charge is still used as originally given, but more often is carefully refined for modern usage. Doreen Valiente rewrote a beautiful version of it. Starhawk gives one version of it in *The Spiral Dance;* Janet and Stewart Farrar have another in *Eight Sabbats For Witches.* Even the fantasy writer Andre Norton gives a version of the Charge in her book *Moon Called.*

The Charge of the Goddess gives ancient instructions of when to meet and what to expect from Moon energies and powers. No one knows for certain how old the Charge really is; Leland thought it to be an authentic part of ritual secretly carried down from ancient times by Pagan worshippers in the Mediterranean region.

It begins with "Listen to the words of the Great Mother, who of old was called Artemis, Athene, Diana, Cerridwen...." A list of Moon-goddess names follows. It continues "Whenever you have need of anything, once in the month, and better it be when the Moon is full, you shall assemble in some secret place...." The Charge promises that celebration of the Goddess will free the devotee from slavery to other people and Christianized laws, and the Goddess will teach Her followers mystical secrets.

Each coven, group, and individual may have a slightly modified version of the Charge of the Goddess, often a compilation and rewording of other versions. The following is the version which I use; it is part of the original, parts of others, and part my own.

> *Listen to the words of the Great Goddess, who in ancient times was named Artemis, Diana, Astarte, Ishtar, Aphrodite, Venus, Cerridwen, the Morrigu, Freyja, the White Lady, and many other names.*
>
> *Whenever you have need of My aid, assemble in a secret place at least once a month, especially at the Full Moon. Know that My laws and love shall make you free, for no man can prevent your worship of Me in your mind and heart. Listen well when you come into My presence, and I shall teach you of deep mysteries, ancient and powerful. I require no sacrifices or pain of your bodies, for I am Mother of all things, the Creatress who made you out of My love, and the One who endures through all time.*
>
> *I am the One who is the beauty of the Earth, the green of growing things. I am the white Moon whose light is full among the stars, soft upon the Earth. From Me all things are born, to Me all things, in their season, return. Let My joyous worship be in your hearts, for all acts of love and pleasure are My rituals. You see Me in the love of man and woman, the love of parent and child, the love of humans to all My creations. When you create with your hands, I am there. I blow the breath of life into the seeds you plant, whether of plant or child. Always I stand beside you, whispering soft words of wisdom and guidance.*
>
> *All seekers of the Mysteries must come to Me, for I am the True Source, the Keeper of the Cauldron. All who seek to know Me, know this. All your seeking and yearning will avail you nothing unless you know the Mystery: for if what you seek you find not within, you will never find it without. For behold, I have been with you from the beginning, and I will gather you to My breast at the end of your earthly existence.*

The Charge is usually read early in the ritual. Hearing or speaking it helps an aware, devoted worshipper to open doors into the collective unconscious, even if it is only a crack. An understanding of the ritual, psychic phenomena, dreams, and paranormal abilities can then be more fully achieved through the access to ancient knowledge buried deep within the collective unconscious of every human. The high tide of Full Moon energy strengthens the ability of the worshipper to make this connection.

We have no information as to whether there were once also "charges" for the crescent and Dark Moons. There may well have been, for the goddesses symbolizing these phases of the Moon were held in high regard and had groups of devoted followers.

Although once many of the Moon rituals were for women only, there is no reason that men cannot join in the worship. Even in ancient times some men chose to break away from the male-oriented religions and worship the Great Goddess.

The Great Goddess archetype, in Her three Moon aspects, has outlasted persecution, ridicule, attempted theft of powers, and abandonment. No human or religious laws can prevent the emotions, minds, and bodies of humans (female and male) from responding to Her symbol, the Moon. Individually, we must follow the moonbeam path that leads within to the secret, inner door of Her ancient knowledge. We must learn to become aware of the Moon's phases and flows of energy; we must understand how the Moon's energies flow through the lunar year. When we can do this, we will have the key to that inner door.

BIBLIOGRAPHY

Angus, S. *The Mystery-Religions.* New York: Dover, 1975.

Avalon, Arthur. *Shakti & Shakta.* New York: Dover, 1978.

Bachofen, J. J. Edited by Joseph Campbell and translated by Ralph Manheim. *Myth, Religion, & Mother Right.* Princeton, NJ: Princeton University Press, 1973.

Baring, Anne, and Jules Cashford. *The Myth of the Goddess: Evolution of an Image.* New York: Viking Arkana, 1991.

Bennett, Florence Mary. *Religious Cults Associated With the Amazons.* NY: AMS Press, 1967. Originally published NY 1912.

Bierhorst, John. *The Mythology of Mexico & Central America.* New York: William Morris & Co., 1990.

Blavatsky, H. P. *Isis Unveiled.* Pasadena, CA: Theosophical University Press, 1976.

Bodde, Derk. *Festivals in Classical China: New Year & Other Annual Observances During the Han Dynasty, 206 BC-AD 220.* Princeton, NJ: Princeton University Press, 1975.

Branston, Brian. *Gods of the North.* UK: Thames & Hudson, 1957.

Brasch, R. *How Did It Begin? Customs & Superstitions & Their Romantic Origins.* New York: Simon & Schuster, 1969.

Breasted, James H. *Development of Religion & Thought in Ancient Egypt.* New York: Charles Scribner's Sons, 1912.

Briffault, Robert. *The Mothers: A Study of the Origins of Sentiments & Institutions. 3 vols.* New York: Macmillan, 1952.

Briggs, Katherine M. *Pale Hecate's Team.* UK: Routledge & Kegan Paul, 1962.

Budapest, Zsuzsanna E. *Grandmother Moon.* San Francisco: Harper & Row, 1991.

———*The Grandmother of Time.* San Francisco: Harper & Row, 1989.

Budd, Lillian. *Full Moons: Indian Legends of the Seasons.* New York: Rand McNally & Co., 1971.

Budge, E. A. Wallis. *Amulets & Superstitions.* New York: Dover, 1978.

———*Babylonian Life & History.* New York: Dorset Press, 1992.

———*Dwellers on the Nile.* New York: Dover, 1977.

———*Egyptian Magic.* New York: Dover, 1971.

———*The Gods of the Egyptians. 2 vols.* New York: Dover, 1969.

Butler, Francelia. *Skipping Around the World: The Ritual Nature of Folk-Rhymes.* New York: Ballantine, 1989.

Campbell, Joseph, and Charles Muses, eds. *In All Her Names: Explorations of the Feminine in Divinity.* San Francisco: Harper & Row, 1991.

Campbell, Joseph. *The Masks of God: Primitive, Oriental, Occidental & Creative Mythology.* UK: Penguin Books, 1968.

Carlyon, Richard. *A Guide to the Gods.* New York: William Morrow & Co., 1982.

Cavendish, Richard, ed. *Mythology: An Illustrated Encyclopedia.* New York: Rizzoli, 1980.

Cirlot, J. E. *A Dictionary of Symbols.* New York: Philosophical Library, 1978.

Conway, D. J. *Ancient & Shining Ones.* St. Paul, MN: Llewellyn Publications, 1993.

———*Celtic Magic.* St. Paul, MN: Llewellyn Publications, 1990.

———*Maiden, Mother, Crone.* St. Paul, MN: Llewellyn Publications, 1994.

———*Norse Magic.* St. Paul, MN: Llewellyn Publications, 1990.

Cooper, J.C. *The Aquarian Dictionary of Festivals.* UK: Aquarian Press, 1990.

Cotterell, Arthur. *A Dictionary of World Mythology.* New York: Perigee Books, 1979.

Cotterell, Arthur, ed. *Macmillan Illustrated Encyclopedia of Myths & Legends.* New York: Macmillan, 1989.

Crawford, O. G. S. *The Eye Goddess.* New York: Macmillan, 1956.

Cumont, Franz. *The Mysteries of Mithra.* New York: Dover, 1956.

D'Alviella, Count Goblet. *The Migration of Symbols.* New York: Aquarian Press, 1979.

———*The Mysteries of Eleusis: The Secret Rites & Rituals of the Classical Greek Mystery Tradition.* UK: Aquarian Press, 1981.

Davidson, H. R. Ellis. *Myths & Symbols in Pagan Europe.* Syracuse, NY: University Press, 1988.

de Lys, Claudia. John Philip Lunden, translator and editor. *The Giant Book of Superstitions.* Secaucus, NJ: Citadel Press, 1979.

Diner, Helen. *Mothers & Amazons: The First Feminine History of Culture.* New York: Doubleday/ Anchor, 1973.

Durdin-Robertson, Laurence. *The Goddesses of Chaldea, Syria & Egypt.* Huntington Castle, Clonegal, Enniscorthy, Eire: Cesara Publications, 1975.

——*The Goddesses of India, Tibet, China & Japan.* Huntington Castle, Clonegal, Enniscorthy, Eire: Cesara Publications, 1976.

Eclipse. *The Moon in Hand.* Portland, ME: Astarte Shell Press, 1991.

Eichler, Lillian. *The Customs of Mankind.* New York: Nelson Doubleday, 1924.

Eliade, Mircea. Willard R. Trask, translator. *A History of Religious Ideas. 3 vols.* Chicago, IL: University of Chicago Press, 1978-85.

Elsworthy, Frederick. *The Evil Eye.* New York: Julian Press, 1958.

Evans, Sir Arthur. *The Earlier Religion of Greece in the Light of Cretan Discoveries.* UK: Macmillan, 1931.

Evans, Ivor H., editor. *Brewer's Dictionary of Phrase & Fable.* New York: Harper & Row, 1981. Originally published 1894.

Frazer, James G. *The Golden Bough.* New York: Macmillan, 1963.

Gayley, Charles Mills. *The Classic Myths in English Literature & in Art.* New York: Ginn & Co., 1939.

George, Demetra. *Mysteries of the Dark Moon: the Healing Power of the Dark Goddess.* San Francisco: Harper & Row, 1992.

Gimbutas, Marija. *The Goddesses & Gods of Old Europe, 6500-3500 B.C.* Berkeley, CA: University of California Press, 1982.

——*The Language of the Goddess.* San Francisco: Harper & Row, 1989.

Godwin, Joscelyn. *Mystery Religions of the Ancient World.* UK: Thames & Hudson, 1981.

Goodrich, Norma Lorre. *Priestesses.* New York: HarperCollins, 1989.

Graves, Robert. *The Greek Myths.* UK: Penguin Books, 1981.

——*The White Goddess.* New York: Farrar, Straus & Giroux, 1980.

Gray, Louis Herbert, editor. *The Mythology of All Races. 13 vols.* Boston, MA: 1918.

Guirand, Felix, editor. Richard Aldington & Delano Ames, translators. *New Larousse Encyclopedia of Mythology.* UK: Hamlyn, 1978.

Hall, Manly P. *The Secret Teachings of All Ages.* Los Angeles, CA: Philosophical Research Society, 1977.

Hall, Nor. *The Moon & the Virgin: Reflections on the Archetypal Feminine.* San Francisco: Harper & Row, 1980.

Harding, M. Esther. *Woman's Mysteries: Ancient & Modern.* New York: G.P. Putnam's Sons, 1971.

Harley, Rev. Timothy. *Moon Lore.* Rutland, VT: Charles E. Tuttle Co., 1970.

Harrison, Jane Ellen. *Prolegomena to the Study of Greek Religion.* UK: Merlin Press, 1980.

Hays, H. R. *In the Beginnings.* New York: G. P. Putnam's Sons, 1963.

Hazlitt, W. Carew. *Faiths & Folklore of the British Isles. 2 vols.* New York: Benjamin Blom, 1965.

Herzberg, Max J. *Myths & Their Meaning.* Boston, MA: Allyn & Bacon, 1928.

Hooke, S. H. *Middle Eastern Mythology.* UK: Penguin Books, 1963.

Jobes, Gertrude & James. *Outer Space.* New York: Scarecrow Press, 1964.

Johnson, Buffie. *Lady of the Beasts: Ancient Images of the Goddess & Her Sacred Animals.* San Francisco: Harper & Row, 1988.

Jung, Carl G. *The Archetypes & the Collective Unconscious.* Princeton, NJ: Princeton University Press, 1990.

——*Man & His Symbols.* New York: Doubleday & Co., 1964.

Jung, Carl G., and Kerenyi, C. *The Myth of the Divine Child.* Princeton, NJ: Princeton University Press, 1973.

Katzeff, Paul. *Full Moons: Fact & Fantasy About Lunar Influence.* Secaucus, NJ: Citadel Press, 1981.

——*Moon Madness & Other Effects of the Full Moon.* Secaucus, NJ: Citadel Press, 1981.

Kerenyi, Karl. Murray Stein, translator. *Athene: Virgin & Mother in Greek Religion.* Houston, TX: Spring Publications, 1978.

Kerenyi, Karl. *Eleusis: Archetypal Image of Mother & Daughter.* New York: Schocken Books, 1967.

——*Goddesses of Sun & Moon.* Trans. Murray Stein. Dallas, TX: Spring Publications, 1979.

Kinsley, David R. *The Sword & the Flute: Kali & Krishna. Dark Visions of the Terrible & the Sublime in Hindu Mythology.* Berkeley, CA: University of California Press, 1975.

Knight, Richard Payne. *The Symbolical Language of Ancient Art & Mythology.* New York: J. W. Bouton, 1892.

Knightly, Charles. *The Customs & Ceremonies of Britain.* UK: Thames & Hudson, 1986.

Koltuv, Barbara Black. *The Book of Lilith.* York Beach, ME: Nicolas-Hays, Inc., 1986.

Kryder, Rowena Pattee. *The Faces of the Moon Mother: An Archetypal Cycle.* Mt. Shasta, CA: Golden Point Productions, 1991.

Krupp, Dr. E. C. *Beyond the Blue Horizon.* New York: Oxford University Press, 1991.

Larrington, Carolyne, editor. *The Feminist Companion to Mythology.* UK: Pandora, 1992.

Leach, Maria, editor. *Funk & Wagnalls Standard Dictionary of Folklore, Mythology, & Legend.* New York: Funk & Wagnalls, 1972. First published 1949.

Leek, Sybil. *Moon Signs: Lunar Astrology.* New York: G.P. Putnam's Sons, 1977.

Leland, Charles G. *Aradia: Gospel of the Witches.* New York: Dr. Leo L. Martello, 1971.

Levy, G. Rachel. *The Gate of Horn: A Study of the Religious Conceptions of the Stone Age & Their Influence upon European Thought.* UK: Faber & Faber, 1946.

Lurker, Manfred. *Dictionary of Gods & Goddesses, Devils & Demons.* New York: Routledge & Kegan Paul, 1987.

MacCraig, Hugh. *The 200 Year Ephemeris*. Richmond, VA: Macoy Publishing, 1949.

Manning, Al. *Moon Lore & Moon Magic*. West Nyack, NY: Parker Publishing, 1980.

McLean, Adam. *The Triple Goddess: an Exploration of the Archetypal Feminine*. Grand Rapids, MI: Phanes Press, 1989.

Meyer, Marvin W., editor. *The Ancient Mysteries: A Sourcebook*. San Francisco: Harper & Row, 1987.

Mikalson, Jon. *The Sacred & Civil Calendar of the Athenian Year*. Princeton, NJ: Princeton University Press, 1975.

Monaghan, Patricia. *The Book of Goddesses & Heroines*. St. Paul, MN: Llewellyn Publications, 1990.

Mookerjee, Ajit. *Kali: the Feminine Force*. Rochester, VT: Destiny Books, 1988.

Morrison, Lillian, compiled by. *Touch Blue*. New York: Thomas Y. Crowell Co., 1958.

Murray, Alexander S. *Who's Who in Mythology*. New York: Bonanza Books, 1988.

Mylonas, George. *Eleusis & the Eleusinian Mysteries*. Princeton, NJ: Princeton University Press, 1961.

Neumann, Erich. *The Great Mother: An Analysis of the Archetype*. Princeton, NJ: Princeton University Press, 1963.

O'Flaherty, Wendy Doniger. *Hindu Myths*. UK: Penguin Books, 1975.

Olson, Carl, editor. *The Book of Goddess Past & Present*. New York: Crossroad, 1989.

Opie, Iona & Peter, editors. *The Oxford Dictionary of Nursery Rhymes*. UK: Clarendon Press, 1952.

Patai, Raphael. *The Hebrew Goddess*. New York: Avon, 1978.

Pennick, Nigel. *The Pagan Book of Days*. Rochester, VT: Destiny Books, 1992.

——*Practical Magic in the Northern Tradition*. UK: Aquarian Press, 1989.

Pepper, Elizabeth, and Wilcock, John. *Magical & Mystical Sites*. New York: Harper & Row, 1977.

Perera, Sylvia Brinton. *Descent to the Goddess: A Way of Initiation for Women*. Canada: Inner City Books, 1981.

Potter, Carole. *Knock on Wood & Other Superstitions*. New York: Bonanza Books, 1984.

Purce, Jill. *The Mystic Spiral: Journey of the Soul*. New York: Thames & Hudson, 1974.

Radford, Edwin & Mona A. *Encyclopaedia of Superstitions*. New York: The Philosophical Library, 1949.

Rush, Anne Kent. *Moon, Moon*. New York: Random House, 1976.

Sargent, H. C., and Kittredge, G. L. *English & Scottish Popular Ballads*. Boston, MA: Houghton Mifflin, 1932.

Sharkey, John. *Celtic Mysteries: the Ancient Religion*. New York: The Crossroad Publishing Co., 1975.

Sjoo, Monica, and Mor, Barbara. *The Great Cosmic Mother: Rediscovering the Religion of the Earth*. San Francisco: Harper & Row, 1987.

Sobol, Donald J. *The Amazons of Greek Mythology.* Cranbury, NJ: A. S. Barnes & Co., 1972.

Spicer, Dorothy Gladys. *The Book of Festivals.* New York: Woman's Press, 1937.

Spretnak, Charlene. *Lost Goddesses of Early Greece: a Collection of Pre-Hellenic Myths.* Boston, MA: Beacon Press, 1992.

Starhawk. *The Spiral Dance.* San Francisco: Harper & Row, 1979.

Stein, Diane. *The Goddess Book of Days.* St. Paul, MN: Llewellyn Publications, 1988.

Stone, Merlin. *Ancient Mirrors of Womanhood.* Boston, MA: Beacon, 1984.

Suhr, Elmer G. *The Spinning Aphrodite: The Evolution of the Goddess from Earliest Pre-Hellenic Symbolism Through Late Classical Times.* New York: Helios Books, 1969.

Swanhild. *Holiday Folklore.* Green Man Press, 1990.

Thomas, William, and Pavitt, Kate. *The Book of Talismans, Amulets & Zodiacal Gems.* N. Hollywood, CA: Wilshire Book Co., 1970.

Thompson, William Irwin. *The Time Falling Bodies Take to Light: Mythology, Sexuality & the Origins of Culture.* New York: St. Martin's Press, 1981.

Turville-Petre, E.O.G. *Myths & Religion of the North.* New York: Holt, Rinehart & Winston, 1964.

Vermaseren, Maarten, J. A.M.H. Lemmers, translator. *Cybele & Attis: The Myth & the Cult.* UK: Thames & Hudson, 1977.

Walker, Barbara G. *The Crone: Woman of Age, Wisdom & Power.* San Francisco: Harper & Row, 1985.

———*The Woman's Dictionary of Symbols & Sacred Objects.* San Francisco: Harper & Row, 1988.

———*The Woman's Encyclopedia of Myths & Secrets.* San Francisco: Harper & Row, 1983.

Waring, Philippa. *A Dictionary of Omens & Superstitions.* New York: Ballantine Books, 1978.

Weigle, Marta. *Spiders & Spinsters: Women & Mythology.* Albuquerque, NM: University of New Mexico Press, 1982.

Wilde, Lady. *Irish Cures, Mystic Charms & Superstitions.* New York: Sterling Publishing, 1991.

Willetts, R. F. *Cretan Cults & Festivals.* UK: Routledge & Kegan Paul, 1962.

Wimberly, Lowry Charles. *Folklore in the English & Scottish Ballads.* New York: Dover, 1965.

Wolkstein, Diane, and Kramer, Samuel N. *Inanna, Queen of Heaven & Earth: Her Stories & Hymns from Sumer.* UK: Rider & Co., 1983.

Zimmer, Heinrich. *Myths & Symbols in Indian Art & Civilization.* Princeton, NJ: Princeton University Press, 1946.

INDEX

On the following pages you will find listed, with their current prices, some of the books now available on related subjects. Your book dealer stocks most of these and will stock new titles in the Llewellyn series as they become available. We urge your patronage.

To Get a Free Catalog

You are invited to write for our bimonthly news magazine/catalog, *Llewellyn's New Worlds of Mind and Spirit.* A sample copy is free, and it will continue coming to you at no cost as long as you are an active mail customer. Or you may subscribe for just $10 in the United States and Canada ($20 overseas, first class mail). Many bookstores also have *New Worlds* available to their customers. Ask for it.

In *New Worlds* you will find news and features about new books, tapes and services; announcements of meetings and seminars; helpful articles; author interviews and much more. Write to:

Llewellyn's New Worlds of Mind and Spirit
P.O. Box 64383-167, St. Paul, MN 55164-0383, U.S.A.

To Order Books And Tapes

If your book store does not carry the titles described on the following pages, you may order them directly from Llewellyn by sending the full price in U.S. funds, plus postage and handling (see below).

Credit card orders: VISA, MasterCard, American Express are accepted. Call us toll-free within the United States and Canada at 1-800-THE-MOON.

Special Group Discount: Because there is a great deal of interest in group discussion and study of the subject matter of this book, we offer a 20% quantity discount to group leaders or agents. Our Special Quantity Price for a minimum order of five copies of *Moon Magick* is $59.80 cash-with-order. Include postage and handling charges noted below.

Postage and Handling: Include $4 postage and handling for orders $15 and under; $5 for orders *over* $15. There are no postage and handling charges for orders over $100. Postage and handling rates are subject to change. We ship UPS whenever possible within the continental United States; delivery is guaranteed. Please provide your street address as UPS does not deliver to P.O. boxes. Orders shipped to Alaska, Hawaii, Canada, Mexico and Puerto Rico will be sent via first class mail. Allow 4-6 weeks for delivery. **International orders:** Airmail – add retail price of each book and $5 for each non-book item (audiotapes, etc.); Surface mail – add $1 per item.

Minnesota residents add 7% sales tax.

Mail orders to:
Llewellyn Worldwide, P.O. Box 64383-167, St. Paul, MN 55164-0383, U.S.A.

For customer service, call (612) 291-1970.

THE ANCIENT & SHINING ONES
World Myth, Magic & Religion
by D.J. Conway

The Ancient & Shining Ones is a handy, comprehensive reference guide to the myths and deities from ancient religions around the world. Now you can easily find the information you need to develop your own rituals and worship using the Gods/Goddesses with which you resonate most strongly. More than just a mythological dictionary, *The Ancient & Shining Ones* explains the magickal aspects of each deity and explores such practices as Witchcraft, Ceremonial Magick, Shamanism and the Qabala. It also discusses the importance of ritual and magick, and what makes magick work.

Most people are too vague in appealing for help from the Cosmic Beings—they either end up contacting the wrong energy source, or they are unable to make any contact at all, and their petitions go unanswered. In order to touch the power of the universe, we must re-educate ourselves about the Ancient Ones. The ancient pools of energy created and fed by centuries of belief and worship in the deities still exist. Today these energies can bring peace of mind, spiritual illumination and contentment. On a very earthy level, they can produce love, good health, money, protection, and success.

0–87542–170–9, 448 pgs., 7 x 10, 300 illus., softcover $17.95

CELTIC MAGIC
by D. J. Conway

Many people, not all of Irish descent, have a great interest in the ancient Celts and the Celtic pantheon, and *Celtic Magic* is the map they need for exploring this ancient and fascinating magical culture.

Celtic Magic is for the reader who is either a beginner or intermediate in the field of magic. It provides an extensive "how-to" of practical spell-working. There are many books on the market dealing with the Celts and their beliefs, but none guide the reader to a practical application of magical knowledge for use in everyday life. There is also an in-depth discussion of Celtic deities and the Celtic way of life and worship, so that an intermediate practitioner can expand upon the spellwork to build a series of magical rituals. Presented in an easy-to-understand format, *Celtic Magic* is for anyone searching for new spells that can be worked immediately, without elaborate or rare materials, and with minimal time and preparation.

0-87542-136-9, 240 pgs., mass market, illus. $4.99

Prices subject to change without notice.